HOME SCHOOL
BURNOUT

Other books by Raymond and Dorothy Moore

Home Grown Kids (Word Books, 1981)

Homespun Schools (Word Books, 1982)

Homestyle Teaching (Word Books, 1984)

Homemade Health (Word, 1986)

Homebuilt Discipline (Thomas Nelson, 1987)

Better Late Than Early (Readers Digest-Moore, 1975)

School Can Wait (BYU-Moore, 1979)

HOME SCHOOL BURNOUT

What It Is. What Causes It. And How to Cure It.

Raymond S. Moore, Ed.D
Dorothy N. Moore, M.A.

with

D. Kathleen Moore-Kordenbrock, A.B.
Dennis R. Moore, M.A.
Robert Moon, Ph.D.
Robert Strom, Ph.D.

and

A few of many highly
successful home educators

Wolgemuth & Hyatt, Publishers, Inc.
Brentwood, Tennessee

Unless otherwise noted, all Scripture quotations are from the
New King James Version of the Bible, copyrighted 1984 by
Thomas Nelson, Inc., Nashville, Tennessee.

Wolgemuth & Hyatt, Publishers, Inc.
P.O. Box 1941, Brentwood, Tennessee 37027.

Printed in the United States of America.

First printing, October, 1988
Second printing, August, 1989

Library of Congress Cataloging-in-Publication Data

Moore, Raymond S.
    Home school burnout : what it is, what causes it, and how
    to cure it / Raymond S. Moore, Dorothy N. Moore with
    D. Kathleen Moore-Kordenbrock . . . [et al.]. — 1st ed.
    p. cm.

Bibliography: p.
Includes index.
ISBN 0-943497-35-3
    1. Home schooling—United States. 2. Burn out
    (Psychology) I. Moore, Dorothy N. II. Title.

LC40.M66   1988   649'.68'0973—dc19   88-27658

CONTENTS

PROLOGUE

During the last year of World War II, I was forced as a medical soldier general staff officer in New Guinea and the Philippines to watch as men destroyed each other. And some of the worst destruction was not of the body, but of the mind. Although this was an experience in anguish for me, what I see happening to children in our society makes that destruction pale by comparison. Many educators and parents today are destroying innocent children, and by their stifling routines are themselves being destroyed. The cattle-car care often provided children does not give them even the dignity offered to soldiers.

Home education, both full- and part-time, is in crisis. Thousands are turning their children over to others, burning out when victory is within their grasp. Our understanding of children—and parents—is being tested. Are we disciplined? Or irresponsible and uninformed? We will show you how many parents and the state are guilty of child abuse (our definition being "using a child wrongly or improperly"), sometimes aided and abetted by some members of the home school community. We have set out here to be all things to all home educators and their critics, hoping that by all means we might help some. We work with all races, colors, creeds, and national origins, yet realize that by our determination to help we may neglect or offend some. Forgive, if we do. That's the chance we had to take. Eliminating mental, spiritual, emotional, and physical burnout of parents, teachers and students is the dish many parents have put on our front burner. We are Christians; you may be Muslim, Hindu, or Jew or prefer no religion at all—but burnout respects no creed. If your curricula and methods work for you, bless you! Too many are dissatisfied, worried, crying "Help!" Besides, education is much more than any curriculum.

Burnout can be addressed in many ways—mind, emotions, stress, parents, children, stages, preventives, cures. We have chosen to give you a research-and experience-based book which uses stories and facts to help parents and children cope with stress at home and at school. We offer simple, practical answers in both prevention and revitalization or cure. We will do this as graciously as we know how, realizing that inevitably we must step on some toes if we are to give answers that rightly challenge destructive interests and ingrown practices.

It seems that we have received a mountain of letters and appeals to hurry this book. Unexpectedly, but happily for us, a small army has also helped. And coordinating their bright talents has been no small job. Their answers really are worthy of another book. So Parts 4 and 5 are your bonus. All are highly successful parent-teachers from coast to coast and overseas. Although we used no criteria except success, and although few of them, if any, know their co-authors, their agreement on goals and methods is remarkable. They richly flavor this book and give you a variety of perspectives Dorothy and I alone couldn't possibly provide.

Two associate authors are our children, Dennis and Kathleen, whom we home taught thirty to forty years ago and who helped pioneer the home schooling movement. Both are child development specialists. Dennis is a doctoral student in educational psychology and counseling at Arizona State University; Kathie was formerly with the Sacramento City Schools and now teaches her three boys. She lives near Washington, D.C. with her husband, Lt. Col. Bruce Kordenbrock, who is Director of Operations for the U.S. Air Force Intelligence Reserve.

Two distinguished educators and authors complete our author crew: Dr. Robert Moon is a former assistant director of the Council For Exceptional Children, Washington, D.C. Over the past eighteen to twenty years Dr. Moon has been a key Hewitt investigator and co-author. With his wife, Louise, he has established one of America's finest records in "healing" exceptional children.

Dr. Robert Strom is a well-known author and professor of child psychology at Arizona State University. He and his wife, Shirley, are world authorities on grandparenting, and head the Office of Parent Development International at ASU, where Dorothy and I are honored to be charter research associates. They provide our chapter on grandmas and grandpas.

We are also passing this manuscript by a distinguished panel of university professors. They include Dr. Russell Doll, professor of education, University of Missouri, Kansas City; Dr. Donald Erickson, University of California, Los Angeles; Dr. Margaret Hafner, recently retired from the State University of New York; Dr. Sam Peavey, professor emeritus of the School of Education, University of Louisville; Dr. Ralph Scott, director of the child clinic at the University of Northern Iowa; and Drs. Larry and Gail Walker—Larry is a state university political science professor, and Gail was a research professor in education until she began teaching their boys at home.

We make no attempt here to go deeply into remedial techniques, but offer simple, proven ways to do master teaching while enjoying your young. I alone accept ultimate responsibility for this volume. If you need further help or lists of our books or believe we've erred in anything, please send a self-addressed, stamped envelope (SASE) to the Moore Foundation, Box 1, Camas, WA 98607. We ask, in fairness, that you require the same quality of research or experience from our critics.

—Raymond S. Moore

HOW AND WHY THIS BOOK CAME ABOUT

In late 1987, Robert Wolgemuth and Mike Hyatt of Wolgemuth & Hyatt, the well-known educational and religious publishers, took me to lunch where I found the conversation even more stimulating than the smorgasbord. I expected to talk about manuscripts we had discussed over the last several years. Dorothy and I had written several books under their guidance in two other publishing firms. Robert had given the name *Home Grown Kids* to one of our flagship books. Yet I was unprepared for Mike's proposal.

"Ray," he said, jamming his index finger into the tablecloth, "thousands of parents are burning out, and we've got to do something to help them."

A home schooling father was confirming what I knew well! "You must give us a book that will heal burned-out parents," he persisted, "and show others how to avoid this sickness! We are destroying thoughtful mothers by the thousands."

I reminded them that some editors, publishers, and workshop speakers might make accusations of "scare tactics" or "vested interests" even though Dorothy and I take no money from home education.

"We'll take that chance," they insisted. "Tell it like it is!"

Where to Begin

There is no perfect sequence in a book of this kind. If you are impatient to "get down to points," go directly to Parts 4 and 5 where you will quickly see how clear-thinking parents turned potential disaster into high success. Otherwise, bear with us as we, with the help of some of the nation's leading educators and our own research and experience, lead you systematically through a proven burnout prevention formula.

The "Qualification" Issue

The biggest single excuse for not teaching at home is "I'm not qualified; I don't know if I could handle it." This book is designed to make you confident instead of fearful. It shows that for the great majority this fear is ill-informed or exaggerated. Some professionals may have made you feel this way, but if you're a loving parent, you have some special qualifications that can make you a good teacher!

Another concern of most "authorities" and laymen is that women can't remain at home these days for financial reasons. We take that issue up briefly and with surprising evidence in our chapter on working mothers.

When we invited parents to tell in this book how they beat or avoided burnout, we deliberately avoided asking them which curriculum or method they used. We knew only that their students were very high achievers or otherwise honored. Yet, we discovered that a good many of them used similar methods and materials. Nearly all the parents started formally, yet most have forsaken that approach, becoming more laid back as their children's creativity excites them and their success relaxes them.

We urge our readers to deal cautiously with promoters. Our overriding affection is for young children and their parents who are trying to get, or keep, their families together. So you will find that we have less sympathy for (1) those with vested interests or whose ethics we question or who fail to look before they leap or speak, and (2) for individuals and groups who make money with seemingly little concern for the real needs of children.

Our Goals

In responding to the challenge that Robert Wolgemuth set before us, we agreed on a book that would accomplish six major goals: (1) provide a background for home education; (2) tell how to avoid burnout in parents and children; (3) suggest the quickest and most effective ways to cure burnout when parents and children are already sick from it; (4) give examples—mostly in their own words—of parents who have followed sound formulas and have become highly successful home teachers, some of them after having been badly "burned"; (5) back up this counsel with chapters in such needy areas as basics, organization, lesson plans, home industries, certification, etc.; and (6) repeat facts often enough throughout the book to drive them home in the face of standard practices that contradict them.

We did not write this book for only full-time home teachers. Its principles and methods were written for a number of reasons and with a number of people in mind: They can bring maximum change with minimum effort:

First, to help parents who love their children enough to help them be the best they can be, especially those who feel overwhelmed by teaching their own children or helping them with homework, those perplexed by unusual behavior, or frustrated by educational systems which destroy cherished cultures. Second, to help children, whether they are schooled at home or in formal school settings. Third, to help classroom teachers, legislators, school officials, social workers, book and curriculum publishers, lecturers, consultants, and others who love children, whether these professionals have jumped on the home teaching bandwagon or sit in the critics' den. Fourth, to strengthen individuals who work in the literacy movement, including immigrants and those in prison who are doubly imprisoned by illiteracy. Fifth, to lay down a system of principles and methods which will work with great effectiveness among other races and tongues overseas—where some of home education's most destructive forces are at work!

We do not, however, insist here that *all* parents are qualified to teach their children at home! But our reasons for this caveat are largely different from those of educators who judge by credentials and degrees. The only parents we view as *unqualified* are those who have little use or appreciation for their children or are not fit patterns morally, psychologically, or emotionally, or those who do not themselves have minimal skills. In other words, there are home situations which are not as good as available local schools.

For example, in Champaign, Illinois, a six-year-old child was taken from his mother when she was placed in a mental hospital. During the previous year or so the boy had been helped by

Dr. Sam Kirk and other University of Illinois staff who had taken an interest in him, raising his IQ from 75 to about 86. He then was placed in a foster home and put in a rural school where by age seven and a half his IQ jumped to 104. By the midpoint of the second grade, he was performing normally. Dr. Kirk was pleased that the combination of rural home and rural school had done more for him than the university preschool (which had an adult-child ratio of one to five). Yet, when he was about eight, the boy's mother was released from the hospital and regained his custody. When measured again at age ten, his IQ was back to the original 75, from normal to retarded.

This caution in no way demeans home education. But it does suggest that parents should not be careless or viewed as infallibly good influences on their children in all cases.

Virtually all the honored or high-scoring home schoolers we know have been taught by a three-point real-life learning formula: (1) they have warm, responsive parents who minimize structure, (2) they spend much more time with their parents than with peers, and (3) they have been given generous freedom, under parental guidance, to work out their own ideas and explore for themselves.[1]

These three factors flower best in a context of *readiness* (letting your children develop naturally) and of *balance* (allowing your youngsters to spend at least as much time in manual activities and service opportunities as in study).

The three-point recipe is not only for home-taught children. The best public and parochial schools also enjoy informal approaches to education, as we will show later. Parents of conventionally schooled children can give a great boost to their creativity, achievement, behavior, and positive sociability by (1) having them spend as little time in formal education as possible, (2) eliminating conventional homework as much as possible, (3) working with them in family industries at home and in church or other non-school activities such as 4-H, Scouts, AWANA, Pathfinders, and pinstripers, and (4) utilizing phenomenally successful skill programs or games such as Math-It and Winston Grammar or other curriculum programs which capitalize on writing, singing, or otherwise combining skill building with fun.

We repeat this theme several times in this book from one angle or another. It counters the conventional school approach which we call "the educational extrusion process" in which we pressure children through a narrow form, largely limited to textbooks, workbooks, and tests. Such extrusion presses down curiosities and creativity (which otherwise sprout like antennae from children's brains).

Rooted in Research

From his studies of genius through the centuries, Smithsonian researcher Harold McCurdy put together a recipe for genius and leadership very similar to the three-point formula which threads through this book.[2] He suggests that mass education is, in its way, a vast experiment on reducing all three factors [fond responsiveness, family closeness, and free exploration] to a minimum; accordingly, it should tend to suppress the occurrence of genius.

As of this writing we have well over 150 masters, doctoral, and other independent researchers working with us in one way or another who with little or no contact among them have come up with remarkably harmonious findings. And studies made by states themselves are consistent with our research reports.

Some researchers sampled locally, some statewide, and others nationally. Some concentrate on religious groups, others on the population at large. Some study socialization and some cognition, while others explore student achievement or parental effectiveness as teachers, or a combination of these factors. At least one has taken a historical approach. Yet, despite their wide range of backgrounds and institutional orientation (from Princeton to East Texas State University and from Bob Jones University to Stanford), their findings thus far are harmonious.

For Careful Consideration

Please bear these things in mind as you go through this book:

Don't buy high and sell low. Before you start home teaching or decide to quit, consider this warning from Wall Street. Build on your joys. Profit from your woes rather than scuttling them, and see if ideas from this book might bring some happy surprises.

Don't expect all to be a journalistic delight. The stories in this book are offered to encourage and teach more than to entertain. At times you may think it a surgeon's scalpel; if so, it wounds to heal.

Don't get caught by those who do a lot of expounding with very little research. Whether you believe in the Bible, Torah, or Koran, remember that lecturers reciting quotations will not get you far in education at home without a sound understanding of your children and some elements of the learning process. Check your instructor's, author's or speakers credentials carefully. Many from coast to coast feel they have been ripped off.

Know the difference between an authority and one who acts like one. We know promoters who are good people. Others offer a striking first impression, a slick organization, and a well-turned sentence in exchange for your entrance fee or a book mixture of good, bad, and doubtful sources, along with scant professional experience. Real authorities — whether in universities or in household kitchens over the land — will demonstrate creative ideas based on *professional* experience and research facts.

Verify the quality of your literature before you buy a book or curriculum. None is perfect, but there is a vast difference between warm, responsive experiences tailored to your child and conventional formal school at home. Ask around. Don't take *any* recommendation unless you are certain of your source. Some parents have found later that their friends were too proud to admit they made a mistake. You may be more naive or gullible than you think and find out later that you were well on the way to burnout before you started. Be independent. Part 3 will give you hints on this. And we will on occasion refer you to some of our more specialized books.

Remember also, as you read this book, that you and your children are each at least as unique as your creeds and states. You can go into a shop and buy an adjustable cap that will fit *on* any head. But you can't possibly find a *ready-made, packaged* educational system which will fit *into* any head. Salesmen may be persuasive, and it may sound as easy as taking a sugar pill, but one day you may be sorry when that pill burns out your insides. That is the pain we are trying to help you avoid — or to cure.

You and your youngsters deserve the considerations we suggest here. If you reasonably follow these simple educational diets and cures, based as they are on over fifty years of research, successful experience and common sense, your blisters from stress, frustration, and other burnouts will largely disappear.

PART ONE

WHY DO PARENTS AND CHILDREN BURN OUT?

ONE

SO THIS IS HOME SCHOOLING?

BACKDROP: Some methods used in home education are reflections of the same bad practices which have proven to be unproductive in conventional schools. All wrong ideas are hazardous, not only for burnout, but also for other maladies. We decided to pass several of them on as horrible examples, though more common than one would suppose. Yet home schoolers—parents and children—may need to be reminded that there are far more burnouts among their "regular school" comrades than there are in home schools.

We also share this chapter with parents who send their children to conventional schools, and we applaud them as they supplement their youngsters' formal school lessons with creative activities. The child who is taught *more* or *less* at home has a great advantage over the youngster who is not taught there at all. And the record is quite clear that the one who is given more quality adult attention, support, and freedom to explore will be the one who will significantly excel. Note that word *freedom*. Children value it, too.

We begin now with stories we have witnessed.

In an East Coast town a tousled mother grimly confronts her bored or pouting offspring. They are slouched at a messy kitchen table and several desks in a contrived schoolroom in a basement that evokes recollections of Fibber McGee's closet. Sandy McAnn gorges them on rote workbooks and primitive textbooks that formally choke off almost all freedom to think. She is alarmed if they ever interrupt their tedium with a creative question or suspicious if they pursue an idea of their own.

"It just might be," she grumbles to herself, "another trick to get away from their books!"

For five to six hours a day — or more — this misguided mother keeps her flock in academic, behavioral, and social straitjackets, condemned to perpetual isolation from their agemates. They are already indelibly marked as misfits in local society. Outside the back gate the neighbor kids can't make up their minds whether to sympathize or to taunt the captives inside.

So *this* is home education? Try another scene.

In a plush Southern California subdivision Nellie Strickland toils in the wee small hours of the night to keep everything ship-shape so that she can devote the next day "sacrificially" to educating her children. After all, she gave up a perfectly good job to do this, didn't she? A perfectionist who can't stand a speck of dust anywhere, she applies the same sanctions to her flock. For the sake of her driving conscience they must master all those textbook facts and, in their dad's ominous words, "cream the SAT" (Scholastic Aptitude Test).

Yet for some time Joe Strickland has been worried that his wife was "overdoing," although he didn't realize how burned out she was until their family physician warned him that "Nellie must have a rest; she is a candidate for a stroke." Knowing the children well, we could see that they *also* needed a rest.

Is *this* home teaching? Really? Try one more.

Carmen (her friends call her "Carm") is a certified teacher, now "retired," who lives in the heart of America's corn belt. Her state is proud of its school system and fiercely defensive of any interference with its "educational integrity." Its message is "Home-work, homework, and . . . more homework!" And Carmen has heard it well. Her youngsters are settled into grades three and six of Public School 111 where they have been schooled since age five, and where they ride the crest of the homework wave with state SATs ranging to twelve points above national norms.

But every day is a battle and a march: a battle to get her kids out of bed and grudgingly off to school, and a march at the end of the day, away from the playground and cookie jar and down to, guess what — yes, more homework! Little chance for any creative thought or activity, an almost total block on entrepreneurship, and not much opportunity to serve their community.

Carm's message is loud and clear, "Keep at those books until every problem and exercise is done, and don't skip a page!" Her eight-year-old Josie and eleven-year-old Curt get the message: Instead of reveling in the prospects of citizenship in their great grain bowl, their lives, to them, are just "Corn, corn, and more corn."

Sadly, these are the stark impressions too many parents give. We don't bother to characterize truant families who claim to home teach, but in fact do nothing. Television and exercise on the streets is their curriculum. They are counterfeits. Yet all these parents are losing the chance of a lifetime to enjoy and to build great kids. Their programs either degrade their young or collapse. They lose in behavior and creativity. And gossips thrive. Children rebel. Parents burn out. In earlier days, most of you listened to us, or others with a similar message, when we told you that children are better off at home with their parents than in a formal school environment, especially in their early years. So, in the same way, we hope you will be willing to listen to the voices of research and experience, ours and others, in finding the individualized methods your children need for the very best results.

Even one home school failure, we confess, is too many. And the methods of Homework Carm are no improvement on those of Sandy and Nell. But we know that sanctimonious citizens looking on with pristine, conventional wisdom don't help matters much. Even the best home teachers are not risk-free as long as parents and children are less than perfect, and neighbors, relatives, and school officials are nosy—and skeptical! A single black spot on the pedagogical wall or even one weed in the educational garden alarms them. Never mind that otherwise the wall is immaculate and the garden glorious while conventional education's own back yard is marred with educational litter and certain misuse of "special" education.

We have repeatedly heard educators and social workers set up such straw men as poor achievement, behavior, sociability, or even incest and other child abuse as possible problems in home education which they have "heard about." Yet when questioned for specific examples, they usually can't produce any. If such a situation indeed does exist, it more likely is *under the guise of home schooling* but clearly *is not home schooling*.

In some cases, of course, such stories about home schools may be gossip by those who are well-meaning but simply uninformed. Yet often they are a ruse, a crude prank designed to cover their own vested interests. When we question these wishers of doom, they somehow reason that although children, too young even to be in school, are cooped up several hours a day or later chained to excessive homework which cuts them off from real and creative work at home, they are less abused than youngsters who have to work with their parents in the family business or on the family farm.

In reality, putting children out of their home nests and into conventional schools before they are ready is like putting a free bird in a cage. Instead, we should study our children's developmental needs and discover when, where, and how to provide the *very best* education and socialization for them.

What Is the Best Education?

First of all, it is *freely allowing and encouraging* home teaching for those who have the inclination. Then, for all others, pursuing programs that are as "home-style" as possible, always seeking parental involvement. Teachers should follow more closely the parent model in (1) responding warmly to their students, (2) providing a consistent model of good values in a ratio where their influence would count heavily, (3) teaching only tasks for which the child is ready, and (4) encouraging children to explore their own interests and to work out their own imaginations instead of only adult-contrived myths and fairy tales. The closer public, private, and church schools get to this model — and many are trying these days — the brighter and better behaved their school children will be. It is, in fact, a healing balm for families *and* schools.

Chronological age is a poor indicator of readiness — that is a well-established fact. We need to begin making use of the many good indicators of readiness for specific learning tasks.

Because academic achievement in conventional school has been linked to parental involvement, many public and private school educators are waking up to the value of parents and are making efforts to involve them as helpers and even decision makers in their school systems. If your school officials are thinking along these lines, we hope you will encourage and cooperate with them for the sake of those children who do not have a home school choice. Remember, we do not say that all home teaching is perfect, but we do warn those parents who try to teach as they were taught in conventional schools: From fifty years of research and long experience with unnumbered home teachers, we are now certain that they will work harder, worry more, and accomplish less than if they used the simple, informal methods we present in this book. Parents involved in mass education can also learn much from home schooling — the greatest educational method ever invented.

The *true* picture of the effective home teacher is more often a secure and happy mom. She and the children do straightening-up chores the first thing each day so that the home will provide an organized, clean environment for learning. She selects learning tasks for which each child is ready. She requires only enough daily practice or drill to allow her children to progress appropriately to mastery of the basic skills. FUN projects are used to integrate and reinforce basic skills. And much of the day is framed around the children's interests with work and service that builds genuine golden-rule citizens and successful entrepreneurs.

After reading, writing, arithmetic, and spelling are mastered reasonably and without rushing, she lets her scholars explore largely on their own, making herself available to help find resources and occasionally to answer a *how* or a *why*. The older they get, as they move on through the grades and high school, the more they effectively operate on their own.

Family Formula

The procedures many families use for bringing out the best in their kids run something like this:

The parents let their children grow up as naturally as possible. This does *not* mean that there is no guidance, no discipline. On the contrary, for every family it means that they practice *discipleship* and build *self-control* — the kind of building which requires sound parental examples. They don't rush their children into formal studies — as most schools do.

These parents understand that children's brains, bodies, and emotions are as different as their fingerprints. So they study how children develop, how to meet their uniquely individual needs, and when they are ready to undertake additional tasks. They consider manual work at least as important as study and play, depending of course on the age and maturity of their children. They delight to see their kids working out their own unique ideas.

Freedom and Flexibility

As adults, we demand *our* freedoms. Children should have some freedoms, too, within the framework of adult wisdom and love. This is not indulgence, not even close to it! The greatest freedom they can enjoy is a chance to grow naturally under the guidance of their parents who do not create academic or social straitjackets, but rather move with them in creative work, study, and play which make the most of their own inventive genius. And no one usually knows children's individual interests better than loving parents and teachers who care.

These practices are used by the best teachers in all schools and by parents who supplement the classroom by providing appropriate activity for their children after school. The danger, and remedy, may be anywhere and is illustrated by a true story about Tommy's experiences in two *regular* schools:

He was bright, active, and mature for a six-year-old. He was enrolled in a Christian school where there were only fifteen children in his first grade class. About a third of those children were judged as likely to have to repeat. Tommy's teacher was the rigid type. Soon his mother noticed despondency, morbidity. He often isolated himself in his room. He complained that his family liked his sister better than him — something they had never heard before. He noted that his favorite color was black. Finally he wished he were dead.

His alert parents quickly moved him to another school where the atmosphere was relaxed and open to activity. By the end of the year, he was at the head of his class. All his emotional problems had disappeared. Whether at home or at school, freedom and flexibility have a way with children as well as adults!

T W O

OF COURSE YOU CAN DO IT!

BACKDROP: If you can read with understanding, write with meaning, speak clearly, and add, subtract, multiply, and divide, and if you love and respond to your children, you can be a good teacher! Most parents who consider home schooling think they can't do it, and fear that if they do that they will fulfill their neighbors' and relatives' prophecies of failure. They don't realize that with only a good basic education they can bring out the natural talents and mental abilities of their children. Yet many do not look carefully enough before they leap, but take the first curriculum or method suggested, usually trying to teach as they were taught in school. This is all wrong. You may not like to hear us say this, but it is true. *True home schooling is tutorial, hand made, customized to each child. Such parents respond to their children in a loving, informal way, a balance between systematic structure where needed and a great deal of freedom for youngsters to explore.*

My father was a great ice skater. And no wonder: From early boyhood he had played "sandlot ice hockey" around Scotland, in eastern South Dakota, and in Zion City, Illinois, where he worked as a boy in its famous lace factory. But here I was a native Southern Californian, a rank beginner on ice that summer night in Hollywood's old Polar Palace.

And I'd better make the best of it. Only a year or so before, we were caught in the financial crash of 1929 and our few pennies now seldom stretched enough for a night on the town.

"You'll love it!" Dad promised, his big toothy grin followed by a slight tilt of his head as he added, ". . . as soon as you get your confidence. Just have faith!"

Sounded like the preacher in church.

But the first time I stepped out on the ice that warm evening in my rented CCM blades, I had very real doubts about Dad's prophecy. Immediately my feet shot toward the ceiling and my bottom warmly greeted the ice, as he skated away like a song.

"Is this some kind of trick?" I groaned in disbelief, my pride at its lowest ebb. But Dad had the audacity to zing around the rink again to give me more improbable advice. He knew better than to pamper me as he did my sisters, supporting them with his big right arm. He wanted me to learn as he had, like a man. "Of course you can do it!" he barked out when he saw doubt written all over my red face.

Because he said so, I staggered on.

And he breezed by again . . . and again . . . and again.

"Hang onto the railing until you get your sea legs," he would shout as he sailed by. He hadn't mentioned the railing before, but I'd already found it. Besides he didn't overdo things with his headstrong sixteen-year-old son.

My ankles bent and wobbled, and before long they were aching. About that time he once again slowed down around the curve where I was hung up on the rail.

"Relax. Forget about walking. Just glide." And again he added, "Have faith in yourself!"

While I was taking five in the box seats at rink's edge, Dad whirred around yet another time. "Before long," he assured me with his big warm grin, "you will have better balance on the ice than you have on the floor."

That sounded about as preposterous to me as a paratrooper who tells novices it's like falling into a feather bed. Yet within a few months, with Dad's warm guidance, his prophecy came true. My balance on ice became much more stable than walking on a floor. I did "flying-three" jumps and skated backward as fast as forward — something I never could do on a sidewalk or floor.

Yet the habits I had to unlearn were as crucial as those I had to learn. For example, I had to forget about walking while I was in the rink. At least Dad was not after me to "stand up straight" or to "throw your shoulders back." On the ice you lean in the direction you are going. I learned to land on my knees instead of those spine-crunching falls on my rear. And the feeling was much more relaxed: I could actually glide. I couldn't believe it, but it was precisely as Dad had said.

I'll never forget the night he sat in wonder and exclaimed, "You're a much better skater than I!"

Learn to Relax

Whether you are frustrated and stressed or just thinking about home teaching, hang on for a moment. Hang on to the rail we provide you here, and home school support groups which wait to hold your hand. Have you already tried day after miserable day and month after endless month and found yourself staggering? You are trying to walk on ice when you should be gliding! Hang on! There is no need to stumble or plod.

For the beginning parent, home teaching is like learning to ice skate after you have been walking for fifteen or twenty or thirty years. Most home teachers have more to unlearn than to learn. This is particularly true of *certified* teachers, most of whom have been taught to teach via mass production. We know; we trained them! They know little about informal tutoring and many fear the responsibility of teaching their own where there aren't other teachers around to share the blame if anything goes wrong.

Unfortunately many home school curriculum entrepreneur-opportunists know even less. They wreak damage with their conventional classroom "packages," which superimpose classroom techniques on a tutorial program — like insisting that Rolls Royce craftsmen adopt Yugo technology. Parents and children quickly burn out from several hours of dull routine a day with little opportunity for exploration and working out their own creative ideas. This will make more sense once you have seen others' successes and mistakes. Have a little faith!

Don't be concerned about the amount of education you have so much as your attitude toward your children. Almost all highly successful home teachers (who stay with it) eventually move from a *plodding formality* into an *informal glide*. This doesn't mean that they throw all structure and caution to the winds, but that they become encouraging resource people rather than rigid pedagogues. If you have a fairly decent *basic* education, and a warm, responsive heart, you *can* be a good teacher at home!

Most home teachers start out about the same. At first, you are comfortable only in the old ways, the ways you were taught. Unless you are a maverick, you find it hard to imagine any other way. You know how to walk, but have little understanding of how to glide until you see someone else doing it, or have them tell you how they did it. Then you see the fun and success it can be. Unless you overcome the grip of habit, tradition, and convention, you will only bring the institutional school into your home. Such a *school at home* is hardly *home schooling* in the easiest and best sense. Many parents buy school-type curricula and sit down to plod through textbooks and workbooks with their children in simulated classrooms six hours or more a day. One despairing mother told us with open palms that she couldn't "get around to everything in *twelve* hours!" So burnouts sear their children, too.

Peer dependency? If you are an average adult, you are so peer dependent that you're scared sick to stand out from the crowd— your relatives, neighbors, school, and church friends. And Failure's grisly head makes your fears horrific! You are too secure on the floor to take a chance on the ice. Anything but standard practice scares you, unless you see how easily Susie is doing it down the street or realize you're destroying your children's love for learning.

Or you may already be teaching at home, but are at an impasse with your youngsters. Then you may discover (1) how easy it is, (2) what fun it is to glide instead of plod, to have fun as a master teacher of your own children, and (3) how foolish it is to drop conventional baggage on your home as so many curriculum publishers and state departments of education propose today.

We hope you will take a hard look with us at "orthodox" education and see for yourself that there is a better way. It is an enjoyable way to build character and curtail behavior problems while bringing out the best in your children.

A Case Study

To get you started, we'll tell you a recent real-life story of Christine, a Colorado housewife. Our records tell us that Christine's daughter, Jessica, was seven and her son, Jordan, was five. After three years of conventional school Jessica was doing well academically, but not emotionally. Christine withdrew her and started doing "school at home," fondly and excitedly expecting "a smooth continuum of learning." But she "found that's not the way it happens." She describes Jessica's two-month turn-around and the effect it had on her little brother and the family:

I find I have had to modify my expectations weekly, at least! Jessica is extremely resistant to any work that is "assigned" to her. And yet, she will work for hours at projects of her own design. Seeing this, I realized I had two choices: either "crack down" and make her play-time contingent on completing her school work, or simply "go limp." Since communication with Jessica has been a painful deficiency, I chose last week to bow out altogether—I made *no* assignments, or even suggestions, about school work. I presented nothing and required nothing. The results have been astonishing!

Last week she conceptualized and built from scrap a lovely "snack bar" called "the Pilot's Crew." Her father helped with the large construction, but she sanded it and painted it by herself. She has been open for three days, selling cookies after school, and has made eight dollars *after* expenses. It has been a joy to see—she took one idea (from another home schooler we know) and has followed through happily and energetically. The project has incorporated much math, art, carpentry, baking, health considerations, marketing and sales, planning and organizing— the list goes on and on.

In addition, she has, in quiet moments, chosen various lessons to do on her own, improved her relationship with her brother by 100 percent, discovered a half dozen new friends, and is overall exhibiting a cheerful confidence that we've not seen on a regular basis for over a year. As I write this, she is playing school with Jordan, having already cleaned her room before coming downstairs! He is now making progress in behavior, too!

This dramatic improvement only highlights the gradual ones we have been seeing all along. Jessica's nightmares and stomach-aches have all but disappeared. We rarely hear whining or tantrums—and then only when she is *very* tired. She is vastly improved in negotiating skills and self-confidence. Although she is still reluctant to pour out her heart to me, she has begun to speak briefly about her feelings and fears to us and a trusted adult friend. All her somatic [body] symptoms are gone!

Now that I am beginning to get over *my* performance anxieties, I can see as I write this how far she has come in a very short time. I am profoundly grateful for this opportunity to begin again with my children.

Customized Curriculum

Christine's story doesn't suggest that you throw caution to the winds and let your children have their own way in all things, but that you avoid teacher-centered programs in which children are often treated as slaves to traditional schedules and textbooks. Your curriculum should be tailored to *your* child and provide him much more time to pursue *his* interests than *your* workbooks. For many parents a good curriculum provides feelings of security. But parents need to learn how children develop and learn. Spend more of your mental effort on studying and exploiting your children's motivation instead of always confronting them with books.

Notice the unexpected results when Christine dropped the formality and began to relax: (1) Jessica's creativity began to bloom. (2) Her father became involved. (3) Her behavior improved as her creativity became productive. (4) Her brother began to share her enthusiasm. (5) She discovered new friends, yet took charge instead of being so subject to peer influences. (6) Her somatic problems subsided — tiredness, stomachaches, nightmares, even whining and tantrums. (7) She dropped her guard and began to confide. (8) At age eight, she became an independent "businesswoman," making, selling, and earning — a neat way to learn arithmetic, stewardship, and human relations.

All children are different from all others, yet principles don't change. We remind you that we don't suggest you wipe out all assignments or have *no* formal work. When children are developmentally ready, they should spend enough quality time to master their basics. Most parents use a few textbooks for reading, writing, spelling, and arithmetic and also for subjects such as art, music, advanced math, and some of the sciences. We encourage you to use proven, largely self-teaching "efficiency" courses such as Basic Math-It, Winston Grammar, and the

Moore-McGuffey Readers which provide excellent results without exhausting you.[1] Basic Math-It has a readiness course called Pre-Math-It for familiarization with numbers, and a follow-up Advanced Math-It course which includes percentage and basic algebra and geometry. But Basic Math-It is the crucial program if you want your child to be the fastest figurer in town. Winston Grammar is a fun way to make your child love grammar instead of hating it, as most do. The *Moore-McGuffey Readers* are the only complete readers in color and cloth which carry the 1836, 1838, and 1843 stories which do not offend groups today. We substituted later McGuffey stories for those which said that Indians are savages or that God doesn't love little children who are naughty or that tend to glorify the killing of whales. And once a child learns them, he can save *you* stress by teaching your other children.

Some of these courses can be exciting, assuming that teacher and student follow directions carefully, and that the child meets the Math-It readiness test. For example, Mark Rosenquist, then thirteen, came to our seminar in Cincinnati and told us he had completed Math-It. So we invited him to the podium and wrote seven three-digit numbers on the blackboard, called out from the audience while his back was turned. He added the column in nineteen seconds, well ahead of a math professor in the third row who used a hand calculator. In Sacramento, when a contractor-candidate came to be examined for his license, the clerk warned him that without a hand calculator, he would fail. He said he would try, and was the first one through with nearly a perfect paper. He had taken Math-It! When a Math-It-trained, second-grade home schooler visited a conventional fourth grade, he was embarrassed because the students applauded him for being "faster than us."

More Ideas for Shaping Your Children

There is much more to home-based education than a tailored curriculum. Besides teaching the basics, you need to build character in your children. We present here more ideas to help you succeed. We'll cover these areas in greater depth throughout the book.

- Seldom, if ever, begin *formal* study before age eight to ten.
- Yet read and respond to your children from their earliest years.

- Rely more on discussion at all levels: warm responses and project (i.e., unit or block) learning more than structured formal work, although there will be drill during the skill-learning years with mastery of basic skills as your goal. Live and have fun with your children as they learn. Be sure materials are effective, simple to teach.

- Consider getting master teacher counsel.[2] Experience suggests that such counsel helps most parents get over the humps in the first year or two.

- Share family management; make your children regular officers in a family industry or corporation — making and selling goods and services; utilize this experience in math and science.

- Involve them in service, letting them understand that they learn to serve *first at home* without pay (unless it is out of the ordinary), and *then others* — the needy, ill, poor, aged.

- Share your fellowship and sound example all day.

- Be selective about materials you choose or workshops you attend. Are they genuinely proven, professional, and worthy educationally? Are the materials as good as they are expensive? Are conclusions based on research?

- Have fun and effective learning on field trips.

- Perhaps you should consider reducing their reading of myths and fairy tales; the Apostle Paul said to teach what is true, honest, noble, and pure.[3] True epics and allegories tend more to stir positive change than reading matter which is not true.

We have systematically laid down such principles, methods, and resources in other books based on nearly forty-five years of home teaching, twenty years of intensive research and experimentation, and thousands of years of historical examples, over three centuries of them in America.[4] We do offer you more than opinions here! We set the stage for the play and counterplay between the family and the state in establishing your educational "homestead." The thoroughly researched facts, state-of-the-art responses, and carefully selected story examples we give you will probably answer most of your questions as any blue book like this should.

Although Christine's early experience was the most common route to burnout, there are many causes such as fears of the law, certification demands, achievement testing, behavior, family health, organization, sociability, pressures from lecturers and publishers, and successes and failures of other home teachers. When you have finished this book you should be able, with few possible exceptions, to say convincingly to yourself, "Of course I can do it!" and go on to do it very well. Seldom can any "outside" teacher match parents in teaching their own children, particularly when those mothers and dads teach them as friends.

THREE

HOME SCHOOLING'S FIFTH COLUMN

BACKDROP: One of Germany's most feared devices during World War II was the fifth column. Where normally the army marched in four columns, there was the invisible column of local helpers for the enemy — citizens of the invaded country who could be depended upon to help the invaders while pretending to be loyal to their own government. They also became known as "Quislings," after the notorious Norwegian traitor. Yet not all were *deliberately* traitorous. Many thought they were loyal heroes and heroines for truth when in fact they were being used by forces which would take away their freedoms, then destroy them.

As a group, home educators boast the strongest families that we know. Many are so intrepid that heaven will certainly mark them for its Medal of Honor. So it will come as a shock to some to learn that they have been used by some forces within the home education movement that appear to be bent more on personal gain than strengthening families. Others, poorly informed, may be as dangerous. *If you are a tender spirit who disdains the dark side of a book, skip this chapter. This is one of our "caution" pieces.*

In our federally sponsored research that led to our public advocacy of home education nearly twenty years ago, we were naively unprepared for the problems we were to face — dangers that still harass parents and teachers today. We saved carefully and planned retirement outside of an institutional setting that would give us freedom to try to change American schools in a small way.

What audacity, you say, to think that our research might clean up some of America's educational litter! And you're right! Yet, the last thing on our minds was sharing in a home teaching trend that would become America's largest educational movement. After investing years of time and millions of dollars in the movement and seeing what home teaching could do, we became determined to do our best to insure that home teaching never be used wrongly. How little we understood! At first we feared public officials most. Yet we soon found that although a few were genuinely opponents and many were skeptical, there was much more understanding among rank and file public educators than some home educators like to think; many have been genuinely friendly, some even home teaching their own. We still share an ominous parent fear — the joint venturing of school officials and social workers who threaten to take children from their families. Yet that has happened only a few times to our knowledge among home educators over the last twenty years. Now that our leaders and lawyers are experienced, much of the former panic has subsided.

Creating more stress, we believe, is a column that works among us as the fifth column did throughout Europe during World War II. Christians, who constitute the largest segment of home schoolers, are also the most vulnerable. Often naive, gullible, and totally trusting of their "brethren," they are sure prey to a variety of ill-informed entrepreneurs.

Others of these "enemies" are actually unselfish, but poorly informed people who think they are performing a great service. We have listened to some who make emotional appeals for family unity in the name of Christ, yet the losses we have traced suggest that these people are more responsible for burnouts than are public officials. Claiming sound experience in home education, *they have just enough learning to make them dangerous.*

Christians aren't alone here. We face five or more negative, destructive forces: curriculum rushers, anti-staters, zealots without wisdom, bandwagoners, and pretenders.

Curriculum Rushers

Betty and Frank (not their real names) are conscientious parents of three, ages three, seven, and ten. They've been less than happy with peer words and manners their seven-year-old Eric is bringing home from school. His teacher suggests the possibility of something called "special education" for his "attention deficit," and possibly Ritalin because he is "antsy." Betty has become increasingly disturbed at behavior she hasn't seen in her son before: bed-wetting, nightmares, and appetite loss.

Her ten-year-old Mimi, on the other hand, has been doing well in her studies, but seems to be withdrawing more and more from family conversations and association with her neighbor friends. Often she curls up silently on the living room carpet or Betty finds her upstairs in a fetal position on her bed.

About this time the Sunday newspaper begins an attractive series on home teaching. Then Monday, Betty sees a sparkling home school family on the evening news. Like a new car owner who sees cars like his everywhere, she now notices conservative magazine ads that have actually been running for months. An especially promising one describes a home education package "which any parent can teach" and for a price that just can't be turned down.

Betty is hooked. She jerks her youngsters out of school so fast that even she is surprised. She picks up a couple of old used desks down at a second-hand store, and is in business before you can say "I pledge allegiance."

Soon reality begins to show its ugly face. Although Mimi reads at high school level, she is frustrated with the math package that imprisons her at fifth grade. The curriculum people assumed she was in about fifth grade in everything. After all, she passed fourth grade at the local public school, didn't she? But in the village school she never got past third-grade math.

Eric is bored with workbooks. His hands prefer bread dough. He creates great things in his sand pile, but he's not ready to read! The three-year-old? Well, Nels has chicken pox.

Betty assumes from the way she was taught that she must mimic the six-hour program of the local public school. And perfectionist that she is, she must do a little extra. What if she were to fail? So she grimly hangs on for dear life, attempting a juggling act that would stun a circus clown.

She somehow clings until she is almost a physical and nervous wreck, and then the day of reckoning comes—the annual achievement tests. If she had chosen a competent curriculum tailored to her child, which included personal master teacher guidance when she needed it, she would have nothing to fear. Hasn't she read about those great records home teachers are making across America and Canada, and in Europe, Africa, Central and South America, the South Pacific, and in the Orient? Small comfort to a beginner! Late that afternoon our home teacher goes to bed exhausted, instructing Mimi to "have supper ready at six, before Daddy gets home." At least Betty accomplished something: She had a daughter who could prepare a balanced and nutritious meal! Yet even this was little comfort. She was burned out, the victim of hurry-up-and-wait: Hurry up the process and wait for her doom.

"I don't like to remind you, Betty, but I told you so," Frank needled her gently that night, laying a cold wash cloth across her fevered brow.

"I know. I know."

Betty's mistakes? Carelessness in jumping onto unfamiliar ground: ordering the first program she saw, without examining its validity for her family and its requirements for formal teaching of slowly developing Eric before he was ready.

Fortunately, before all was lost, Betty and Frank got in touch with local home school leaders and with specialists who had some understanding of curricula and the developmental needs of children. Yet thousands like them simply give up. They hardly become good salespeople for home education!

Anti-Staters

Although there are some who actively preach "Hate the state," their number appears to be waning as more parents and home school organizations win in courts and legislatures. They are astonished at how much integrity and common sense most legislators have despite pressures of vested groups such as publishers and teacher unions. Yet there are parents who see the state as their enemy instead of a servant to help and protect them and over whom, as responsible citizens, they may have more control. These parents need to learn that quietness and confidence often produce better results.

Last week we received contrasting calls from Massachusetts and New Jersey, an attorney and a housewife. The attorney quickly saw the Golden Rule sense of not jumping on his state if the problem could be solved in a more tactful and permanent way. The other was from "Lynn," a New Jersey mother complaining that she was due in court through no fault of her own.

I was curious, for once I had interceded in a similar case. Judge Isaacs of New Jersey was a straight-thinking jurist who listened carefully and questioned me closely, then threw the case out of court. His decision also had a salutary effect on New Jersey policy which is currently among the best in the United States.

How, I wondered, could we be in trouble now?

Although not bitter, Lynn placed all the blame on the school district when she was partly at fault. She told me she was a Christian with no obligation to the state. While expressing as much sympathy as I conscientiously could, I reminded her of Christ's admonition to render unto Caesar that which is Caesar's and unto God that which is God's.[1]

I further advised her that top constitutional lawyers insist that states *do* have a "compelling interest" in assuring that children have reasonable understanding in three areas: (1) basic skills (reading, writing, math, spelling, etc.) so they can earn a living, (2) health and safety, and (3) American citizenship.

She was adamant, even though she had delayed giving the state notice of her home school curriculum until after the reporting deadline had expired. She also argued that the local principal had lied to the court in preparing the state's case; and the evidence did point in that direction. Yet she could have done more to ensure that her skirts were clean in all respects—avoiding all carelessness and all indifference to the law. Fortunately, we again had a New Jersey judge with common sense and a heart for parents who cared enough to teach their own. He dismissed her with a warning to be prompt next time. Some of these cases don't end so sweetly.

Zealots Without Wisdom

A few workshop and seminar speakers or authors are making every effort to revive an old myth which says that since children "grow faster" in their first months and years, we should rush them into formal reading. Nothing will burn out parents or children faster than trying to teach an unready child. It is like trying to make him shovel sand or snow with an untempered tin-foil shovel.

Among the more radical proponents of this view are those who suggest rushing little children into formal reading so that they can read their Bibles sooner and become Christians faster. These speakers and authors pitifully ignore developmental principles which they have apparently not gone to much trouble to explore, yet which are at least as unchangeable as the Rock of Gibraltar. And ambitious parents drink it in without questioning a word, even paying substantial sums for this nonsense. This may sound harsh, yet the damage which these self-acclaimed specialists are perpetrating demands more than a gentle nudge.

Most critics don't dare say these things publicly. As those who are largely held responsible for the movement, we *must*. Since we take no money from this business, our only vested interest is children. So we offer our research and counsel to all, and we're glad that some curriculum purveyors and workshop speakers have consulted with us. Since most families assemble their own materials in terms of their own philosophies and goals, we feel we can better serve them by assisting them rather than by obligating them to any one program or curriculum. Extraordinary success with minimal friction, and fun without frustration is the usual result.[2]

You'll pay if you ignore the maturity levels at which children naturally integrate their vision, hearing, taste, touch, smell, physical coordination, brain development, and reasoning ability. Children's abilities mature at widely different rates. Some read well at five, yet for most children, integration of maturity levels (IML) does not come before ages eight to twelve. For children who go early to school, adult-type reasoning ability usually comes much later, for many not until ages fifteen to twenty.

Many of the proponents of early learning often also misinterpret children's learning *speed*. They're right when they say little children learn fast. But if what they make of this weren't so tragic, it would be a joke—like a chamber of commerce executive who brags that Hometown is the fastest growing in the state: It grew at the rate of 1000 percent in one year, from a population of two to twenty!

These individuals miss the *big* point: A young child, of course, learns very fast. In his first day of life he learns at least ten times as much as he knew when he came out of the birth canal, which was one thing only: He came into a big, noisy world. In quick succession he learned about his mother's warm caresses and how to drink her milk, and about bath oil and diapers and cribs. Yet never again will he learn at his birth learning rate, percentage-wise! As his *number of experiences* increase, his *learning percentage rate* declines — just as Hometown's growth rate dropped from 1000 percent to 100 percent the next year when its population had about the same increase, this time from twenty to forty residents.

When your child has a few thousand learning experiences under his little belt at ages ten or twelve, he learns faster than ever. As you give him time to grow naturally, to develop thousands of "learning hooks" — bits of information — under your sure and loving guidance, and to *explore freely*, encouraged and informed by your *warm parental responsiveness*, he will hang many more new learnings than those who are formally rushed. He will be much happier and more creative. Children are not little buckets to fill up, but little trees to grow. Give them a chance with all the love and patience your heart can muster.

Those Bandwagoners

Many writers, lecturers, and curriculum publishers offer excellent programs, materials, and counsel. Yet some, in their inexperience, are destroying home education. And these include some of the most prominent in the business. Some think formal teaching must dominate. Some sell "organizers" that stress mothers out just trying to keep records. Some talk about home industries as if it is not good for fathers to have work out of the home. Some seem preoccupied with money and influence. They fear or ignore simple, responsive, free, balanced home teaching which virtually never burns out!

Some promoters don't know better; others do, but find it more expedient and saleable to advertise curricula that teach as most parents were taught, bad as that may be. We don't see how opportunistic workshop speakers and profiteering publishers are any less guilty of misusing children than are those school officials and social workers they so often accuse.

The very day we wrote this we received a call from Penny Fox, a top leader in West Virginia, asking for help in a court case. The parents chose a curriculum from a school in another state with a large clientele. It promised the parents protection "under its umbrella," but apparently offered no help to this beleaguered mom and dad. This curriculum accommodates early school entry and is highly formal — one of the most certain routes to parent and child burnout.

We made a serious mistake a number of years ago. We were given to understand by this school, and others, that they were in harmony with our findings. So we gave them wide publicity in our books. Before long, perceptive parents asked why we gave names of curricula that did not measure up to the standards we had outlined in those very books. They taught us a lesson, a dear one.

We suggest that other leaders learn from our mistake: Check out carefully all who want to exhibit at your seminars. It is tempting to skip this step, for you make money on each table you rent. While some exhibitors will be very good, there will almost invariably be some who are unprofessional and unreliable. It is like putting several drops of cyanide into a jug of apple juice. The juice is sweet, but the cyanide is deadly! This happened to us once at a seminar six years ago, so now we accept only exhibits for which we accept responsibility.

The Pretenders

The pretenders proclaim themselves authorities or claim expertise in their brochures or books, yet offer unprofessional counsel and materials based more on assumption than on careful investigation.

At least two curriculum producers claim to protect members from the state. With one, the state is hardly a threat; in the other the "protection" offered is doubtful, yet clients pay the price of a curriculum — much more than membership in the Home School Legal Defense Association.

The pretenders somehow know that by acting authoritatively they will be accepted by many as authorities, and many gullible parents will go along. But seldom, if ever, do they help in courts or legislatures. They offer ideas and for a moment may inspire, but seldom do they provide *substantive* help to make life easier for those who teach at home. We have intensively researched home education for nearly twenty years and reported in the nation's top professional journals. We have practiced what we preach for over forty years. Yet we do not pretend to offer across-the-board evaluations such as offered with alacrity by some excited freshman home school authors.

Intolerance

And finally in this chapter, one of our most dangerous of burnout traps is bigotry, that stubborn and complete intolerance of any creed, belief, or opinion that differs from one's own.

While some of us sweated for years to develop legislative unity among all creeds and wrote laws that protected parents' rights, other writers and speakers touted home schooling as an *organic* Christian movement and set out to divide home teachers in a self-serving effort that ruined effective coalitions.

These inexperienced and misguided writers and speakers— *none of whom helped in legislatures and courts*—have preached their divisive gospel to earnest, but naive Christians. Although a conciliation effort put the divisiveness substantially to rest, there remain serious groups who view anyone other than their religious or philosophical persuasion as an untouchable. There is neither love nor Christianity in such bigotry—which must be forever buried in the interest of understanding and unity if home schooling is to reach its highest and least stressful potential.

The best expression we have heard of this ideal, except for the Golden Rule itself, is the little four-line trinket which, though only a thimbleful of verse, somehow holds eternity:

> He drew a circle that shut me out—
> Heretic, rebel, a thing to flout.
> But love and I had the wit to win:
> We drew a circle that took him in!
> —Edwin Markham, "Out With It."

Learn to identify those in the fifth column. Keep your distance instead of blindly supporting them. And pray for their change!

Christianity in such bigotry—which much be forever buried in the interest of understanding and unity if home schooling is to reach its highest and least stressful potential.

The best expression we have heard of this ideal, except for the Golden Rule itself, is the little four-line trinket which, though only a thimbleful of verse, somehow holds eternity:

> He drew a circle that shut me out—
> Heretic, rebel, a thing to flout.
> But love and I had the wit to win:
> We drew a circle that took him in!
> —Edwin Markham, "Out With It."

Learn to identify those in the fifth column. Keep your distance instead of blindly supporting them. And pray for their change!

GETTING OFF
THE TROLLEY

BACKDROP: Often our own egos, influenced by others around us, tend to make us believe that somehow, if we can just endure, we'll come out all right. Such presumption, combined with our own peer dependency—the compulsion to do a thing the way everyone else around us seems to be doing it—is an effective blinder, and binder of our creative ideas. Tradition, good as it is in many ways, can also be a road block to great learning. Conventional wisdom and practice in any society, unless unselfish and wise, build the surest freeways to its doom.

Did you ever go to a party where you were supposed to recite your favorite poem? You anticipated it breathlessly for weeks, and rehearsed it with all your most dramatic gestures until you knew it backwards and forwards and upside-down. You were dressed in your go-to-meeting best, with shoes shined better than new. Then just before your turn arrived, the cutest girl in town stepped up to the platform and presented an award-winning performance of—you guessed it—your very own poem! And you half tiptoed and half ran out of the auditorium in tears, never to be quite the same public performer again. It is just such a latent fear that we will be upstaged or embarrassed by ridicule or questions from relatives or colleagues that keeps most of us from stepping out in creative ways. Some call it ego. And men have no corner on it. Irv Janis called it "groupthink" and described how President Kennedy's White House think-tank made monumental errors because they were afraid to challenge the President's thinking or that of one of his favorite aides.[1] From such White House thinking came the Bay of Pigs and Vietnam catastrophes.

It is well known among psychologists—and statesmen— that one of the most precarious tasks in the world is to alter conventional wisdom and practice. It is safer to allow a Brahmin bull in a New Delhi china store than to introduce a new idea into tradition-bound heads, especially if there is a vested interest or ego to protect.

Professors and publishers are no different from other people. In some cases they have even more egotism or vulnerable power structure to justify and protect. So educators are sometimes even slower than laymen to respond to sound ethics and common sense. In states where we have defended parents in court, we usually find legislators more ready for change than many public and church educators.

If we think there is only one poem we can learn, and if someone does it better, it is easy to fear that all heaven will be lost. If we are comfortable with one way of doing things, we fear almost anything different. So we ride along on our conventional trolley, thinking others' thoughts after them, afraid to get off at a different station and explore for a while.

Guided Freedom

I was like that. Although teachers considered me creative enough to be troublesome, I only toyed with the questions of why and how people like Thomas Edison and George Washington Carver developed such marvelous talents with apparently such limited backgrounds and so few immediate school resources. I was too conventional to realize that they had the greatest of all assets: They had loving adults who understood their needs and with appropriate guidance gave them freedom to explore.

Young Tom was dunced out of school into the warm, responsive climate of his home. His teacher called him "addled," an old-time word that rested roughly between "retarded" and "crazy." Never mind that his mother was not highly educated; she knew how to love and spent a lot of time giving her "bemuddled" son a foundation for genius. She encouraged him to explore! Although her son never did learn to spell very well, she loved him and had unlimited confidence in him. And he justified her faith. Soon he was running paper routes, selling snacks on the trains, and, before long, employing other youngsters to help him. The more he

got around, the more his curiosity abounded. He was a classic il-
lustration of one of the best kept secrets in Western education:
*Students who work with their hands develop common sense and practical
skills and do much better with their heads*. Like handles of a wheelbar-
row, he accomplishes much more by using the two together than
by using one alone.

Young George W. Carver worked, too. Like his namesake,
he was taught by a loving family at home. When he was about
twelve he went to school, but not the year round. Although
black, he was in no sense a slave. Yet, like George Washington
and Benjamin Franklin and Abraham Lincoln, he did his share
of the chores. He was encouraged to have bugs and plants and
books all over the house.

Little mention is made today of George Washington's big
brothers who were sent to England to grammar school; nor is
much heard of George Washington Carver's contemporaries.
But the two home-taught Georges are authentic American
heroes on the lips of kids of all colors and creeds. Why not
emulate them? Why not teach our children work as well as
sports? Most of us are too busy to consider anything new, especially when it may place us at risk with conventional practice or
the law. I was one of those. Busy variously as a public school
superintendent, university professor, college dean, president,
and federal educational officer in Washington, D.C., I thought
little of the unnatural nature of our schools until my reading-
specialist wife asked some hard questions: why little boys and
girls were forced into school at the same ages, even though boys
develop later than girls; and why almost all of her slow learners
were very young. Politics being what it is, I saw the hopelessness
of the government's efforts to answer those questions.

It was in 1933 at age seventeen that I was first asked to teach —
a college remedial English course. I was astonished! As a college
freshman the year before I apparently had done well, mostly because of my ninth-grade-educated father. It was no big thing.
They simply needed someone of lesser maturity than a professor,
who was simple enough to help freshmen who were struggling
with grammar. It was the sound old idea of cross-age teaching —
using the older to teach the younger and the stronger to help
the weaker.

For fifty-five years since that time I have been learning-conscious, watching mystified as the free learners develop expressive originality while many pipeline learners have that potential stagnated. For over thirty of those years I didn't fully understand, even though Dorothy and I instinctively practiced "guided freedom" over forty years ago with our children.

Recouping the Past

So today when parents ask me, "Where were you twenty years ago?" or "Why haven't you told us before?" I bow my head and apologize. And other professors are doing it with me. One of America's most distinguished educators, Dr. Sam B. Peavey, who is professor emeritus of the University of Louisville School of Education, wrote this recently to a newspaper editor in his native state of North Dakota:

> I have had a long career as a public school teacher, administrator, and university professor of education. A major part of my work has dealt with the education of teachers and the evaluation of schools. In recent years my university assignment has provided extensive opportunities to observe and evaluate the newer Christian schools and home schools.

> I can testify that as a whole they are providing a sound and usually superior education for children. It is unfortunate that the general public has a very limited and often negative view of what these dedicated parents are doing for their children at great sacrifice and expense. In an era when homes and families face tragic deterioration, the home school evidences those values that once held homes and families together.

> The public school will continue to serve the majority of parents and children. However, there is a mounting need to understand and respect the widespread search for alternative forms of educational programs throughout the nation. A sheltered and defensive monopoly in the hands of a powerful coalition of professional educators and politicians acts to stifle educational freedom and initiative. *I have been an active member of that coalition over many years.*

> Let's hope that the legislature and the people of North Dakota are now ready . . . to allow all parents the educational and re-

ligious freedom enjoyed by the citizens of almost all states today. The Supreme Court has stated clearly and forcefully, "The primary role of parents in the upbringing of their children is now established beyond debate as an enduring American tradition."[2]

I must admit having had many second thoughts as we have carried the banner for delayed school entrance and home schooling over the past forty years. The most consistently hostile opponents in our early days were our colleagues in Christian schools who feared that we might somehow destroy enrollments. Sadly, in some cases enrollments were more important to them than their children's welfare. Indeed, we were vulnerable to such accusations, for some of them did lose students to home schools. They wouldn't listen to our suggestions, however, on how to cope with these apparent losses. Eventually, many discovered that if they would "mother" home school families by providing counsel, testing, and specialized courses, they could *multiply* enrollments and substantially increase cash income.

Some of us are now becoming bold in the certainty that something must be done or our Western society will not long survive, so we have set out to make up for lost time. Are our days of genius gone? We act like it, but perish the thought! They are yet with us in America and in any other culture or nation. But we must open our minds, retrieve the true picture from research, learn from our forebears, and give a little of ourselves.

We know there are many more Alexander Graham Bells in Canada, more Winston Churchills in England, more Konrad Adenauers in Germany, more Ninomiya Sontokus in Japan, and more Thomas Edisons, George Washington Carvers, and Douglas MacArthurs in America if we will only let them spend more of their time growing naturally as *their* parents did—at home. Although it has taken a long time, some of us have come to realize that it's time to be more serious about placing the needs of children ahead of our egos, enrollment concerns, fears of criticism, and even sometimes the risk of financial loss.

PART TWO

PREVENTION AND REMEDY: HOW CAN WE PREVENT BURNOUT?

WHY ARE TRUE HOME SCHOOLERS SO BAL-ANCED AND BRIGHT?

BACKDROP: Does research mean anything to you? Carefully done, conclusive studies which stand the test of history and common sense? Take a look at the famed eight-year study. Does shoving the books at your kids make them bright? Or do they do better when you confront them less and give them a chance to use their own initiative and creativity? Why do you teach the way you do? Is it because you were taught that way? Or because your children learn better? Are you willing to take a chance on an old-fashioned method? Consider a few examples of how successful parents are doing it and why. In this chapter we will give you an overview, and in Parts 4 and 5, the personal experiences of some of America's most successful home teachers.

Fifty years ago, in one of the most remarkable studies ever made, Carnegie, the Progressive Education Association and others spent $4 million to find which children learned more, those who were taught by teachers or those who were left to develop and learn for themselves. This Eight-Year Study reported findings many educators prefer to ignore.[1]

Researchers compared fifteen hundred children who were taught in conventional elementary school classrooms with fifteen hundred who learned in very flexible situations or who were not taught at all—where adults were available only to answer questions or help the children find materials or information. The children were paired by age, sex, social background, aptitude test scores, vocational interests, etc. They were followed through high school and college for over eight years.

The results astounded the researchers and study sponsors. On every variable, on every parameter, including their grades in high school and college, academic honors, leadership capacity, and even attitude on the job, the children from the flexible classes outperformed those in the conventional pressured class-rooms. But the children who were not formally taught at all had the highest scores of all in all areas measured.

Because of our long experience in schools and colleges, we have been convinced of the validity of this research. Yet now, as we see creative parents applying the principles and methods of this research with great success, we are witnesses to a beautiful and unusual drama which overwhelmingly illustrates the possi-bilities for average parents. Sometimes those parents, who them-selves are products of formal schooling, trudge through trial and error when they can't quite get past their conventional back-grounds, but when they do, they have great success!

Success Stories

Many home schoolers have demonstrated that the recipe of the Eight-Year Study can produce talented children. Home-taught Jeff Larsen of Booneville, Mississippi, in 1986 had the highest GED score in his state.[2] Said eighteen-year-old Jeff, "I attribute a lot of my doing well . . . to the home environment my parents worked to create for me." He described that environ-ment as "relaxed" with lots of "independent study." He and his sister, Angie, studied textbooks and other books. Yet, "We pur-sued our natural interests," Jeff observed. "When we had ques-tions, we went to our parents for help." When the Larsens visited us, we learned that in 1987 Angie scored 30 points higher than Jeff did the year before!

Home schooler Dale Holmes of Saginaw, Michigan, dropped out of school at age twelve. He then began to teach himself for the most part, adding to the basic subjects he had learned in school. In 1987, at age nineteen, he graduated from the local state college with highest honors in his class—a 3.91 average out of a possible 4.0.[3] Three years ahead of the average student his age, he began a three-year doctoral fellowship the next year at Syracuse University.

Dale's formula: "People will work incredibly hard on things they are interested in. It was my problem what became of me." Scoffing at suggestions that he was exceptionally bright, he added, "I was left alone to do what I wanted to do." He does not suggest that his parents gave him license to go wild, but warmly responded to his questions and gave him freedom to explore.

In Atlantic, Iowa, fourteen-year-old home schooler Heidi Roland wanted to enter the State spelling bee, but had to have the local superintendent's permission. He granted it on the condition that she would give Schuler Junior High credit if she won. Heidi won, and, although the schoolmen did not share her enthusiasm, her public school friends were her most enthusiastic supporters. The high average performances of home-schooled children measured against the national norms suggests that Heidi is not unusual. Home taught Jed Purdy won the 1988 *state* spelling bee in West Virginia.

In a local home school support group in Madison, Wisconsin, we found three boys, ages thirteen, twelve, and eleven, enrolled part-time in the University of Wisconsin taking courses in aeronautics, chemistry, and biological sciences: Shane Alme, David Purvis, and Andrew Groth. They were, in order, sons of a cement finisher, a youth worker, and a pastor. Andrew's brother, Peter, age seven, excels him in math and in entrepreneurship.

Does Parents' Education Affect Performance

The educational level of the parents does not seem to make much difference in the performance of their students, assuming of course that they can read, write, count, and speak clearly. I found that court-accepted standardized achievement test scores of home-schooled children whose parents were arrested or arraigned for teaching averaged 80.1 percent.[4] Nearly all parents were from lower socioeconomic levels and well below educational levels of average home educating parents, for seldom do school officials or social service personnel confront middle-to-upper socioeconomic classes who school at home.

The history of home education suggests that it is not necessary for children to be tutored by parents who are scientists, artists, politicians, writers, or other professionals in order to become bright in those fields. For example, as far as we know, George Washington, Abraham Lincoln, Thomas Edison, and Grandma Moses were not so endowed. And in the 1930s Harold Skeels found that retarded orphan teenagers transformed orphan infants into bright, normal children by responding often and warmly to them.[5]

And it seems to make little difference in the 1980s: Neither David nor Micki Colfax of Boonville, California are physical scientists, and both of them deny any special interest or ability in math. Yet their oldest son, Grant, recently graduated from Harvard with high honors in the biological sciences, and their second son, Drew, is a junior there in physics and their third son, a Harvard sophomore in math, received full scholarships.

"Nor," said Mrs. Colfax, "do we consider them especially gifted." Dr. Colfax, a sociologist, added that Grant didn't begin reading until he was nine and a half. "Yet," notes Mrs. Colfax, "he was reading fluently before he was ten." If California school officials had insisted on early achievement testing at age seven or eight, the boy would likely have been in special education.

From still another learning perspective, two younger Colfax sons, Reed and Garth, both adopted and schooled in the same free-wheeling combination of "good books and practical experience," may be showing even greater promise, says Dave Colfax. At age sixteen Reed taught himself college-level calculus and analytical geometry. And Garth has a remarkable artistic talent.

All concerned believe that the reason for this success is warm, educationally responsive parenting along with the positive influence of brothers Grant and Drew, and a work-study balance that provides great freedom of exploration.

"What is your secret? How do you get all your boys to study?" some of us asked the Colfaxes.

"We live on a working ranch, and it is a real pleasure," she grinned, "for them to come into the house and read."

In Escondido, California, two boys from different families recently began reading at age ten and a half and were reading up to grade in a few weeks. Such stories challenge the wisdom of those states who demand early testing for children, many of whom are relegated to special education (or what the kids call "the garbage pile") for any of a variety of problems, when in fact the problem is usually a lack of readiness. If we waited a few years we could save millions of children from frustration and failure.[6]

Common Characteristic

Many new findings are being reported by more than 150 masters and doctoral researchers whom the new Moore Foundation is helping to probe home education.[7] A consensus of the studies suggests that (1) home-educated children are highly competent socially, seldom age-segregated, and generally respectful of their parents; (2) the children study a full range of conventional and enrichment subject matter; (3) the average annual family income is around $25,000; (4) most parents have some college education; (5) most have definite philosophical or religious convictions and high moral values, although home school rationales reach far beyond religious views to include family integrity, desire for children to excel, and examples of successful neighbors and friends; (6) there are nearly three children per family; (7) curricula vary widely from extremely flexible programs to quite formal teaching; (8) materials vary widely; and (9) children taught with a great deal of warm parental responsiveness and comaraderie in study, work, and service develop an adult level of reasonability five to eight years sooner than conventionally schooled students.

Recognizing Proven Results

These results of family responsiveness in developing cognition are astonishingly consistent with Smithsonian research and a number of recent studies.[8] This may also be a reason for the mathematical superiority of many home-schooled children.[9] Dr. Hassler Whitney of Princeton's Institute for Advanced Study, notes School Superintendent L. P. Benezet's 1929-1930 experiments in connection with Columbia University in which he found if math is delayed — even as late as the seventh grade when children are more mature in their reasoning — they will learn much faster and easier and will outdistance others.[10]

The excellence of the home as an educational nest enjoys the support of leading psychologists and researchers who once advocated early schooling. Says Chicago's Benjamin Bloom, once a powerful proponent of Head Start, "There is no question in my mind that a mother who is really interested in her child teaches that child so much more than the child could learn with a group of twenty or thirty other children."[11]

When *Education Week*'s interviewer suggested that this may be so "if the mother is home," Bloom wasn't deterred by the specter of the working mother: "I am only trying to say that what we have done is to take the child away from almost a tutoring pro-gram — the mother — and the mother is enormously more suc-cessful than a group program. There is no way you can avoid that." It might be observed here that in many home schooling families these days, fathers are happily joining the teaching staff.

Yet many parents turn their youngsters at an early age over to schools and to peer dependency. The mass education methods restrict exploration more than encourage it. Thus schools share accountability for declines in learning and behavior obvious to all, and for decaying literacy levels: No more than half of Ameri-can adults have the ability to handle a bank account or make out a job application without help.[12]

The price for bright, well-adjusted children is within the range of nearly all: warm parent responses, high family values, and a lot of opportunity to explore. To ignore children and to limit their creativity is a great loss!

SIX

WHEN ARE THEY READY FOR FORMAL LEARNING?

BACKDROP: If there is any story which reflects a generation's sense of balance and wisdom, it's the way it treats its children.

If there is any explicit demonstration of ignorance, it is when parents give their children something to do without handing them tools. "Go out and hoe the garden," you shout, but the handle is broken and you are too busy to fix it. "Tie your shoes!" you tell your four-year old, but his little fingers are unready, unsure. "Read those letters," you insist, yet his immature eyes see an upside-down blur. When we send our very young children off to school, are we perhaps demonstrating that same ignorance?

Replicable research on readiness of young children for learning and for institutional life out of the home is comprehensive and conclusive academically, behaviorally, and socially in warning parents not to rush their children into *formal* learning before eight to ten or (say some of the world's most experienced research psychologists) age twelve. We have done one of the world's most extensive research analyses on school readiness in a fruitless search for some justification, *any* justification for sending *normal* children away to kindergarten or school at four or five or six or seven. We've found absolutely none!

In *Acres of Diamonds*, Russell Conwell's most famous Chatauqua story, Al Hafed sold his farm to finance his quest for a legendary diamond mine. He searched the world over until his fortune was gone and he died hungry and penniless. Then one day came the news that a vast diamond deposit had been discovered in the river sands which snaked through his own backyard, now the famed Golconda Diamond Mines. America's quest for excellence—for healthy, self-directed students—very well could have the same ending.

A Wisconsin family offered us an explicit example of a child's readiness for learning. Their daughter, age five, was given a bicycle, yet had no interest in riding, even with training wheels. Over a year the bike was a frame for her "tent." When nearly seven she decided to ride, took off the "silly" training wheels, declined her mother's offer to "push" her, and rode blithely away.

Results of Early Formal Schooling

From the White House to the humblest home, Americans are groping for answers to declines in literacy, ethics, and general behavior. Yet they seem to be trying everything *except* what history, research, and common sense suggest, even for the most common and easily understood problems. For example, a surprising ignorance or indifference exists in terms of peer dependency, a mental health nemesis that is rampant even in preschools.[1]

Yet, instead of studying how best to meet our children's needs, we simply do what everyone else seems to be doing, and often put our little ones out of their homes, *their homes*, and away from environments that best produce outgoing, healthy, happy, creative children. Hewitt researchers concluded from their federally sponsored studies that America is placing its little children in formal settings long before most of them, particularly boys, are ready. The effect on their mental and emotional health is devastating. Dropout rates also are mute testimony to the problem.

From Piagetian specialist David Elkind in Boston to William Rohwer in Berkeley, California, top learning and development authorities warn that early formal schooling is burning out our children.[2] Teachers who attempt to cope with these youngsters are also burning out. The learning tools of the average child who enrolls today between the ages of four and six or seven are neither tempered nor sharp enough for the structured academic tasks that increasingly are thrown at them. Worse still, we create *negative* sociability.

The sequence for the average child these days often spells disaster for both mental and physical health: (1) *uncertainty* as the child leaves the family nest early for a less secure environment; (2) *puzzlement* at the new pressures and restrictions of the classroom; (3) *frustration* because unready learning tools — senses, cognition, brain hemispheres, coordination — cannot handle the regimentation of formal lessons and the pressures they bring; (4) *hyperactivity* growing out of nerves and jitter, from frustration; (5) *failure* which quite naturally flows from the four experiences above; and (6) *delinquency* which is failure's twin, for the same reason.

Indifference to the mental and emotional health of children is not new. The pages of history outline great cycles that began with vigorous cultures awakening to the needs of children and ending with surrender of family ties and the death of societies and empires as children were rushed into formal learning *either at home or in an institution.* This is a tragedy now happening, and startlingly is even endorsed by some in the name of religion!

Research provides a link from past to present and provides a moving perspective on children today. Persuasive reasons exist for (1) declining literacy, (2) academic failures, (3) widespread delinquency, and (4) rampant peer dependency which combine to bring us ill-mannered, badly-behaved, drug-and-sex-oriented youngsters who are often disrespectful and sometimes violent. All four reasons act in concert to deny our goal of happy, confident children who are healthy in body, mind, and spirit. Whether or not we can be conclusive about causes, America's decline in literacy from the estimated 80 percent to 90 percent in the last century to the 50 percent of today parallels the parental scramble to put children in institutional settings at ever younger ages.

Delaying Formal Instruction

Our research analyses concluded that, where possible, children should be withheld from formal schooling until at least ages eight to ten.[3] Elkind warned against student burnout which has become pervasive in our schools. Rohwer agreed, basing his conclusions in part on investigations in twelve countries by Sweden's Torsten Husen.[4] Husen subsequently confirmed Rohwer's perceptions in a letter we received from him November 23, 1972. Rohwer, with deep concern for conceptual demands of reading and arithmetic, offers an answer:

All of the learning necessary for success in high school can be accomplished in only two or three years of formal skill study. Delaying mandatory instruction in the basic skills until the junior high school years could mean academic success for millions of school children who are doomed to failure under the traditional school system.[5] This solution would delay school entrance at least until the child is eleven or twelve, ages which become critical.

In face of present practice, how can these remarks be justified, bearing in mind that the present and future health of the child is at stake? First, children normally are not mature enough for formal school programs until their senses, coordination, neurological development, and cognition are ready. Piagetian experiments have shown repeatedly that cognitive maturity may not come until close to age twelve. Interestingly, the ancient Orthodox Jews, known over the world for their brilliance, provided little or no formal schooling until after age twelve for girls and thirteen for boys when children were considered able to accept full responsibility for their actions.

When Dr. J. T. Fisher, later "dean" of American psychiatrists, started school at thirteen, unable to read or write, and graduated from a Boston high school at sixteen, he thought he was a genius until he found that any "normal" child could do the same. He added, "If a child could be assured of a wholesome home life and proper physical development, this might provide the answer to . . . a shortage of qualified teachers."[6]

Nearly a century ago, John Dewey called for school entry at age eight or later.[7] *Seventy-five years ago*, Arnold Gesell counseled parents to take their children out on the hilltops and in the valleys and let them be taught by a singing bird and an insect humming on a leaf, instead of textbooks.[8] *Twenty-five years ago*, Marcelle Geber demonstrated that mothers in the African bush brought up children who were more socially and mentally alert than youngsters of the elite who could afford preschool.[9] Warmth was the key. Still later, Mermelstein and Shulman proved that, at least until ages nine or ten, children who went to school did no better than those who did not attend school.[10] Daphne De Rebello reported that in India dropouts who find employment are ahead of their peers in mental and social perception.[11]

The only conceivable negative aspect of delayed school entrance we have found involved parents who delayed entrance into conventional schools *in first grade*, then, when their children were older, made them begin at first grade instead of allowing them to skip grades.

Problems with Formal Instruction

Few conventional educators understand this situation—the damage of frustration, the denial of free exploration, the value of warmth as a learning motivator, or the tutorial method which historically never has been equaled as an efficient teaching device. A UCLA study of 1,016 public schools found that teachers averaged a total of about seven minutes daily, all day, in personal exchanges with their students. This would allow for no more than one or two personal responses for each student. In contrast, our counts of daily responses in typical home schools ranged from more than fifty to nearly three hundred.[12]

We feel sad as we see parents crippling along and burning out instead of having fun and getting great results teaching their own. Educators *talk about* individual differences, but often pay little attention to them in practice. They don't appreciate that some children read at age three while others with a different profile but just as bright, don't read until ten.

Dr. Robert Moon, one of our co-authors and former assistant director for the Council of Exceptional Children, makes a two-pronged comment here: "Parents who (1) rush their little children into formal schooling and/or (2) wrongly school them at home, border on child abuse. Instead of using common sense, they let the process become an extension of their own ego. They're so sure they're right. Their children are virtually in prison for twenty-four hours a day. They simply won't give them enough freedom to let them blossom. If children were not so beautifully malleable and did not naturally bond so much better with their parents than at school, they wouldn't survive."

Don't Rush Your Children

Parental ego can be dangerous. As little tykes face flash cards almost from birth, they are cut off from truly happy, creative, and noble lives. And they nearly always suffer—neuroses, ill health, social loss, or delinquency. We recently received a letter from Rick, a young man who visited us fifteen years or so ago. He was having early teen problems at the time, yet his folks had little idea of his needs. He was obviously bright, so they did what most ambitious parents do: They rushed him into school. Now he was suffering for it. I lost track of him until a few weeks ago when his mother wrote that he was in a Tennessee jail for murder. He reportedly had killed a man while under the influence of liquor and drugs. His mother asked if I would write him. Rick responded promptly and lucidly to my letter:

> I've been reading some of your material you sent; I've found it fascinating. I recall being labeled hyperactive; I also recall being given drugs (Ritalin) to "help me concentrate." I don't know that it helped me. . . . I do think that it gave me a taste for popping pills. I still neglected my assignments and read an entire set of encyclopedias as I found them more interesting.

Such is the early history of many delinquents today. School failure leads to bad behavior. Any kind of pill carries dangerous potential for drugs, simply from the habit of "popping" them.

We reemphasize: *The best early "academics" are your responses to your children*—giving yourself to them in warm fellowship, conversation, travel; reading and telling stories with moral values; working at home chores and cottage industries together; teaching them by example how to serve others (in the home and down the street); being alert to their highest motives and interests; and encouraging them to develop their own creative ideas in the sand pile, with kitchen dough, with a telescope, in a diary, and with tools in the garage or garden.

The idea that parents should hurry reading, spelling, writing, or math ahead of children's normal development is not supported by a single replicable research study in the world or by any clinical experience in history. All history, research, and common sense points in the opposite direction! We repeat: Any who push the three R's early, deny the readiness factors the Creator built in—reasonably mature vision, hearing, taste, touch, smell, reason, brain growth, coordination—as clearly documented in our books *Better Late Than Early* and *School Can Wait*.

One day I was startled while visiting Burton White, the noted authority on children's first three years. He had written, to my surprise, a supportive guest editorial on my cover article in the *Phi Delta Kappan.* [13] We were discussing childhood studies and research analyses I had directed under federal grants when he said, "The only thing I don't agree with in your reports is your data on the young child's vision." He referred to our findings that young eyes are not ready for formal tasks until at least eight to ten. I insisted that we had more evidence on that than on anything else.

"I know," he replied with a twinkle, "but children's eyes were not made to read at all." And when he saw my quizzical look, he added, "They were made to enjoy everything around them!"

Nevertheless, we seem willing to rush our little ones into schools though we wouldn't think of sending our pets to the cages of a kennel for any length of time. *America is not the only nation pushing its children. From Japan to Sweden, the rush is on.* In France's famed "mothering school" system, we found little tots as young as two and a half, sometimes with more than sixty children in the care of a teacher and custodial aide. Even in pristine Switzerland we found unready tots in school. Such rushing may be to you something to brag about, but it is only a matter of time until you will have something to cry about.

SEVEN

HOW CAN THEY POSSIBLY BE SOCIALIZED?

BACKDROP: In recent years, since most alert educators have found that children taught some or entirely in the home average much higher in achievement, they have been compelled to find another bone to pick. It was quite a task, but most of the critics finally settled on *socialization.* And they have been busy picking the old bone, blanched and white, almost to the marrow. Yet if they are honest and still listening and reading, they eventually discover, usually to their surprise, that the socialization picture in the home is even more dramatic and consistently encouraging than achievement. And the evidence from both research and history, is powerful.

Dr. Robert Moon tells of a tiny four-year-old black boy in Benton Harbor, Michigan, who was so malnourished that he looked the picture of death. He seemed hard of hearing and oblivious to all attempts to reach him. Yet on the third attempt, he was found to have normal hearing.

While carrying on a community development project in the city, Moon asked an eighteen-year-old female volunteer to take the little boy for an hour or two each day.

"Take all precautions to see that his needs are safely met," he instructed, underscoring the word *safely.* Then he added the key direction: "Don't give any attention to anyone else while you are with him, not even a glance or a word! He is to have your total devotion for that hour or two each day."

Three months later when the volunteer came to visit his care center, Moon noted a dramatic change. The little tyke ran to the young woman as soon as she appeared in the doorway. "That's my teacher. That's my teacher," he murmured as he grabbed her legs tightly and snuggled his head in her skirt.

After a total of six months, Moon reports, the little boy was approaching normal behavior. Whenever the volunteer would arrive, the child would shout in the classroom, "That's my teacher."

Yet how sad that his love object was temporary! His greatest need and that of all children is a significant relationship with one or more adults, especially his parents or grandparents or other family members, if possible and if those persons are supportive examples. The common assumption these days is that to be well-socialized children require the association schools afford. Replicable evidence clearly points the other way.

Two Texas teenagers are poignant examples. Both have been taught at home about five years. While a bit shy, Amy has generally gotten along well with her peers. Melissa, also a bit shy, didn't get along with anybody until she was taken out of school and her creativity allowed to flower. Today, at fifteen, both of them make an excellent living by baking, babysitting, house cleaning, and sewing. Last summer Amy was voted best camper by leaders of a four hundred member girls camp. Melissa was voted best camper by the teenage campers themselves.

Peer Dependence

Dr. Urie Bronfenbrenner and his Cornell teams found that children who spend more elective time with their peers than with their parents until the fifth or sixth grades — about ages eleven or twelve — will become peer dependent.[1] Such knuckling under to peer values incurs four losses crucial to sound mental health and positive sociability. These losses, stated in lay terms, are self-worth, optimism, respect for parents, and trust in peers.

From their earliest years children learn manners, habits, language patterns, and actions by observing and then imitating. Yet they do not clearly establish these values until around ages ten to twelve. Your consistent example provides the best model, but in its absence children mimic their peers — even at the preschool level.[2] Young children demand Nike shoes or Jordache jeans because all the kids have them. In another school it might be Reeboks and Lees.

Instead of learning strong family values where possible, children knuckle under to peer pressures which range from clothes, language, music, and food and on to grosser things. Remember! They adopt these values as readily as the measles or any other contagious disease. This is why Dr. Bronfenbrenner calls it "social contagion."

Do you think it wise to give your child as good a chance in life as you would a cherished pet? Take dogs, for example, for at our house we know them best: How would you socialize or obedience-train your precious pup, whether pedigreed or not? You know, of course, that two dogs may be friends, but three make a pack. And a pack is usually up to no good purpose. So how would you feel if local laws required that you bring your pup to the bus stop each day to join other dogs in a yellow cage that wheels down the road to the kennel or pound for socializing exercises? You know for sure that association with the pack is the fastest way to destroy any obedience training *you* have planned. Yet that is the very thing we do daily to our children, only with imponderable risks.

Does anyone who knows children believe that the yellow school bus takes children down the road to a constructive, positive sense of society? Or returns them in the afternoon or evening more loving creatures than when they left in the morning? This happens only when the home is worse than the school! There is absolutely no evidence to support the prevailing assumption by parents and educators that the average school is more of a positive socializing agency than a good home—certainly not an altruistic one. And there is powerful evidence that we are schooling our youngsters today to be young narcissists. The ultimate result is recorded in the daily papers—failure, delinquency, asociability, drugs, sex, and often even violence. Values are being destroyed.

Every child needs an adult or adults to whom he can consistently relate over the long term of his development, who models the right values and who cares enough about him to guide him by precept and example into adopting these values. A paid daycare person is here today and gone tomorrow. A teacher may not understand what a child's family *should* mean to him. It is wise to understand this principle *before* your daughter comes home pregnant or you learn that your son is on drugs.

And the separation into age groups which our schools largely assure today is a desocializing phenomenon that few educators consider. Begin talking about friends of their brothers or sisters in the fifth or sixth grade or their parents' buddies, and children will give you short shrift. They are so peer dependent and narcissistic that they are actually *negatively* socialized.

Contrast this picture with the average home-taught teen or preteen youngster at a church or community activity, and you will find quite a different reaction. One of the many joyous outcomes of home education is that your children will likely get along well with people of all ages. When occasionally they are ridiculed by other children, they usually take it in stride. The fact that they have long felt needed, wanted, and depended upon has given them a sense of personal competence. They subconsciously cherish this desirable independence, and it translates into *positive*, outgoing, altruistic sociability. At almost any gathering of home-educating families, you will quickly note the curiosity of home schoolers about adult conversation. You will also usually observe older youngsters caring for the younger. Such behavior is seldom found in meetings of families whose children are conventionally schooled.

This exciting, exquisite quality is lost among most youth today. They have little use for younger children or adults. They run only with their agemates; they get along only with their peers. But even that is not a genuinely happy sociability. They are willing to give in to peer values in order to get peer recognition. They are imprisoned in social straitjackets. This is not a private domain of the disadvantaged; among the most obvious are children of the idle rich who are more interested in their professions, clubs, or another dollar than they are in building a heritage for their offspring. They amuse them instead of working them, serve instead of being served, indulge instead of loving, and ignore instead of sharing. Their behavior will, of course, precisely reflect their parents' examples.

Since youngsters these days commonly begin school six or eight years before their values have jelled, it is of little wonder that Bronfenbrenner blames these "socially disruptive develop-ments" on the schools. Yet he does not leave the parent without indictment. He vows that "the peer-oriented child is more a prod-uct of parental disregard than of attractiveness of the peer group!"

The loss to boys is of particular concern academically, be-haviorally, and socially. It is well-established and generally assumed that boys trail girls about a year in overall maturity at five or six, two years at twelve, and three years at twenty-one. Despite their widely-acknowledged delay in maturity, we de-mand their enrollment in school at the same ages as girls. Among the most ominous are findings in American high schools that there are eight boys for each girl in classes for the emotion-ally impaired, and thirteen boys for each girl in remedial learn-ing groups.[3] Self-worth, male identity, and respect for women are lost — unfortunate outcomes, especially in today's society.

Self-Concept

Parents who work with their children, sharing the manage-ment of the home and making them actual officers in the family corporation or industry — making and/or selling anything from pink lemonade to cookies, muffins, or wooden toys (which pref-erably *they* have made) or providing services such as lawn mow-ing, paper routes, or baby-sitting — have little trouble of this or-der. When they combine this work with community service they come to feel even more needed, wanted, and depended upon and develop a very certain self-respect which has little relation to the typical "me-first" ego orientation of today's youth. We believe this combination of study, work, and service is the simplest, easiest, and most enjoyable route to great families.

Notice that we say children who feel needed, wanted, and depended upon at home are those who develop self-confidence or self-worth. We don't say "self-esteem." In a modern I'm-okay-you're-okay context, self-esteem is often equated with self-confidence and self-respect. We think this may be a trap. It may lead us to think in terms of egotism, inappropriate pride, and immediate satisfaction with ourselves rather than to strive for intrinsic self-respect or worth and self-confidence.

The power of the home as a positive socializing agency is dem-onstrated by the recent national sampling by J. W. Taylor V.[4]

He found that (1) 77.7 percent of all home-tutored children rank in the top quartile on the *Piers-Harris Children's Self-Concept Scale*, with more than half of all home schoolers placing in the top ten percent; (2) the longer they are taught at home, the higher their self-concept; and (3) the child's self-concept is unrelated to the parents' educational levels.

This study comes at a time when scholars across the nation are finding, quite uniformly, a serious self-concept decline in conventionally schooled children. This in turn may be another reason for increased peer dependency with all the social contagion it brings in its train.

A Common Sense Solution

It might help to offer here some proven and practical answers for both achievement and socialization. Our goal is to get your thinking going on an even broader base, for there are neat and enjoyable solutions to building sound self-concepts in our children, and in ourselves.

First, we need more parent education and less conventional schooling of young children. *Second*, in the home school renaissance, many thousands of parents have discovered their need to know how their children grow and learn. Their study has resulted in higher-achieving, better-behaving, self-directed children.

Some demur, pointing to Head Start as demonstrating need for out-of-home care. Yet the Ypsilanti study, the only long-range experiment consistently upholding Head Start, involves the home far more than typical programs. Even such key Head Start founders as Bloom and Nimnicht now laud the home as the best learning nest and parents as the best teachers.[5]

In physical health and behavior—in exposure to disease and to negative-aggressive acts—the home is fifteen times as safe as the average daycare center.[6] Even the directors of the Ypsilanti study admit it isn't a cure-all for normal children, and will help those children most who are helped most in the home rather than the commonly conceived storefront Head Start operation.[7]

Here are well-proven ways to improve the mental and emotional health of our children:

1. More of loving and consistent parents, and less of formal school — at home *or* in the conventional school setting;

2. More free exploration with the guidance of warm, responsive parents and fewer limits of classrooms and books;

3. More concern about readiness for learning and ability to think and less training to be simple repeaters;

4. More and higher priorities to child-rearing and fewer to material wants;

5. More old-fashioned chores and family industries — children working with parents — and fewer rivalry sports and amusements;

6. More genuine humor in your daily affairs. We do not mean jesting and joking; these do not build. But pleasant ways to solve family dilemmas. In our home when we were working to save on our utility bills, someone would occasionally call out, "Who left the light on in the bathroom?" If there was any doubt, the answer was always predictable: "It was Schmitty." Blaming it on this imaginary character saved hundreds of confrontations, yet was always a gentle reminder to all of us to be a bit more careful next time; and

7. More down-to-earth socializing with your children, not only at picnics and games to which you sometimes invite their special friends and *their* families, but also in the home.

For some parents, this issue of socialization is at the head of their decision to home school. It was for Tim and Terry Mohr who wrote to us about their daughter:[8]

It was Melissa's numbness with the institutional school that drove us to alternatives. A year behind in math by fifth grade was bad enough in our family, but much worse was the cruel and vicious verbal harassment by classmates. So we decided on home schooling. The next year she easily made up her math, but her self-concept was our big worry. Often depressed, cranky, and even withdrawn, we had more than a little concern.

But being with her family more than her peers has brought a dramatic change. She has become self-confident, is stable, and is in demand throughout our neighborhood for her skills in child care . . . and assisting neighborhood mothers with household tasks. . . . Lest anyone doubt the carry-over into community life with her peers, four hundred girl campers voted her "Most Outstanding Camper" at youth camp a year ago. Her experience has made a joke out of the hackneyed question, "But what about their socialization?"

EIGHT

THINKING: IF YOU WANT TO HURRY IT, WAIT!

BACKDROP: We have trouble with teaching methods and materials which seem designed to insure that our children will do as little thinking as possible. "Dumbed down" readers with "scientifically limited" word lists dominate the educational field. Too many teachers accommodate this idea of science by asking only *whats, whens, wheres,* and *how muches.* Not enough are asking *why?* and *how?*

We are missing a very big bet, speaking in gamblers' terms. But this is no gamble. We are throwing away a sure thing when we crowd young children's minds with educational litter and pedagogical garbage before they are ready, instead of giving them time and freedom to think, explore, and create for themselves. Let's put away the pedagogical pabulum and give them something to chew on! Here are some ideas of *how* that might happen and *why.* If you still really want to hurry their thinking, just wait!

Before you decide if you want to go the hurry-up route, consider what you seek in the long run. Is it the temporary approval of your neighbors and friends? Or is it long-term achievement and stability that will one day give you and your children great satisfaction (and perhaps make your neighbors wish they had done the same)? It is a matter of being far-sighted—willing to sacrifice present pleasures for future benefits. If you want bright and balanced children, *you must help them be thinkers, not mere reflectors of others' thoughts.*

David Quine, until recently a counselor in the Richardson, Texas, public schools has joined two University of Oklahoma professors in studying cognitive maturity in children — the ability to think things through maturely and consistently.[1] They find that children schooled at home or delaying school entry develop this ability from five to eight years earlier than conventionally schooled children. This confirms and updates what world cognition authority Jean Piaget made clear to some of us at Geneva many years ago. When he once was asked if the child's brain can be speeded up, Piaget suggested that was an "American question." He added, "It probably can but probably should not be speeded up."[2]

Yet Quine has found, as we have long held, that no matter how earnestly you counsel home teaching parents to go easy on their children, to respond to them warmly and give them a lot of opportunity to explore, most parents "take school and implant it in the home." He adds, "Then later, as they become more comfortable, they begin doing things *with* their children" (instead of *at* them).

Understanding a Child's Cognitive Ability

Quine tells how in a 1974 study, Professor Jack Renner of the University of Oklahoma applied Piagetian tasks to thirty-three randomly selected sixth graders about equally divided from two public schools in the same system. Twenty-nine of the thirty-three were twelve years old, and four were thirteen. Yet only six of the thirty-three (18 percent) successfully demonstrated that they were close to adult-level "formal" reasoning or cognition.

Piaget estimated that the average child moves into this level of cognition between ages fifteen and twenty.[3] Yet recent studies of *home-taught children only eight to ten years old*, found that eight out of ninteen (42 percent) were successful. Piaget repeatedly told students his concern that the age at which children reach formal, or adult-level, reasoning is becoming delayed.

This inability to think, to solve problems, is affected by (1) "soft" textbooks and workbooks which require only short answers with analyses, are dumbed down in vocabulary, and don't require children to grapple with *why* and *how* issues; and (2) by equally "soft" television which is designed to amuse more than to challenge a child's brain.[4]

Often parent enthusiasts ask, "But how about Japan—where they school so young?" Educators are coming more and more to the conclusion that Japan also suffers seriously, and often disastrously, from this pressure syndrome with young children; they are finding that as a nation they do not generally produce creative adults.[5] Some of us who lived for years in the post-World War II era of Japan, and have witnessed this pressure building for many years, are particularly aware of how anxiety, frustration, and frequent failure breed for that nation the highest child suicide rate in the world, down even to age four.

The parent who understands children will know (1) why they sometimes do some strange things, and (2) that when parents *understand* how children develop, *they in turn breed patience that will keep them from burning out their young.* How does this work?

When I was around eight or nine, Mother gave me the privilege of making and baking a cake. What a treat! I carefully assembled all the ingredients, laid the recipe thoughtfully out of the way, (because Mother's recipe cards were always neat as a pin), and began measuring. First the flour; it had to be sifted two or three times if my chocolate cake was to be light enough to be a great surprise for Dad's birthday. He was a connoisseur! Then came the baking powder, salt, and other dry ingredients, which I poured into the sifter which was now nearly filled with studiously sifted pastry flour.

Next came the eggs and the liquids. I carefully broke the eggs into the sifter, careful not to drop any eggshells, and quite skillfully poured in the buttermilk. Didn't the recipe say to "add eggs and buttermilk"?

When I was well into my final "sifting," Mother happened by. I was struggling with a mess in that sifter that soon had her yelling with laughter. Then she understandingly explained. What was my problem? My ability to reason from cause to effect, otherwise known as cognition, was yet immature. I hadn't asked myself what would be the effect if I added liquid to dry ingredients in a utensil which was designed to process only fine dry foods. I didn't realize that some knowledge was assumed in the recipe. In fact I simply wasn't thoughtful. In those few moments

I learned from my mother one of the most important lessons of my life, one which relates more to people than to flour and sugar and chocolate.

We recently received a cute story (which you'll understand has special meaning to me) from Meg Bartlett whose son Kristofer is nine, the oldest of three children. Meg decided wisely that giving her boy something constructive to do was the best preventive medicine for avoiding the disease of rebellion, so she set him to baking, using a brownie mix for his first adventure.

"You must follow the recipe exactly," Meg instructed.

Kristofer assured her that all was under control, and the "sound of kitchen clatter" was music to her ears as she turned to other chores, delighted and self-satisfied that her heir was "budding" as a responsible young man.

After a little while, however, all was too silent for any good purpose. About the moment Meg began to panic, Kristofer's voice broke the silence.

"Mom, I think you had better come here." There was no shouting or calling, but the phrasing was ominous.

"Why?" she inquired as deliberately as any scared mom could.

"Just come here," was the courteous if troubled reply.

As Meg walked into the kitchen, there stood Kristofer with a look of bewilderment on his face, the bowl of brownie batter cradled in his left arm, and suspended over the bowl, his right hand hung—COVERED—with brownie batter.

As calmly as she "could muster" Meg asked, "What are you doing?" She didn't even stress the *are* or the *doing*. "Just like you said, Mom. I'm following the directions, but it just isn't working right. . . . Look here, it says . . . beat by hand 'til smooth and shiny." So kids are still kids in the 1980s!

Yet another account of how and when and to what extent children develop cognitive readiness was Dorothy's experience with our grandson Brent, then three. She had spread a slice of bread with peanut butter and cut it into four pieces so that his little hands could grasp them easily. When he picked up one piece to eat it, he took it almost all in one bite.

"Brent," Dorothy carefully and clearly admonished him, "your bites are too big. Please eat each piece in four bites."

The little fellow adores his grandma and wanted to please her, so he picked up the next piece gently, and with his eyes rolled up to her, proceeded to stuff it into his undersized mouth.

So grandma patiently reminded him again with her nodding forehead as well as her words.

"Why didn't you eat that piece in four bites, as I told you?" She looked down on that winsome but clownish little mug.

"I don't know how to make four bites," he replied, looking quizzically up at her.

And indeed he didn't. The concept of even small numbers was still beyond him. He simply was not capable of granting her request. *He wasn't ready.*

The strong and stable bridge here, like those at the Golden Gate and in Brooklyn, New York, cannot be built in a day. At home *and* at school, children need the warm, patient response by parents and other adults—rather than pressure for early formal learning—which takes into consideration the materials at hand and how well the learning tools are tempered.

When parents warmly respond a lot with their children from their earliest years, reasoning more and more maturely with them as they grow in cognitive ability, they develop thinkers. A simple way to do this is to use *whys* and *hows* frequently in your conversation, and encourage them to do the same. Most of today's education is based on short, non-thinking repetition: *whats*, *wheres*, and *whens*.

The Principle Approach

Several curriculum publishers, to our delight, make a good use of what they call "The Principle Approach." This is a sacred idea at the Moore Foundation. With some publishers this is presented in the context of American government and social studies. We support their worthwhile efforts. Yet we would like to go on a bit further, for we learned this in college and it has been a deep concern of ours for over fifty years.

First we must ask, What *is* a principle? The answer is crucial to your and your childrens' quality of thought. A principle is always a foundation for thinking in any area of discussion—in philosophy, nature, religious or political doctrine, or scientific constituents such as in chemistry. A short definition is "the basic reason why" or "the basic why." For example, *love is a principle*, not an emotion or an embrace or a kiss or a sexual act, although it may be expressed through those acts. Love (not to be confused with lust and its selfish meanings) is *the basic selfless reason for those acts.*

You may apply such principles to all aspects of life. One example is stewardship. In some churches and synagogues this is all wrapped up in the word *tithe* or 10 percent which the people return in the offering plate before all other offerings. Yet that is not principled thinking at all. True stewardship recognizes the ownership of another—employer, church, family, government, shopkeeper, or God. And at its highest principled level, stewardship means bringing the highest returns possible. This is how the founders of J. C. Penney stores and of the Colgate Company eventually returned tithes of more than 90 percent!

Sound education at school or in the home is principled in everything. Any knowledge or use of that knowledge which is not based on principle is not absolute in truth.

The *principle* approach should be the *standard* approach for everything. Think about it, use it, and live it in the broadest, richest sense in your daily responses and in your encouragement (and where necessary, guidance) as your children freely explore.

But one caution here: In their early years children are more instinctive than reason-*able*. With all respect to their humanness, they are less like reasoning beings when they are born than like little animals. A little chicken out of the egg *six minutes* is more ready to forage for itself than your child is at *six years*!

Yet, while animals and fowl grow rapidly in instincts and very little in reasoning ability, children grow cognitively—in reason-ability, all the time refining their instincts, also. Yet they will be dominated by reason, not instincts. They will never need the relative level of instincts on which the average animal or fowl depends, for they have a higher tool called "reason." They gradually will understand whys and hows, but will not usually be deep into them before seven or eight, as Quine notes, and often not until much later, especially if they have to go through the force-feeding process of most conventional schooling.

Unfortunately many teachers in conventional schools are so pressured with records, behavior problems, forced curricula, regimentation, mass production techniques, and educational litter that they allow no freedom for children to create from their own imaginations.[6] If the pressured child ever turns out well-balanced and happy, he is the exception that proves the rule. And the Creator quite obviously suggests, as any psychologist should know, that *by their very developmental nature* you should let your children grow naturally close by your side.

DO YOU WANT
SUPER BABES
OR SUPER CHILDREN?

BACKDROP: Among the most commonly used "cures" many years ago were mercury, strychnine, and bleeding. They may or may not have demonstrated some merit. But by any sound medical standard, in most medical cases today they are dangerous. Even more dangerous in this modern age is the yuppie obsession with developing genius-by-flash-card. It makes no sense from any point of view and is much less likely to bring genius than is blood-letting likely to reduce a fever or cure the flu. No worthwhile research supports it one iota. Yet many of these young parents are willing to sacrifice their children on the altar of ego. And sooner or later mothers and dads tire—burn *themselves* out in the process. How can we avoid these results, or find a cure?

Our frantic obsession with "preparing for Harvard" at age four is not a new idea! Yet this uneducated idea prevails in the hearts of most fond mothers and dads in one form or another. Their hopes for genius jump out in their zeal to overteach their little lambs in a covert obedience course only to have it backfire more often than not.

Creating Early Burnouts
Frank Edwards tells the story of Harvard psychology professor Boris Sidis who at the turn of the century became captivated with the idea of making superbabies.[1] Sidis could make himself a famous man, the captain of his own ship. His first exhibit would be his infant son, William. Daily he hung letters and

figures over the baby's crib and called out their names. Sure enough, by six or eight months the tiny boy could recognize some of them. By age two he could read high school books, at four he was writing articles in French and English, and by five he was writing about anatomy. But by the time he turned eight, William developed a hysterical giggle when placed under stress, giving more the impression of idiocy than brilliance. At fourteen, Will's father insisted on his first Harvard lecture where the boy received resounding applause, only to turn from the podium with hysterical and uncontrollable giggles. At the sanitarium to which he was quickly dispatched by an embarrassed father, he told newsmen he wished only to live like a normal person. He called a halt to his father's experiment, but when he finished at Harvard and joined the faculty of Texas' elite Rice Institute, he found he couldn't get along with others.

While trying to establish himself with his peers and students at the Institute, he was convicted of inciting a riot and given a suspended sentence. He vanished and was later discovered clerking in a common store. Accepting an invitation at the urging of a friend to speak on the probability of life on Mars, his mind without judgment led him instead through an hour's lecture on street car transfers. America was too busy with war in 1944 to notice when William Sidis died at forty-six in a Brookline, Massachusetts, boarding house, unwilling to have anything to do with his father, even to accept his substantial inheritance.

Superbaby *group* efforts have resulted in similar catastrophes. Thirty years ago a notable program was initiated in elite and affluent Grosse Point, Michigan, a city known for its high ratio of brilliant executives. The program was sparked by the Sputnik hysteria in 1957, when the first Russian satellite panicked America, afraid of losing scientific leadership.

Public school Pupil Personnel Director Paul Mawhinney tried responding to Sputnik's urgent calls for better, faster learning by experimenting with early enrollment of children, from age four.[2] He and fellow psychologists expected to produce well-adjusted youngsters who would be more aggressive learners and excel Russia's children. Parents were bitter if their offspring were rejected.

Yet after only four or five years of the projected fourteen-year experiment, Dr. Mawhinney's committee of psychologists became disenchanted. About a third of the early entrants turned out to be poorly adjusted; nearly three out of four were found to be entirely lacking in leadership, and only one child in twenty was judged to be an outstanding leader—far below normal performances. And the school dropout rate skyrocketed.

The staff declared not only that the experiment was a failure, but also that for many children it was a very personal experience in failure, destroying self-worth. They concluded that if the youngsters had been allowed to develop normally, they likely would have been outstanding. Yet parents were so consumed with the superbabe gospel that it took school officials nine more years for the staff to wind down the experiment!

In every study we could find over a fifteen-year period which compares early and later school entrants, not one gave the nod to early formal schooling.[3] And more than eight thousand related studies which we analyzed in our literature reviews pointed in the same specific direction.

During the 1987 annual conference of the National Association for the Education of Young Children (NAEYC), a panel concluded that "parents trying to rear 'superbabies' may be creating a generation of early burn-outs."[4] NAEYC President David Elkind observed that "twenty years ago, people thought that precocity was bad. . . . the feeling was 'early ripe, early rot.'. . . Now the motto is 'early ripe, early rich.'" He decried the markets filled with an increasing number of books and programs urging pregnant women to talk or sing to their unborn babies.

Dr. George Sterne, chairman of the American Academy of Pediatrics' Committee on Early Childhood, Adoption and Dependent Care, added that the trend is most noticeable among the yuppies who use books, flash cards, and music lessons "to try and get them [children] on the fast track. They're tired . . . irritable . . . have bellyaches. . . . It's obvious they're on overload." He suggested normal living: "They don't need high-tech curricula to do this."[5]

Child's Play?

When a leading concert artist and university professor asked what I thought about Suzuki music lessons for his children, I told him of the specific research in this area, particularly in violin which was his interest. I gently warned that while early violin may work sometimes, it seldom brings children much musically. Parents who pursue these exercises often find that their little ones eventually become tired or nervous under the stress. They often want to change to another instrument, anything to find relief.

Some parents try to kid themselves and their young ones by calling it "play." But formal music lessons are not child's play no matter what they are called. They are often expensive both in money and nervous energy. Natcha Sonnenberg, a young woman considered by many to be today's foremost female violinist, and by some to be the greatest of all, started early. But her parents soon found from her behavior that this was not wise and waited another five years or so until she was close to her teens when she quickly picked up a violin and became its master.

A few years after asking my counsel, my professor friend confessed that my prediction had come true. He experimented with Suzuki lessons on both his son and daughter, but neither of them "took to the violin." His son eventually did well at piano, but his lovely daughter did not do much with any musical instrument.

One evening when we were sitting with this artist at a concert by an internationally known New England string ensemble and chorus, the audience gave a standing ovation to a thirteen-year-old cello soloist who had been saved for the finale. All of us were entranced by the brilliance of his tones and the speed with which his fingers traveled over the strings. After several encores, we went up to ask the prodigy the same question: "How long have you been playing?"

"Three years," he answered with a boyish grin. My concert-artist friend turned to me with a meaningful nod. It now became increasingly clear to us why more than fifteen hundred professional violin teachers polled in a national survey placed the most effective age for starting violin at between eleven and twelve.[6]

We all have friends who will defend early lessons, particularly if they are parents who have invested in them or are teachers who take the tuition. Yet our experience is that the very young child who begins formal lessons in any sophisticated instrument seldom does well. Some of these parents, like those of Grosse Point, do not awaken to their mistake until too late.

Better Baby Business

In 1966 when I was with the U.S. Office of Education, I was invited to inspect Glenn Doman's Better Baby Institute of Philadelphia. While there was not enough time to make an in-depth evaluation, our team was impressed with case studies and parent testimonies on Dr. Doman's work for brain-damaged children. Some, for example, had become "vegetables," in Dr. Doman's words, from having their heads bashed against an automobile dashboard in a sudden stop or collision.

Yet later when the Doman family began urging parents to pressure *normal* infants at ages one to three or younger, we were deeply concerned. In the first place, Doman has offered no verifiable and replicable comparisons between superbabies and children reared in normal homes. And, in our opinions, the superbaby proponents have not been able to offer the social and self-worth balance lacking in the Sidis and Grosse Point cases. Furthermore, the Doman claims have been discredited by at least seven prestigious scientific groups, including the American Academy of Physical Medicine and Rehabilitation and the Canadian Council for the Disabled as reported in the *Archives of Physical Medicine and Rehabilitation*.[7]

We worry that Doman's "sensory input" may be abusive to little children. (In this book our definition for "child abuse" is "using a child wrongly or improperly.") It places unreasonable demands on vision, hearing, taste, touch, and smell—senses which are not reasonably mature until around ages eight to twelve and sometimes later, even in very bright children. This involves stress on young brains before they have lateralized, that is, before their two hemispheres are working together in a mature way.

Time to Grow

No wonder William Sidis was unbalanced. No wonder the Grosse Point children were burned out. Children need time to grow like flowers, chickens, kittens, puppies, and foals. Who of you would prick a tadpole to make him hop before he had legs? Which of your pets would you put into obedience training before he was ready?

So let's not bother with flash cards at six months or math at two or formal reading lessons at three, or even four, five, six, or seven. You may elevate your ego, but you will likely pay a large price in creativity and normal development of your young.

Read to your children from the time they suckle at your breast; some *will* be reading by four or five. Their brothers or sisters, just as bright, may not be reading until eight or ten. Just be sure your physician checks their vision and hearing, and don't worry. Read to them several times a day, respond to them warmly, and give them license to explore anything that is not dangerous to them. Don't let them read more than fifteen or twenty minutes at a time at age five or six, even if you have to give them a timer or distract them with errands.

Let them help you from the time they start to walk. As the years roll on, let them learn to clean up after *you* instead of your always cleaning after *them*. Respond warmly always, using many whys and hows to trigger their creative thinking as they grow cognitively mature. Ask them questions, but especially by the warmth of your responses, encourage them to question you. Their highest form of play is working *with* you.

In another of her poignant pieces on children, Dr. Selma Freiberg writes:

> I worry about babies and small children who are delivered like packages to neighbors, to strangers, to storage houses like merry mites. In the years when a baby and his parents make their first enduring human partnerships; when love, trust, joy, and self-evaluation emerge through the nurturing love of human partners, millions of small children in our land may be learning values for survival in our baby banks. They may learn that the world outside the home is an indifferent world, or even a hostile world. Or they may learn that all adults are interchangeable, that love is capricious, that human attachment is a perilous investment, and that love should be hoarded for the self in service of survival.[8]

Whether you study Sidis or Grosse Point, or look to history, research, or common sense, you will find no sound source that tells you to hurry your babies. The slower boat with *you* as the captain is the surest voyage to bright, well-balanced children, with the family keel cutting deeply and surely in today's troubled water.

GREAT FAMILY HEALTH

BACKDROP: Because physical, mental, and emotional health is crucial to avoiding—and healing—burnout, we give you a synopsis of the NEWSTART system of total health, from top medical authorities in our new book *Home Made Health.* NEWSTART means Nutrition, Exercise, Water, Sunshine, Temperance, Air, Rest-Regularity-Recreation, and Trust in God. It combines science's and faith's best answers for vibrant health. It is not faddish, but practical and sensible. We *know* from experience that it works! Some of you have told us that a lifestyle change was all that was necessary to cure a serious case of burnout.

In the mid-1970s when the growth of home education was beginning to develop speed, we realized that a college-level model was needed for follow-up. We searched for an institution that would bring together a complete experience in education and health to youth who were conscientious enough to want one, but our search proved unsuccessful. Our Hewitt Board agreed that we should start one. Thus was born the Weimar Institute, located in the Lower California Sierras between Sacramento and Reno. Under an outstanding faculty and highly skilled physicians, it prepares creative students and brings amazing healing to Weimar "guests" suffering from arthritis, diabetes, heart disease, hypertension, weight problems, and stress. *NEWSTART* is a Weimar acronym. Weimar's east coast sequel is Hartland Institute near Rapidan, Virginia.

Health is a newsworthy topic these days. Magazines and newspapers closely cover the American Heart Association and the American Cancer Society. They tell us that cancer will at some time strike 30 percent of Americans, affecting three out of four homes, and kill more children between the ages of three and fourteen as the years go on. Other news warns of heart disease, diabetes, osteoporosis, and other degenerative diseases.

Although prospects of freedom from these frightening maladies provide a valid reason for lifestyle changes, many people are interested in health for even better reasons — in order to live longer and more vibrantly. Family members who care about each other are also concerned, particularly about their children: The basic habits for a lifetime are laid in those early years.

Many home schooling families are courageous enough to make those lifestyle changes, knowing that by doing so they have a better chance to develop intellectual power, excellence in character, self-discipline, and self-direction, as well as a better quality of life.

Nutrition

What we eat seems to have the most direct bearing on the length of our lives and our general well-being as well as the risk of developing any of the diseases we've mentioned. The same lifestyle affects both. The villain which plays the most havoc in destroying our goals is most often identified as fat, which comes in various forms.

The loud, clear message from all organizations promoting good health in this country is that not more than 30 percent of our daily calories should be in fat. Health professionals in *preventive* programs and conservatives are recommending 15 percent to 25 percent. For relatively rapid improvement or recovery of serious health problems, *therapeutic* diets, with as low as 10 percent of the calories in fat are recommended. Yet the average American diet is 40 percent to 45 percent fat!

Remarkable Results

Controlling our intake of fat and increasing our intake of natural foods can make remarkable differences in family health and happiness. Since publication of our book *Homemade Health*, the letters have been pouring in.[1] Here is an excerpt from Joanne Wolf's of New Jersey:

My family and I have suffered from hypoglycemia, multiple food allergies, horrible eczema, fatigue, depression, and from being overweight. . . . We tried the traditional high protein/low carbohydrate diet which helped with the sugar problem but left us with worsening allergies. Then we tried elimination diets and rotation diets, but found we soon became allergic to just about everything we ate. Last winter I watched as my face, arms, legs, and chest puffed up with itchy, oozy eczema. It was an awful experience and everything I tried made it worse. . . .

I read a review in your newsletter on *Homemade Health* and promptly sent for a copy. Today my eczema is *totally* gone and my husband and I are each thirty pounds lighter. (I went from a size 20 to a 12!) For the first time in my life I can control my appetite — no more overwhelming cravings. We can eat just about all the "allergic" food that gave us so much trouble last year and no more low blood sugar blues either! I have energy like I never had before and exercise is no longer a chore. This is also the first winter we haven't caught every illness that's come round.

In a sequel written just last week, Joanne tells us they are still on track and "can't imagine ever going back to the way we used to eat."

Studies of Japanese Diets
An epidemiological study on Japanese women has helped to underline the importance of a low-fat diet in regard to breast cancer which has become the leading cancer killer of women. In the United States breast cancer is estimated to be four to five times as common as in Japan where women eat a traditional Japanese diet with about 20 percent fat. Granddaughters and great-granddaughters of Japanese families who now live in Hawaii and the mainland of the United States and adopted the standard American diet have the same breast cancer rates as other U.S. women. With these women, as with women of Polish descent, it took only a couple of generations for the increase to occur.[2]

A similar study of Japanese lifestyle in relation to heart disease found that the Westernized Japanese in Los Angeles with a dietary fat content of 40 percent had nine times the relative death rate of those in Japan.[3]

Interestingly enough, the recommendations are relatively consistent: Eat fewer items that are high in fat and cholesterol; select breads, cereals, and pastas where the words *whole wheat* or *whole grain* are listed first in the ingredients; and eat many fruits, vegetables, legumes, oat-based products, and nuts in moderation. It's a good idea to keep track of your diet on a chart, especially if you have any health problems or have inherited any family tendencies to any of these diseases.

Exercise

But even diet isn't the whole answer. Exercise is significant as an aid in the prevention of all the diseases mentioned. In spite of fads in exercise, such as high-impact aerobics, bicycling, or jogging, ordinary walking has been declared the best exercise, because almost anyone can do it, almost anywhere at almost any time. Such weight-bearing exercise is more vital in the prevention of osteoporosis, for example, than are other types of exercise. Walking also improves cardiovascular functions, makes your muscles stronger and more limber, burns calories, trims physique, builds strength and endurance, and because it is more moderate than some, is virtually injury-free.

The assurance of better *mental health* by exercise may be as important as physical health. Individuals who regularly exercise report that they feel more relaxed, have less fatigue, more discipline, and a sense of looking better and being more productive in work. And such response has been normal since the beginning of time. Great teachers of the ages used to walk while thinking or lecturing students.

Even some of you have noted what Oliver Wendell Holmes observed that "in walking, the will and the muscles are so accustomed to working together and performing their task with so little expenditure of force that the intellect is left comparatively free." Now many studies have shown that even extreme life stresses, such as divorce, moving, surgery, and death, have minimal impact on your health if you are physically active.[4]

Significant to parents who want thoughtful children is a study of twenty individuals who exercised three times a week for six months. They were not only 20 percent more fit, but they were also 70 percent better at making decisions than they had been before exercising.[5]

Water

We have already had excellent responses from encouraging everyone to drink *at least* six to eight glasses of water a day, starting with a pint to a quart of water a half hour or more before breakfast — a great tonic and cleanser! Also, as much as possible, eliminate unnecessary liquids *with* meals, or for an hour or so afterward, so as not to dilute your stomach's digestive juices. Beware of caffeine — in tea, coffee, colas, etc. Its effect on the body is negative in almost every respect — contributing to hypertension, heart attack, irregular heart beat, heartburn, stomach ulcers, colon cancer, and especially for women, a loss of iron from meals. This drug causes excretion of valuable minerals through the urine, creating illusions that all is well when, in fact, the body often suffers from fatigue, hunger, or illness.[6]

Sunshine

The scare of skin cancer from sunshine has caused many people to avoid sun like the plague. Sunshine is a friendly ally in the prevention and healing of many health problems, *if used in moderation.* It strengthens our bones, kills germs, soothes the nerves, builds the immune system, helps to reduce blood pressure, tends to normalize blood sugar in hypoglycemics, and generally energizes the body.

Our distinguished consultants feel that skin cancer is caused in part by (1) a high-fat diet, including refined fats (as used in margarine, mayonnaise, cheese, etc.), (2) oils on the skin while literally "frying" in the sun, and (3) *intemperate* use of sunshine. Overexposure to the sun is always dangerous. Light-skinned people are more vulnerable than dark-skinned. It is better to be temperate, even cautious, than to be exposed to the sun for a long time, even with so-called protective lotion, some of which is said to be dangerous to skin cells.[7]

Temperance

There are few good things in life that cannot in some way be perverted or, when out of control, do damage: fire, water, food, exercise, sunshine, even work and rest! So temperance is best defined as abstinence from things that are harmful — tobacco, alcohol, caffeine, and all unnecessary drugs — and moderation in using all that is good.

Air

Vigorous exercise is bound to force deep breathing, which in most unpolluted air brings oxygen into the lungs. This renews the brain and body functions. Yet if your normal breathing habits are poor the rest of the time, your vitality may be reduced, making you tired, depressed, even anemic and decreasing your mental capacities — memory, creativity, and concentration. So train yourself and your family how to breathe from the diaphragm and develop good posture so as not to cramp the lungs. Try to live in the most healthful air possible and get plenty of fresh air at night.

Rest, Regularity, Recreation

What mother is not tired much of the time? But does she have to be? The answer is a resounding "no." All she or anybody needs is to allow the body to renew itself with rest. Every cell and every organ in the body has a rhythm of rest and activity, from the heart to the kidneys. If you allow that natural rhythm to synchronize as it should, your body will respond with energy that will surprise you. The secret lies in *regular* hours of sleep, *regular* times to eat (with nothing between meals), *regular* periods of relaxation and recreation. Help your children establish habits of regularity, too, for a wonderful heritage of health. While lecturing with us in Germany, Dr. Gunther Hildebrandt, world authority on body rhythms, observed that sleep is worth more than twice as much before midnight as after!

Trust in God

Stress can be very negative, or it can be positive. Without it, life would be boring, for it motivates us to achieve, to interact, and to adapt. Negative stress involves fears, threats, disasters. It may also be caused by negative emotions, intemperance such as overwork, or even our perceptions of things. We need to know that God is faithful and will help those who trust in Him to overcome stressful situations. By resting in Him we can renew ourselves and develop proper mental attitudes, enabling us to be secure and productive.

PART THREE

WHAT CAN WE DO ABOUT BURNOUT?

ELEVEN

HOW WELL DO YOU KNOW YOUR TEENAGERS?

BACKDROP: We have talked about attitudes of parents, publishers, and schools. What about children, especially teens? Whom or what do they most cherish? Their parents? Their peers? Things? Do parents and teachers and neighbors know? And what is the result when we come up with the wrong answers? Where parents are even moderately responsive, children prefer their company and are much more secure and socially mature in the security of their family values than those of their peers. We start out with a little experiment that surprises most adults. And we close with a recipe that will do more than anything to produce noble, secure, high-achieving, well-socialized teens.

Suspicious that parents knew little about the down-deep feelings of their children, we began a direct and very simple series of studies fifteen years ago, and still do them today. Any parent or pastor or teacher or other group leader can do the same — evaluate youngsters' values on the one hand and the perceptions of their parents on the other. The experiment is easy to replicate in your church or other group. We have visited the children in some twenty early teen church school classes. Their ages are usually about twelve to fifteen — standard junior high school groups. We studied this segment of teen attitudes, for if you do well with your kids at that age, they are usually yours for life. We usually question parents in church congregations or classes, although we receive similar responses in other settings.

Conducting the Test

We address a basic six-part question first to children via a secret ballot, and then to parents in groups. We carefully prepare the students to respond with their true individual feelings without the influence of their peers: We try to arrange them so they are not sitting close together, and always give them written ballots instead of asking for oral or hand-signal responses. The groups have ranged from 8 to 300 youngsters and from 50 to more than 1000 parents. The total number of children involved in all group interviews has been about 630; the total number of parents and friends, about 8000.

The instructions and question to early teens go like this: "Think carefully; which of the following rewards are most important to you? Please, *with your eyes only on your own ballot*, mark only two of the six possible answers!" (Repeat this instruction.) "Mark those two choices like this: If your first choice is to be liked by your agemates, mark it with a *1*; if your second preference is to be rich, mark it *2* — mark only two choices out of six." (Repeat this instruction also.)

☐ To be rich

☐ To be happily married

☐ To graduate well

☐ To be liked by your agemates

☐ To get along with your parents

☐ To be saved eternally (or never to die)

We tabulate the results under supervision of their teacher or teachers by using three or more teens elected by the group. The questions to parents (and others of the adult groups) are as follows. *First*: Do you think you know your children and their values well? And *second*: If we were to ask your early teens about the most important things in their lives, in what order do you believe they would respond to these six values? We slowly recite the values and repeat the list before asking for a hand vote on each item which the deacons count.

Interpreting the Responses

No two groups are identical, of course, but results from all have been so similar as to provide significant conclusions. We were not particularly surprised at parental and other church member responses, but the children's reactions told us that adults have a lot to learn about their kids' values: Most among the parent groups invariably thought that the teens' first choices would be *riches* or *agemates*. After that, they guessed that the early teens' preferences would be *salvation* or *parents*. They conjectured that *graduation* would follow, and, for this age, *marriage* would be last.

The parents were generally correct only on the last two. More than 97 percent of the early teens place salvation first, and the majority place parents second. Agemates are usually third, and riches are a tossup with graduation. Many parents and grandparents—and pastors and teachers—comment that this is one of the biggest lessons of their lives.

But don't miss a significant point that few catch! If we had taken anything but a secret poll, the results would have more likely been those anticipated by adults. Teens, and younger children, generally strive to give an impression that does not distinguish them from their agemates. Even if they have very high values "down inside," they are unlikely to reveal them to their peers. And parents and other adults misjudge them unless they know them intimately. But few parents do. Rather they estimate their children's values by those they equate with their peers. Children in fact have more faith in their parents than parents have in their children!

You might try this study on *your* church or support group. If you do it precisely as we have described our operation, we believe that you will have similar findings, and happy results in relationships in your church or other group.

We hear a lot about marriage encounters, marriage enrichment, and similar movements—far more good things than bad. But we don't hear much about child-awareness or understanding children's development as central topics in marriage renewal programs. Yet no marriage can truly excel without this understanding.

Meeting Your Children's Needs

What should you do, then, if you find your children wanting to go back to school or otherwise becoming restless? Or if you find some loneliness among your teens or others whom you have withdrawn from school to teach at home? Occasionally the situation is too difficult for you to control, and school it must be. Yet you will likely do well if you (1) take your children into your plans from the start, (2) put your best foot forward (e.g., show them how *they* can manage the family industry, make money, possibly hire friends and former schoolmates, have freedom for vacations with you, and enjoy much more freedom to explore in their studies), (3) make clear the true advantages of home education historically and currently, (4) get them involved with wholesome children their age, (5) keep them busy, and (6) don't sway easily with their momentary emotions. Listen to Gayle Butler's wisdom, writing for Lee Gonet's Alabama *Voice*:

> Since hindsight is said to be 20/20, I can now look back at last year — our first attempt to home school — and declare it not so bad.

> The needs of every home schooling family are unique. Indeed, no two homes or families are identical, and I soon realized that this is not "Little House on the Prairie." When we finally worked out a schedule to meet the needs of all five of us, it was November.

> By January, our youngest daughter was beginning to miss being around other children her age (ten). Her loneliness is genuine. There are no other children in our neighborhood and only one girl her age at church. Ashley simply misses having thirty friends in class with her. I think an "in state" pen pal will help and have encouraged her to write her own letter to the *Voice* requesting such friends-by-mail.

> Our eldest daughter will be a junior this year. Last spring she realized that this is the year her peers in public school will get a class ring and have a prom. She saw all the ceremony of graduation and wonders how solitary her "graduation" will be. She remembers the sheer fun of band trips and panic of concert solos and misses that aspect of public school. Of course, it may be easy enough for us as adults and parents to determine that

these concerns of a teenager aren't very important in the full scope of life and eternity, but teens see things in a different light. They live TODAY! We continue to seek ways to minister to her needs for companionship and fun.

Our three girls were in fourth, eighth, and tenth grades when we began to home school. I know it would have been much easier for us all if they had not already formed their own ideas regarding how school works, how the teacher is supposed to teach, what the student can get by with—like "Why can't I turn in the same research paper I did last year? It was so good!" and "What do you mean I have to read another book? Can't I write this report on a book I've already read? Just this one time . . . PLEASE!!" No one would have been the wiser in public school, but Mom knows! It was an adjustment to have both parents fully informed about what was required in each subject. That meant no putting off assignments until the last day.

I said that to make this point: If there are any parents who have young children and haven't quite made the commitment to home school, I want you to know that the earlier you begin the easier it will be. I wish I had made the decision when my sixteen-year-old was seven—so many wasted years and unpleasant situations ago.[1]

Here is a mother who thinks her daughters' thoughts after them—and sometimes before! It takes character, ingenuity (and for many, prayer) to work out problems like Gayle Butler's. We congratulate her, for many just lie down and give up. They may never be appreciated one day like this mother who knows the difference between indulgence and love.

Do you want to know how your children really feel? Do things *with* them. Set aside unnecessary work, television, sports pages, and clubs. Don't use that "quality time" excuse. You wouldn't do that to your boss or favorite pet. Quality time for children is when they need you! And that can be *any* time, *all* the time. Work *with* them, play *with* them, plan *with* them, talk *with* them, and if you do as we do in our home, pray *with* them. Don't judge them by their peers. Become their peers (with obvious reservations)—during their most challenging years.

TWELVE

THE SPECTER OF STANDARDIZED TESTING

BACKDROP: Many parents and children view standardized testing as "a ghost of a terrifying nature"—which is the *Random House Dictionary* definition of *specter*. And for good reason. In the first place their standardization is in doubt, not only from a statistical viewpoint, but also because so many school systems, in their efforts to "beat the test" are requiring their teachers to teach to tests, i.e., go through the questions on old tests (and sometimes current ones) to condition children to right answers. Years ago this would have been cheating. But in many schools it is endorsed practice today. Such practices skew any standardization process, and to some extent the breadth and depth of a child's education becomes as narrow as the items on the test. Add to these problems such test day factors of health, attitude, experience, teacher instructions, and the child's general familiarity with areas covered by the test, and you have something to be terrified about if official approval is at stake and there is a risk of court or intervention by social workers.

No matter what your philosophy about your children's maturity, your teaching style, or their learning styles, a state regulation which demands testing before ages ten to twelve puts unfair pressure on both you and your children. Even though we do not know of a single instance where a child has been forced back into school because of low achievement, it does cause burnout for parents and children. So we are satisfied with only those state laws that (1) don't require standardized testing at all or (2) don't *require* testing before ages ten to twelve and preferably later or (3) allow evaluation by a certified teacher in place of testing.

Alleviate the Pressure

Meanwhile, in order to eliminate as much stress as possible, we make some suggestions. We assume that testing is most traumatic for (1) young students, (2) those who originally burned out from early pressure in conventional school, (3) students who have a bona fide learning disability, and (4) the occasional student who simply freezes up at a test.

First, be sure that you know your state statutes, including substitute options, grades to be tested, and standards required. These vary greatly from state to state; being familiar with the requirements of your state may save you unnecessary suffering. Especially note the minimum standard required. Fifteen percentile, as in Oregon for example, is not very high. So, relax, if that is your case. *School officials should not expect any more of home schools than they do of public schools* — where fifty students are below 50 percentile and fifty above. If testing is not required, don't test unless you and your child feel comfortable about it and want it for your own information.

But, if your child must be tested, think it through. What is your attitude? Are you the one who is really in panic? Are you likely to transfer that pressure to your child? How necessary is your concern? Remember, testing is seldom a definitive assessment of the child's abilities. It merely gives you an idea of what has been accomplished only in *school-type tasks*. It says nothing about other abilities or qualities which may be much more valuable for life than merely reading and math. So satisfy yourself that life after testing will go on. If you *aren't* uptight, your child won't be either. Besides, why share the test results with those not legitimately concerned?

Next, explore ways to take off the pressure, especially in the early years. One way is to consider your child at kindergarten level at age six or seven, as far as state reporting is concerned. Almost every educator understands "immaturity." If this isn't the case, have a friendly certified teacher or psychologist provide an evaluation of your child's readiness. Now that schools are testing kindergarteners to see if they are ready for first grade, you should have the right to make that decision also. Home school normally does not need to pay attention to either grade levels or achievement grades. No child fails either one! So don't allow your child to be a possibility for failure by starting him out at a higher level than he may be ready for. You can always skip a grade or two later on. But you can also decide to have him tested at a lower grade level—primary instead of intermediate, for example—if you feel the other would be risky. Regardless of his age, give him the break he needs as long as you are satisfied that you have been a responsible parent educator. Take charge as his superintendent as well as his teacher!

Be Prepared

Professional teachers feel the pressure, too, because they have discovered that *they* are really the ones being tested and good test scores help to maintain their own standing. They, of course, have learned how to coach their children for the tests. And they can do this legitimately. Then, is it legitimate for you to prepare your children in case you are under pressure to test? Yes. We don't know of any standardized test which is given these days which you cannot prepare for, including the GED, SAT, GRE, etc. Manuals are published for this purpose.

Try to find an old test so that you can check the procedure. Inquire through your support group, a public school teacher, or your school district. Unfortunately, the tests often resemble workbook exercises. Since a child may be confused by something unfamiliar, he needs to know, for example, how to do multiple-choice, true-false, and fill in the blank types of questions, as well as any other particular form of objective checking. You can make up exercises or problems of the *same type* as those given in the test so that they will not come as a surprise to your child. A little practice in synonyms, antonyms, punctuation, and dictionary skills, for example, will raise his overall score considerably in comparison to the time spent in practice.

Most home schoolers do considerably better on reading, vocabulary, and comprehension than they do on math. Yet addition, subtraction, multiplication, and division combinations of math are some of the simplest for children under age ten to learn if they master *Math-It*. At about the third-grade level, they can also become masters of grammar by using the *Winston Grammar Game*. If you need further help, read carefully "Getting the Most from Test Taking and Test-Making" in our book *Home Style Teaching*.

THIRTEEN

THE DISCIPLINE THAT IS DISCIPLESHIP

BACKDROP: Here we look into a pool which may be either troubled or so smooth most of the time that it reflects your happy face and is a joy to your youngsters. *Discipleship* is the name of the game. You are the example, the shepherd. You teach them the difference between *indulgence*, which occupies the moment, and *love*, which graces a lifetime. Consistency, you conclude, is truly a jewel. You discover also that work and service *with* you are the kindest, greatest, and most gentle disciplinarians of all.

"I know I have lost control," writes a mother about her two-year-old son. We'll call her "Nancy."

"I have found this whole business of being a good mother to be totally exhausting." She confesses that his behavior on their walks to the park is so bad that she sometimes doesn't "want to be seen with him. Either Timmy refuses to walk, throws himself on the pavement, screams 'til I pick him up and drag him home, or protests going home when it's time."

Nancy admits being inconsistent. She's firm one moment and lets him have his way the next. Sadly, she also concedes feeling that mothers are basically *caretakers of children*—mostly there to watch out for their safety and physical needs:

"I've always felt early childhood to be a time a mother endures, until her child is old enough to 'relate' to her and she can talk and reason with him."

Nancy simply was not expecting enough of her child—normally a great motivation for him to be worthy of her trust. She sadly has not prepared herself for the most basic care of all—his spirit, his emotions, the cultivation of his love. So she misses the spiritual joy a little one can bring to a household.

Rearing, not Raising

Nancy's worst failing, as she says, is lack of *self*-discipline, though she declares that she is willing and anxious to change and is beginning to see that she has been practicing indulgence rather than love. She didn't realize that love looks ahead, and that children feel more secure when parents set limits and are consistent in enforcing them.

Child *rearing*, as Nancy saw it, is more like *child-raising*. Dr. Charles Weniger, our great English professor, always insisted there *is* a difference. "We raise cattle," he explained, "but we *rear* children."

The farmer needs only to provide physical care and protection. Yet even that involves control. With more intelligent animals, such as dogs or horses, there must be training if the animal is to be useful. So it is with children. Yet the most intelligent animal hasn't much conscience, reasoning ability, or judgment, while your child has great potential!

So you have the responsibility to provide external control over your child during those years when he has little information, judgment, or ability to make choices or to be responsible for his own actions. As he gains in understanding, you gradually teach him the principles of acceptable behavior, giving him practice in decision making and helping him to apply inner control until he has achieved a reasonable degree of self-discipline. And his discipleship will reflect your self-control.

Guiding with Limits

Behavior is like water. It must be controlled by boundaries or it becomes dangerous. Parents must set these limits while training the child to control himself. We think of a mother who confessed that she failed to properly discipline her child as he grew up. Then he, of course, did not learn to control himself, and now his boundaries are set by prison walls.

In the days of horse-drawn carriages, people seldom had to use the reins to direct the horse when they were *on the way home.* The same principle applies to the road of life where the child needs guidance until he knows the way. When he understands self-discipline, responsibility, and obedience to the rules and regulations of the family and of society, he will sense that they bring happiness and freedom to those he loves and admires and will become convinced of their value. On the other hand, if he sees that his parents or other adults use rules and regulations only to bolster their own authority, he gains a distorted picture of freedom. He responds with a strong desire to get away from rules and regulations and becomes a slave of lawlessness and bondage.

Though most parents tell us that home schooling brings their families together, and discipline problems seem to be minimal compared to some others, we don't claim that home schoolers are perfect. Some parents report being embarrassed by problem children on their field trips. Yet thus far these reports are rare.

Some of you complain that your children argue, bicker, and compete for your attention so much that they cannot accomplish as much as you would like. Welcome to the club! Conventional teachers are not without this problem also: Some of our friends in a Midwest school system tell us they spend *at least* half their time in some kind of disciplinary activity.

Unfortunately, problems don't disappear easily when the children are sent back to school. The children simply aren't around as many hours of the day. But soon their *habits* are worse than ever. The social contagion has its day! And you pay the price!

So What's the Remedy?

First, notice *habits*. These traits are formed by repeated actions. If they are *wrong*, they must be reversed by an opposite but sometimes more torturous procedure. Such habits operate automatically in the subconscious part of the brain and must be broken by a series of repeated *corrective* or *positive* actions. Mark Twain once said that habits can't be thrown out the upstairs window, but must be coaxed down one step at a time. Encourage all the good habits you can while working, even contriving, to change the others, perhaps one at a time. And if children have had these habits a long time, you will usually do better not to *impose* changes but to make them *worthwhile* to your child.

So stop and take stock and ask yourself some questions. What about regularity in your home? Are your meals regular or does everyone eat whenever and whatever he wants? Do your children go to bed whenever they feel inclined and get up in the same manner? How about you? Your answers may give you a place to start. No orderly, disciplined home—or any organization—can long exist without regularity. We can almost guarantee that if you can get that under control, your battle will be largely won. (See chapter 18 on "Organization.")

Next, explore your *household methods*. Do you do all the work or are the responsibilities parceled out to all the family team? Do you have a systematic way for each child to check off his personal habits, regular jobs, and family-rotating chores? Are early day duties completed before you start school work? Again the answer is intrinsic in the question. The work must be systematically assigned and completed to have that *clean* feeling.

What about your *teaching methods*, if you are teaching at home? Are you like Sandy McAnn or perfectionist Nellie Strickland who kept their children's noses to the grindstone with the very great possibility of ultimate rebellion or burnout? Or maybe both the household chores and the education is chaotic? Either one may cause burnout.

How is *your example* doing? Do you nag, threaten, scold, ridicule, or scream at the children or are the rules of the household clear and consistent enough so that the children know what to expect without those methods? Do you give your child the silent treatment, withdraw love and approval except when your child is "good"? Or are you just too busy most of the time to listen? Open your heart to your children and demonstrate the constructive discipline and selfless, unconditional love that is so essential for your child's development.

If your children are an age at which they can reason fairly well, from ages six on up, perhaps you need a brief family council once a day or each week to share decision making on home responsibilities. Such a meeting should explore constructive ideas to make the home a more pleasant place for all—it should not be just a time for Dad or Mom to lay down some regulations with threats for noncompliance. Let the children suggest positive actions which could substitute for undesirable behavior. Even parents might need to confess some faults with a commitment to make some changes.

If your children are all young, mostly below the age of reason, discipline generally has to be by consistent benevolent dictatorship, establishing the right habits and always seeking to help the children learn the reasons for obedience and the rewards of happiness when they cooperate. Reward them not with material objects or with too much praise for them personally, but with praise for the things they do. When they misbehave, make it clear that you love them unconditionally, but that you are not happy (and they shouldn't be either) with wrong deeds.

What about punishment? The old saying that you can catch more flies with honey than with vinegar applies here. At any level, rewards of the right kind bring better results than punishment. If punishment is needed, it generally "should fit the crime," in order to help your child understand the law of cause and effect. That is, acts have natural consequences. There is a place for spanking when it is administered in love and approached with reason and control. Especially with young children, unacceptable behavior may sometimes require isolation, apology, restitution, or even spanking. But spanking or switching, if any, should never be beatings or slaps in the face, in anger. Your goal is always to conclude with a right attitude and a commitment for future behavior; otherwise your efforts will be lost.

The true discipline of discipleship for both you and your children is always an ultimate expression of love!

LESSON PLANS—WHY ALL THAT TROUBLE?

BACKDROP: Lesson plans are among the dreariest worries of many home teachers. They shouldn't be. I confess that as a public school teacher mine were so simple as almost to be nonexistent as formal documents. Class records, yes, thoroughly kept. Lengthy lesson plans, no. Yet every home and every state is different. Here we try to make more than adequate provision for those whose education design rests on *more* or *less* formal planning. Dorothy tells you how to keep them simple, very simple, indeed.

One family who experienced a series of illnesses and other emergencies one year admitted they had done little or nothing about any kind of "school." But when the children were tested routinely, they had all gained a grade level or more. The parents wondered if just growing up in an active, thinking household made a difference. While we would normally recommend a little more systematic attention to the children's program year after year, we basically agree that children can learn in such an unstructured environment.

Learning is essentially something the child does for himself. Though he needs a more experienced adult available for feedback, guidance, and stability, the teacher or parent is not to see himself as pouring facts into an empty head. Rather, he serves as an example, a counselor, and a facilitator—a leader in the educational program. The child is the active agent, working out his own thought connections which lead him to the concepts and understandings he needs. Depending on the quality of the process, he also develops his attitudes toward learning, his own values, and his type of creativity—lessons which are more than likely to stay with him for life.

Setting Priorities

Experienced leaders in every walk of life say that "planning time saves time," and parenting is leadership of the very highest order. Whether teaching at home or in the classroom, the teacher is the one who must guide the program to achieve sound growth, balance, subject coverage, and discipline.

The question is, "How detailed, extensive, and rigid does the planning need to be?" Every public school teacher has a class schedule, and the bells require that it be strictly followed in starting, recesses, lunch, and dismissal. In between, however, the "best laid plans of mice and men" are often disturbed by school band practice, girls' chorus, the dental hygienist's visit, assembly, and "you name it." Raymond calls it "litter." So don't get uptight about variations, interruptions, or substitutions. Just plan the best you can and be flexible.

Ask yourself practical questions. You may be an idealist, even a perfectionist, but you know by now you can't do everything, so you'd better think realistically. You have great ideas, but you also have a baby or young child, and it isn't sensible to take your older children on many field trips or to gymnastic, music, and other lessons when the baby must stay with a sitter, delay his feeding, or miss his nap.

Are you worried that there might be gaps in your children's learning? Who doesn't have gaps, hundreds of them? And in order to avoid some great disaster, are you determined to have your children do every page in every workbook in every grade? Sure, there are going to be some drills in phonics, spelling, math, penmanship, etc.—but let's not major in minors.

Workbooks are made to "cut corners" for classroom teachers because they think they can't stretch their time to thirty children any better way. It is also officially accepted as "evidence" on which to base a *grade*. And it makes terrific busywork to keep the children occupied while they have reading groups, do other teaching chores, or have breathing spells. One child brought her workbook home to her mother and asked, "Wanta see my time-wasters?"

Workbooks were a boon to classroom teachers when they first came into use—especially in math, grammar, and spelling—because they saved a lot of tedious copying from the textbook or chalkboard. But they have been sadly overused. Some brighter students "beat" the workbook system by finding the right answers without ever reading the material and then memorizing those facts for the test!

Using many workbooks stifles the development of reason. Just as the physical body requires consistent, even vigorous exercise in order to grow and strengthen, so does the brain. Such exertion consists of analyzing, digesting, organizing, and assimilating information, applying what is learned to practical situations, even stretching the mind to understand difficult concepts. Lack of thinking and reasoning actually weakens your ability to think creatively and independently and makes you dependent on the perception and judgment of others. Don't depend on rote memory or a multiple-choice, fill-in-the-blank mentality—a lower-level skill. It is a kissing cousin to the passive learning of video and television. Children become incapable of discriminating between truth and error, unable to use common sense, and powerless to judge for themselves. Is it any wonder that such a student tends to fall an easy prey to deception and looks to his peers for his values?

Before you even think about lesson plans, know *why* you want to educate your own (your philosophy), *where* you are headed (your goals), *what* you have to teach with (your resources), and *how* you want to teach your children (your methods).

Philosophy

Any teacher certainly needs to know *why* he is doing what he is doing. And the home school teacher is no exception. Your philosophy is *basic* to your commitment and your willingness to follow through. If you decide to teach your children at home because it is popular, or the private school is too expensive, or you don't like the school or the teacher, your commitment is hollow.

On the other hand, if your first conviction is that no one loves and understands your children as well as you do, and you want to be directly involved in their physical, mental, and emotional development enough to make a sacrificial commitment, home schooling's for you! And make sure it is a harmonious balance of study, work, and service.

Goals

You may be tempted to think that your purpose for your child is to help him excel academically. After all, isn't that what school is all about? But such goals, though worthy, are relatively unimportant compared to your basic, long-term goals to help your children (1) develop excellent character and a healthy sense of self-worth; (2) develop high moral and behavioral standards; (3) become responsible members of the family and society; and (4) become friendly, sociable, service-oriented individuals. You may also decide you want to avoid early home separation, peer socialization, and the often unhealthy competition of grades, sports, and materialism.

These are your large, *over-all goals*, equivalent to your basic philosophy of education. There is a lesser set of objectives for the mastery of academics — *Student Learning Objectives* (SLOs) — and a still lesser type used in daily learning sessions and usually referred to as *instructional goals* which we will discuss later.

When dealing with academic goals, you do not have to reinvent the wheel. Typical Courses of Study outline a recommended logical sequence in social studies or other subjects and although they differ almost from district to district, they are generally available. SLOs which guide you and help you assess your students' achievement are available in every school district. Some support groups secure them for their home school members.

Let's look at an example of these SLOs. At the first grade level, two of the many SLOs in math might be for your child to be able to know addition and subtraction facts to ten and to recognize halves and fourths; in reading his SLO's might be to use phonics to decode grade level words and retell simple stories from his reading.

Refer to these, but don't be a slave to them. They are guidelines to the academic goals you want to reach, and they help you determine how well you are progressing. As you review them periodically, you will be surprised at how much you are accomplishing and they will keep you aware of some things which need to be worked on.

Within the SLOs, it would be wise to break them down into quarterly, monthly, even weekly goals. Hopefully, that will not be just to assign certain pages in the textbooks or workbooks so that you can complete them in your school year. Rather these objectives should be much more basic in what you hope your children will accomplish in those time periods.

Resources

Don't worry that you don't have the materials, opportunities, or facilities which the traditional school affords. The home is normally equipped with superior laboratories (the garden, kitchen, garage, or basement) and innumerable real-life experiences. In addition, you have a whole community of learning possibilities, including the store, the bakery, the fire house, etc., and usually parks or woods and the public library. Also you can accumulate your own tapes, maps, and books in lieu of extra school clothes, tuition, or other normal school expenses.

Make a list of your resources and don't forget the talents and interests of people — your own extended family, neighbors, and friends. Brenda Lewis tells about a retired lawyer who helps her fourteen-year-old would-be-attorney son who asks him dozens of questions. And there's a horticulturist who shares his knowledge while he works with his young apprentice neighbor in his orchard and garden.

Methods

Since most of us were taught in conventional schools, we have a strong tendency to teach the way we were taught. This method is generally rigid, detailed, and includes many textbooks, workbooks, tests, and long hours. But if parents are sensitive to the developmental needs of their children and note their response to heavy structure and pressure, they will move toward a more flexible approach. Books will be used as resources more than texts, skills will be used largely in connection with projects or units of study, and meaningful dialogue will abound.

Remember, we are not suggesting that you go to the other extreme — deteriorating into a permissive, spur-of-the-moment, anything-goes attitude which brings chaos. Rather, the program will be systematic, but flexible, with opportunities for the children to explore within reasonable limits. And the teacher will guide, encourage, motivate, and help to maintain balance.

We encourage you to write out your philosophy, objectives, and resources, preferably with your whole family's help. It is valuable not only for use in case it is required by school officials, but for those occasional times when that inevitable question arises: What am I doing this for anyway?

Scheduling

If you were required to present such a document to a superintendent, a schedule would usually be expected also. Besides, both you and your children need a systematic guide. Routine is like the walls of a house — it gives stability to your program. You may shift gears a lot before you come up with something which fits your family, but keep trying. In general, keep sessions short for young children and never go over an hour in academics without a complete change of pace or a work/play break.

We hesitate to set out a *sample* schedule for fear of being misunderstood as suggesting formality. We hope you will consider the following outline simply an *example* from which to make variations, adaptations, and adjustments for different ages, needs, and temperaments, depending on where you are on the vast scale from structure to free project learning. The blocks of time allow for considerable flexibility, but change them as you think best.

6:00 A.M.	Parents — Arise, Dress, Devotions. Children may be awake, but may put on bathrobe and slippers until after breakfast.
7:00 A.M.	Family time or worship, breakfast, children dress, morning chores
9:00 A.M.	Opening exercises, songs, marching, etc.
9:30 A.M.	Skill subjects as needed, individualized (Phonics/Spelling, Reading, Penmanship, Math)
10:30 A.M.	Work/play break
11:00 A.M.	Project learning for all children together, based on a content subject in religion, social studies, or science, ideally incorporating many skills, other

	content areas, art, music, etc. Flexible for breaks, change of pace, etc.
12:30 P.M.	Lunch and quiet time
2:00 P.M.	Cottage industry, service to others, laboratory time, vigorous exercise, free time
5:30 P.M.	Supper and family time
7:00 P.M.	Bath, bedtime routine
8:00 P.M.	Bedtime

If you must account for a certain number of hours of instruction in your state, be sure to think in school-type terms, i.e., agricultural science, woodworking, social work, communication, home economics, business economics, practical arts, physical education, creative arts, etc., in addition to the usual subjects listed above. All *active participation* by your children, such as field trips, work, or shopping, will qualify as "school." So will things that they do independently, such as educational games they play, books or magazines they read for pleasure, tapes they listen to, or informal interviews they have with family or friends.

Lesson Plans

So now how do you plan? Almost everyone recognizes the value of keeping a daily log. It is a safeguard in case of legal problems, is mandatory in some states, provides an over-all record to help you see if your program is well-balanced, and may be a long-term "diary" for posterity.

But why have one book for lesson plans and another for your log? Why not plan your days with the log in mind, using blocks of time as suggested which can be adapted for field trips, projects, or whatever you decide to do? List your plans in a word or two opposite your schedule time slots on the extreme *left*. Then at day's end, flesh out your skeleton plan with more details of what you actually accomplished, on the *right* side.

Allow enough flexibility so that you can drop what you are doing to go and see a rainbow or a cardinal outside the window without "spoiling" your "math time." That does not mean that you stop what you are doing for every bird which comes to the feeder or for endless distractions—just don't be rigid.

A weekly plan is probably most efficient, while keeping in mind your philosophy, goals, resources, and methods. This is the time to evaluate your children's needs and the SLOs which you have yet to meet. Then you decide what learning experiences will contribute best to your program. Make adjustments as necessary during the week.

Let's be specific: You will get so used to the following four steps that you will do them automatically without jotting them down every day. They outline each of your instructional sessions. Carry them out consistently, making sure your goals and amount of learning time fit your children's levels of skill and maturity. We offer skills and projects for each:

1. *Your instructional goal*—i.e., your *stating to* or *formulating with* each child what gains you expect from each session. This provides a *purpose* for the learning activity—why it is useful or important. For instance, using the math SLO above for one of your children as a guide, you may expect that this learning time will result in some progress in the mastery of addition and subtraction facts. His past experience with money or other practical math will help him understand why. Then proceed from where your child was in the last session and give him problems at which he can succeed.

However, your instructional goals for a project with all the children might be to discover certain valuable character traits and apply them to their lives. These may come from a story they read earlier or something that just happened. During these projects you bring in learning ideas and skills.

2. *Your instructional cue—getting them started.* Your cue for your youngest math student might be giving him a mixture of problems in addition and subtraction, working now not only for accuracy but also for speed. Since you are not introducing a new math concept, and you have just been working on increasingly difficult problems up to now, you have no explaining to do.

For your family project, you may have already set the stage by the story you read earlier, but this session should be much less teacher-directed than skill and drill time might be. You may need to ask questions to start a discussion. A child's curiosity, the field trip you went on yesterday, a demonstration of something you saw or heard on the news, or even an approaching holiday — all these are possible instructional cues.

3. *Practicing what is to be learned.* This may be the only item (of the four) which is actually recorded on your lesson plan, though all the other steps will be kept clearly in mind. Using math as an example, let us assume that your child has already worked with *Math-It* or similar basic math. He has learned simple addition and subtraction, but needs some drill sessions to achieve both speed and genuine mastery. Perhaps he has proceeded far enough so that you will choose to have him do speed practice both in addition and subtraction. You no doubt have exercises for this — from books or problems you or others make up — from which you will assign a page or partial page, bearing in mind again his capacity and need to succeed. Make it fun by giving him a stopwatch or kitchen timer and let him time himself, then acknowledge his improvement.

For your project (as compared with basic skill building), your "practice" will involve a much different type of activity. There will be no drill, practice, repetition, even review. Rather you will explore, experiment, or devise ways to broaden the scope of the project appropriately. All should discuss the story, for example, probing the thoughts, feelings, and attitudes of the characters. What traits do they admire and wish to emulate? Challenging their thinking builds understanding and increases reasoning ability. Encourage them to take up other activities, as each is able or can be helped to do, such as additional reading, written stories, oral reports, and map making.

4. *Evaluation.* Evaluate each child's work in skills with him — checking his answers or noting his progress in order to know at what point he should begin the next learning session. Helping him chart his own progress is even better. All should take part in the family project evaluation as it evolves and at its conclusion. Was it worthwhile? What did each child learn? How can we improve, enlarge, or make more practical the next project, and what would we like to do? Be sure to commend each child's best effort.

On your lesson plans for any skill, you may write down only the device, the exercise, or the page number of the book you will use for each student's practice. But don't tie your goals to covering the textbooks or workbooks. Keep your SLOs in the back of your mind and let your imagination — and your children's — help you find exciting ways to bring out learning. You might jot down a reminder to have the children keep a spelling list of all the special vocabulary used in your project, or list related skills or subject areas.

You may feel you need a separate record book for each of your children, yet many parents do well with a combined record for all. A loose-leaf notebook probably is easiest to use. And, depending on your state requirements and your own disposition, you may want to purchase a teachers' record book if you don't want to make a master copy and duplicate it yourself. But there's no need for scores of pages of various forms — keep it simple! Some are frustrated by all the little blocks even on a simple record book; it was even frustrating to me when I taught public school, though in my day I was not required to submit lesson plans as teachers do now. Even now, if the truth were known, many officials would be surprised at how few teachers are actually tied to such plans.

Make your plans fun. Let your children share in the planning. And when you write in your daily log at the end of the day, include their stories about their experiences, poems they have written, flowers they have pressed and catalogued, collections of rocks, shells, and other of their laboratory evidence. Don't forget your home industries and service projects: You will enjoy this planning most of all. And, finally, you'll be surprised to find you have done a lot more than you thought — and officials will, too.

FIFTEEN

WORRIED ABOUT READING AND THE BASICS? TRY THIS!

BACKDROP: Nearly all mothers worry that their offspring might not do well in the all-important basics — reading, writing, arithmetic, and spelling. Almost always they think about teaching the way they were taught or the way they think the state wants them to teach. We ask, Really now, how much *were* you taught? And how much did you learn *in spite of* school?

When our children became school age, we were in Japan and Dorothy was the only American mother-teacher on the college campus where I was president. Here Dorothy gives you the sum of her fifty years of work in education, showing you how to use the unit, project, or block method. Take advantage of her success and the Moores' research, know when your children are ready, and you will do well. Have faith!

Our children had many rich experiences as youngsters, including travel; nature study; music in the home with a piano, records, and tapes; useful work; Bible and other true moral stories, and memory verses. *We found constructive true stories to be more effective in building character than myths or novels, because they help to influence the children's actions and thus their habits, rather than simply amuse.*

We were not concerned about formal schooling until ages eight to ten or later. I already had enough experience with early school entrants in my five years of public school remedial teaching to warn me that children, especially boys, were not really ready for on-going school *at least* until then.

But certain that Dennis at age eight was as bright as any boy, I dutifully got some reputable textbooks and a few workbooks, sat down with him part of an hour or so a day and let him do some work alone. He did well, covering three grades in two years.

BUT he was no eager beaver, and he and I in more recent years have agreed that he might have been more highly motivated if we had waited at least another year. He really didn't take off academically until junior high — the level which Berkeley learning psychologist William Rohwer says is really the optimum time. Dennis later became co-valedictorian in a large school.

By the time Kathie was six and a half, I had accumulated six other English-speaking children whose mothers pled with me to take over. I let Kathie sit in with them — doing her fun things. I made no attempt to teach her formally, but she evidently listened. We never did know for sure how she picked up so much. We had school only in the mornings, yet she was soon moving along with the other beginners. I taught her until age nine and Dennis until thirteen — very late in those days.

What I Learned

Knowing what I do now, I would work with the children even more informally. We had fun, and the children were well-prepared for highly rated schools when they returned to the States, but I would continue teaching my own at home much longer than I did. And though my philosophy, goals, and resources would stay essentially the same, I would use more projects. They are natural, realistic, and practical for children *of all ages and abilities.*

I took three summer classes at UCLA between my junior and senior year in college, one of which was taught by the curriculum coordinator of Los Angeles County Public Schools. She strongly recommended to the whole county the unit or project method for teaching social studies. Skills — reading, writing, spelling, and math — were to be integrated as much as possible into the unit of study. We observed classrooms taught this way.

So I launched out on a project — harbors — in my very first classroom of second and third graders. In our well-to-do school district, we were not limited in equipment or opportunities. So we secured soft wood scrap at the lumber yard, purchased simple carpenter tools, nails, and paint to make little toy boats, and set up a simulated harbor in our classroom. Besides our hands-on experiences, we drew pictures, read stories and books, wrote stories, sang songs, talked, and learned how to spell words about boats. Our closing activity was a field trip to the harbor.

Later our unit was on early California with its history, geography, topography, architecture, vegetation, religion, food, and art. In one corner of the classroom we constructed a California house with simple furnishings big enough for the children to play in. We painted a background of eucalyptus trees and a mission. These particular subjects in the field of social studies allowed integration of most skills except math, but did not include very much science other than plant life and weather. I was really too naive to understand what I now know about standardized testing, teaching to the test, or even to realize that the children's achievement is also a test of the teacher's skill. When my children were routinely tested at the end of the school year and their scores were compared to the previous year's scores and other equivalent grades, the results showed that my children excelled in the basics, especially reading! Of course, we had been fairly consistent in working on the skills needed. Yet we had spent a lot of time with our projects, integrating as much as possible of the other subjects. That first year's record started me on the remedial reading road, with a special class the very next year!

It also taught me that the objectives in all subjects can be successfully achieved with the project method. Executives now tell us that for continuing education, formal courses are a waste of company money. They prefer small real-life, work-related learning projects which are much more efficient than the school "models" and textbooks. Where can this be done better than in your home? To give instruction according to some professor's idea of what is needed conflicts "with everything science knows about how adults learn."[1]

Ingredients of the Project Method

Basic skills involve language arts (reading, including phonics; composition, including penmanship and spelling; and speaking, including grammar and vocabulary) and mathematics. No one denies that these are essential and normally must be mastered to realize our full educational potential. There are certain handicaps in these areas which can be overcome by calculators for those weak in math, typewriters for poor penmen, and word processors with a spelling checklist for poor spellers, but those who know their basics are fortunate.

Content subjects, on the other hand, include social studies, science, religion (or philosophy for those who eschew religion), and even cottage industries. These broad areas are usually chosen for projects because they are inexhaustible in their scope and lend themselves to any level of research and study. They form a basis for exciting practical learning about our world, ourselves, and our past. Basic skill agility advances their study and while using these skills, students learn what valuable, exciting tools they really are. Even creativity is crippled by any lack in the basic skills. A Chinese proverb says that "he who has imagination without learning has wings but no feet."

A teacher who capitalizes on student interest in almost any area at first — even if it's a fourteen-year-old whose only interest seems to be in motorcycles — may find a pathway to motivated learning which has been almost totally snuffed out by the usual regimentation of the classroom. One alert and understanding mother reported that nothing to date had increased her son's reading ability, or created such motivation and opened so many new vistas in his life as much as his temporary devotion to motorcycle magazines. A small home business or industry is also great to help students see the need for improvement, for example, in math computation, reading, or even legible writing.

A day's program is very likely to start with some study, practice, even drill on the basics, especially for those who are beginners, while older students may have to concentrate only on certain weaknesses which unit study helps to pinpoint. This should be followed by work on a unit or project which is launched in any number of ways listed later.

Some simple units may be worth only a few days study, while others can consume several weeks or even months. Sometimes more than one can move along simultaneously. Watching and studying a particular tree and the changes that take place over a year of seasons could be a long-term study while other shorter projects — such as Indians, electricity, insects, the solar system,

Jonah, or lizards—are also being studied. The parent-teacher's job is not to provide all the ideas and activities involved in these studies. Rather she is first of all to discover the children's interests and then to elicit creative ideas from the children. She should also carefully guide to see that projects cover a balanced spectrum as much as possible.

Parents with children enrolled in all curricula that we endorse are encouraged, even before the regular materials arrive, to begin their school year with short projects, such as preservation of food, characteristics of the fall season, or the history of Labor Day, along with a review of the skills. Yet we don't blame parents—and children who have been in conventional schools—if they feel more secure with the traditional method at first, at least until they get their "sea-legs." But we do encourage you to soon launch into short units of study as practice runs for longer projects.

If you have a burned-out youngster or what the school may have called a "learning disabled" child who has just been withdrawn from school, you may not have any choice of method—as Christine experienced with Jessica. (See chapter 2, "Of Course You Can Do It!") This happens often, and projects, mostly involving hands-on activities, are the only acceptable route.

How I Would Start

If I had several children to teach at home, I would first work on my household routine—fitting my program into the family needs. If my husband leaves for work at 7:30 A.M., I would have my children in bed early enough each night to get up at least by 6:30 and have a short worship or family time and breakfast with their daddy to start the day.

Next would be household chores with each one having duties to get the house in reasonable order *before* school. Yet I would try to work daily with one or more not only to teach them *how* to do their jobs, but also to help them understand team work. For example, if my child were just learning to make his bed, I would have him help me make mine, and then I would help him make his. If I had several children, I would also train any older or more competent child to help a little one (in household as well as school tasks) while we all worked toward our common goal. Cross-age and family-team education are important.

Then, for several reasons, I would have "school" at a regular time each day, perhaps 9:00 A.M., with brief opening exercises, probably including the Pledge of Allegiance to my country's flag, a song, and, in our home, a prayer. One reason for the regular time is that it makes you and your children systematic. They are secure in knowing what's next and that Mom is giving her time exclusively to them, at least for a short while. It will also help them feel that it is a real school in terms of social pressure from their friends. If under legal pressure, you can honestly report a schedule of your daily activities, yet stay relaxed, informal.

Under Sevens

If most of the children were seven or under, my "school" would be very informal, and I would try to adapt even to the youngest ones, at least for the first part. I would probably read to them, knowing that children who like to be read to will eventually learn to read; I would do some Scripture memory work and sing some songs. Since children's songs often are repetitious and the melodies simple, we might think up some different words to the songs or make up songs of our own. We might do some finger plays that rhyme and perhaps invent some new ones.

I would include poems in my reading and help them to hear words which sound alike and then play some rhyming games, such as "I see something in the room that rhymes with *fair*" (chair) or outdoors that rhymes with *class* (grass). Or I would play other sound games with them, such as "let's see how many words we can think of that start with *B* as in *baby*." We might make a scrapbook of drawings or cut-out pictures of objects which are classified by their initial consonant letters—*B, C, D,* etc. These ideas only scratch the surface of the informal activities which would make up the "skills" activities of our first session.

If I had a weak background in phonics, I would get a book for myself, but I would be very wary of starting an *intensive* phonics program for any child under seven. Informal, yes. I would start with the initial consonants, then the blends (br, bl, pr, st, sp, etc.), and later the long and short vowels.

Young children who have problems with reading are usually *just not ready.* When they are really ready, even the *difficulty* of the readers is not significant, unless in the meantime they have developed a serious mental or emotional block, convinced that they can never read. Often they can start, as they did in early pioneer days, with the Bible or the McGuffey readers. They were taught the letters and their sounds, often by their own parents, but they had no "controlled-vocabulary" dumbed-down readers contrived to enable teachers to more easily teach reading to young children, ready or not. When phonics are omitted or introduced too early, memorizing sight words, guessing by context or pictures are the routes to reading. A reasonably bright child can easily memorize the limited number of words which are repeated often in the first two or three levels of readers. When they reach the third or fourth grade, however, where vocabulary starts to increase, they can't keep up and if they haven't discovered some tools to unlock new words, they are lost. Many bright children devise systems of phonics, and other attack skills largely by themselves.

While my hands were busy with household duties, I would invite the children to work with me, not worrying about their ineptness. I would tell them stories of past family experiences, give them opportunities to talk, answer their questions, and just mother them naturally.

I would also try to find other times to read to the children and solicit help from Daddy, grandparents, or whomever is willing and able to share in this delightful educational process. My brother visited us in Japan while he was U.S. Army Inspector General during the Korean War. Soon our three-year-old Kathie brought her favorite book, climbed into his lap, and asked him to read to her. After his initial shock, he did. Dennis, a little more shy, would sit beside whomever Kathie "conned" — even Senior Prince Takamatsu, the Emperor's brother!

As I note their interests and need to express themselves, we would stop occasionally to talk about the pictures in the book or discuss their questions. Often I would read stories which have tiny pictures interspersed instead of key words and let each child have a turn reading the "pictures." I might have the older child read some words or parts as he is able. I would call attention to the title of the book or story and key words which may be repeated often, such as the main characters.

Sometimes I might move my finger from left to right to show how the words progress left to right across the page. This is a *learned* technique. Nothing in our brain is built-in to tell us that. Old Hebrew writing was from right to left, and Japanese Kanji may be either vertical, horizontal, right to left, or left to right, depending on its use (hymnal, book, etc.). It is *normal* for a young child to reverse letters and words in his first efforts to write. If the direction taken by words is not learned in the early steps of reading, a bad habit of reversals may be hard to overcome. *Yet this is not dyslexia!* Dyslexia as commonly applied to anyone who cannot read is technically incorrect, though reversals may be a symptom of a truly dyslexic child.

The *Random House Dictionary* says dyslexia is "an impairment of the ability to read due to a brain defect." Such a physical impairment could be caused by an accident, difficult birth, or serious illness. There may be an inherited tendency, though family habits of non-readers influence children also. *Our crucial point here is this: Any children who aren't brain damaged should not be wrongly labeled "dyslexic," simply because their brain and senses are not mature enough at the moment to handle the complete process of reading.* Also when you rush or eliminate phonics in teaching reading, your child may be unable to easily decipher these symbols. In 1975 the Michigan Reading Clinic reportedly examined over thirty thousand allegedly dyslexic children and found only two who were unable to learn to read. Most of them, labeled dyslexic by schools, have been brought home and taught by their parents to recover marvelously. In my "school," I would be much more relaxed about the timing of reading and writing skills.

Richard and Penny Barker of Millersburg, Ohio, are good examples of parents who are definitely not peer-dependent. They let their children develop naturally on their Ohio farmstead where they also take city children in for a week or so at a time to learn about life on a farm. Their Britt learned to read at age four and Maggie at age eleven, yet both were reading the same material by age twelve. Penny observes that Maggie has an easier time understanding what she reads. Penny concludes that

Reading is the footpath to secondary information, in contrast to primary information, which is what we take into our brain through our own experience or through interaction with the source of information. . . . I have found that it is not what he takes in second-hand that a child really *knows*, so much as what he, himself, actually experiences that becomes the foundation of his intelligence. . . . I've noticed over the years I've worked with children that they spend a good deal of time "doing." The experiences they gain from their physical involvement with the environment seem to give them something tangible on which to form their ideas about the world. . . .

When Britt (age fifteen), Maggie (age ten), and Dan (age nine) would go off on birding hikes, only Britt was a reader, so when the others spotted a bird and found a photo of it in the field guide, they would take the guide to Britt so she could help with the identification. Maggie and Dan, who could not rely on being able to read the field guide each time they wanted to recall the information, carefully remembered all that Britt would tell them. This meant that later when the information was wanted, Maggie and Dan had their knowledge with them, whereas Britt was dependent on having the field guide with her for the same information.[2]

A recent letter quite typical of many we have had about "late bloomers" may also give some of you some comfort:

At age nine and a half it was like a light clicking on somewhere inside his head. He no longer wanted all his lessons read to him, but actually *wanted* to read them himself. And he did!

At the end of . . . last school year, he tested at a level of Grade 8.6 in reading. Apparently he had reached his own IML [Integrated Maturity Level]. At the time of this writing, he is eleven, and reading is his best and favorite subject. *Winston Grammar* now makes sense to him and *Math-It* has become a breeze. Last summer he was able, entirely on his own, to write letters to friends and commercial businesses. . . . I used to have secret fears that my children were sub-intelligent, but they were *just little children*.[3]

The length and variety of that first "school" session must be adjusted to the ages, needs, and attention spans of the children.

Young children do best with short quiet periods, interspersed with work or play activity—"recess." If the weather were bad, marching, hopping, tiptoeing, or even fun calisthenics to music could add variety for physical education.

A little later I would involve them in some learning activity— a project, if you please: grocery shopping where they help identify different items by their labels and for which they might make lists, with pictures if not with words; food preparation with measuring; gardening; nature study; a visit to a shut-in; or making greeting cards or mementos for relatives or friends. I would dictate the spelling of some words for the one who knows his letters and help the others copy or even trace over my model of the message they want to convey.

There are very few children who do not want to be involved, so any little one who is really too young to participate must be sleeping, busy entertaining himself, or entertained by one of the family. This is a "management" problem for Mom, but again the teamwork concept must be used—sharing responsibilities appropriate to age and ability.

More often than not, there may be other activities I promised "when we have time," such as digging up ants to make an ant farm, perhaps hunting for the queen ant (without getting bitten!); doing a simple experiment we read about in a children's magazine or book; going to the library or possibly finding some information in our encyclopedia about a praying mantis which the children found yesterday. You may be, in a sense, always teaching, but relaxed. I notice in stores that mothers seem to be naturally responsive to their children about what they see and do.

If my six- or seven-year-old were eager to learn to read or write, I might spend an extra five to ten minutes a day or even twice a day with him in informal phonics, not forgetting these activities (when he is ready for them): (1) phonetic spelling by dictation, an important step in both phonics and spelling (asking him to find words that rhyme with *boy* and then going down the alphabet: coy, joy, soy, toy, etc.); (2) reading, including reading aloud together if he has progressed that far; and (3) writing or a simple math game. Pennsylvania psychiatrist and reading author Robert McKay stresses this "together" reading and singing. And don't ignore your next younger one if he wants to listen in, too.

I would carefully note how much my child really wanted these things, asking myself, "Am I pushing this on him?" Some discover that reading doesn't come by "magic," and lose interest for a while. Be sensitive to this so as not to pressure him and spoil his *long-term* motivation for learning.

I would certainly watch for opportunities which arise during the day which might serve as a springboard for our next morning session. I would also be alert to use counting and measuring for *math* and simple phonics on labels or recipes for *reading.* For example, "Do you hear the *o* in *Ho, ho, ho* in oats?" Then there would be simple *science* (action of baking powder or soda, vinegar, etc., as well as smell, taste, and touch) in my kitchen, and we would discover various creatures, flowers, or plants in our yard or on our walks. Simple map study, directions, and general layout in my neighborhood and community would be our *social studies*; and occasional experiences which the children dictate for "their own book" would serve as creative *writing.*

Now what subject did I miss? None. But these are only a few of the basic learnings which go on naturally within the four walls and neighborhood of a home, for example, manners, dependability, promptness, practical arts, common sense, honesty, compassion. I would do this program not only because it's good preschool education for my children, but also to have a daily log of activities in case I needed it in my state as proof that my six-year-old is indeed being educated. But be careful! Over-anxious mothers can adopt too much of a "teaching-mode" even with this program, pushing her children into *her* ideas of what they should learn instead of being sensitive to their readiness and interests.

After Seven

Depending on the children's needs, ages, and maturity, including secondary students, who are ready for some formal work in skills, we may spend twenty minutes to an hour and a half in practice, drill, and even workbooks, for mastery is your goal. But as project study unfolds and spelling, math, and reading are related to the subject being explored, these skills become more relevant and practical. Many boys are reluctant penmen, even up to ten or eleven. Five or ten minutes a day of *consistent* practice might be enough. If they are writing to a VIP or a pen pal, the minutes go faster. Use *their* interests!

I would train my children to be as obedient and independent of my help as is reasonable for their ages. I would also face the fact that if I had any children under the age of four or five, I could reasonably expect that I would be interrupted by one of them for some needed attention (I might take the phone off the hook for part of the morning). My "schedule" won't go smoothly every day. I can't do all the nice things with or without my children that I would like to do. And I can't have the social life or do what I see other mothers do who send all their children to school.

How a Unit of Study Works

The rest of the morning I would spend on project (or unit) learning, starting with any one of the content subjects, that is, science, social studies, religion. Explore, first on your own, and then with your children, the activities which you can do to integrate the skills and other content subjects into your main topic.

The Bible would be my first choice for its wide range of study, including both skills and other content subjects: language arts; some math; some science; geography; history; economics; government; music; art and crafts; and best of all, the related character qualities developed in the study of Bible heroes and events. For Christians no loftier subjects are available.

However, *if only the facts* of sacred happenings are repeated without the deeper understanding and application of the lessons inherent in the examples given, spiritual study becomes workbookish, dull, and lifeless. Combine your experience with their ideas in devising activities which will make the stories real; talk about their whys and hows — exciting motives and God's purpose in each incident and the lessons to be learned.

Or let's say your youngsters are interested in Iran. Let them study distances, weights, values, topography, products, religions, attitudes, clothes, literature, music, and on and on. Include the wars of the ages, and kings like Xerxes, queens like Esther, and cities like Susa (Shushan) and Babylon. Start with one idea and let it grow — with your own and your children's inventions. It's like starting with small, tightly-packed snowballs, rolling them in the snow, and making them into a big snowman.

Remember that things that are learned by experience last longer and that concepts, attitudes, values, and creativity are lifelong and permanent when facts may be relatively temporary, especially if not reviewed or used often. Remember that your job as teacher is not just to communicate knowledge but to impart that vitalizing energy which is inherent in the mind-to-mind and heart-to-heart relationship of one-to-one teaching.

If your children have been in traditional school, they may at first be at a loss for any ideas of their own. You may have to start gradually to resurrect and redevelop their creativity. It takes some families several months and some a year or two. Allow yourself and your children a little time for creative thought, and ideas will come. *Encourage, answer,* and *ask* whys and hows.

Here are several ways these projects may be launched:

1. A favorite religious, biographical, historical, or other story which may be from a variety of sources — a book; different versions of the Bible, Torah or Koran; the radio or a cassette tape; a video; or a presentation with pictures or felt figures on a flannel board. The story of *Heidi* could inspire the study of Switzerland, then and now; "Little House on the Prairie," could begin a study on the pioneers, and include making butter from cream, learning about their transportation, etc.

2. A particular chapter or section of a social studies or science book which sparks an interest.

3. A local happening such as the electricity being off for a day because of a storm, an accident in the neighborhood, or finding a lost puppy.

4. A current event such as an around-the-world yacht race (weather, ocean currents, time zones, use of the compass and navigation, keeping a log, use of a ruler to find the location of the boats on the world map with fifteen degree divisions, lands and peoples along the way, fish and birds, sailing terminology, etc.), the Olympics, a political election, court case, or legislative action; a disaster, military event, or political upheaval as in Palestine or Iran.

5. A field trip to Sea World or the zoo as a basis for study of oceanography or various animals. There is no limit to the

kinds of field trips that are available, but these can be overdone, especially for very young children.

6. An invitation to view the stars through a telescope at a friend's house or an observatory to touch off interest in astronomy.

7. Holidays or seasons of the year.

8. A family reunion, a visit by relatives, or photographs which begin an interest in family history.

9. A family business already started or one in which the children are active participants.

Working with your children becomes your life. Their imaginations are your inspiration. Trust them, exploit them as love only can. Whatever you do in the normal course of the day, you do it *with* them and watch them flourish beyond your dreams!

SIXTEEN

TRUE CONFESSIONS OF A PERFECTIONIST (PF)

BACKDROP: Dorothy Moore is our surprise among parent burnouts, but for slightly different reasons than most. Her PFism is a phenomenon which I have shared and respected for half a century, yet have only begun to understand in the past few months — as we are about to celebrate our fiftieth wedding anniversary. She always somehow handled the pressures of our busy family, thoroughly supporting a husband who, without realizing it much of the time, was perpetually on the educational frontier. But when she began sharing in our writing nearly fifteen years ago and had to share in answering thousands of letters and calls, her PFism stretched almost to the breaking point. No nervous breakdowns, mental or emotional disturbances, not even any discernible midlife crises, but a blood pressure that rose past the safety point and now must be managed carefully to insure that she never has a stroke. That led to even more lifestyle changes which for the first time she reveals here. Dorothy takes over at this point:

Some of you are PFs. You have told us so and admit that it is burning you out. You may have taken some of your high standards from our books. And we do believe in reasonably organized, sanitary homes, careful management, and well-behaved children. But we know that at times we have expected too much of ourselves, our children, and maybe a few others.

PFism has several basic problems, all with ego mixed in:

1. You wear yourself out reaching your own standards, those of others you love and respect, or even those of God. You try to be perfect by your own strength or increased efforts.

Perhaps if you work harder and longer, you can meet your own expectations. But if you don't make the grade, you are the hardest of all on yourself! You always strive to be better; you never feel good enough.

2. You have a tendency to protect your failures by denying that they are true and often pass the blame to someone else.

3. You believe that no one can do things as well as you can. So it is difficult for you to accept help, and you become critical of others — your spouse, your children, your secretary, or your service man — because they don't do things "right."

4. You are always in demand outside the home because you do things so well! Inside the home, you are a selfless and other-centered mother and wife, generating a *compulsion* to serve. Men get caught in this, too, and may browbeat wife and children.

5. And then there is procrastination. While I have somehow escaped this one, possibly because of some innate drive to tackle almost anything, authorities agree that fear of failure or rejection, especially in PF children, may induce procrastination (the "thief of time"). So they dawdle, are preoccupied about minutiae, often put off tests or delay getting jobs done, usually subconsciously "certain" they will have more time to do a better job later.

In case you wonder how children adopt these characteristics, experts have an answer for that, too. They learn it from adults — often very early in life — by pressures to perform, such as alphabet flash cards around the child's bed (part of a superbaby complex), heavy criticism for mistakes, overemphasis on achievement, too much sports or other rivalry before he is mature, praise of the child or the outcomes rather than his effort, boosting your own ego through your child's successes, reciting his virtues to others in his presence, or by *your* example of PFism — fussiness or work-a-holism. Teachers often add to the problem by commending only the best students or only excellent work.

Why Face Your Perfectionism?
I am a PF. And though not all PFs are alike, we may share some symptoms. If we're not careful, we pass them on to our children. The adults in my life all helped me perpetuate what-

ever PFism I may have inherited. Although they certainly meant well, they didn't do me any favor by indulging me. Maybe I can help some of you by telling you what I learned from the wise teacher called "Experience."

After giving birth to two husky, blond, blue-eyed boys whom my parents loved very much, my mother longed and prayed for a brown-eyed girl. When I arrived according to her specifications, she and Dad were excited, to put it mildly. They named me Dorothy, meaning "gift of God." I was the apple of their eye.

My parents felt that I was perfect—petite, feminine, cute, and smart! These are the words I heard all my young life. Every child wants and needs approval and affirmation, and, of course, I liked it! But it obviously was too much for me. As I see it now, I became dependent on it almost as if it were a drug. When I was older, my mother laughingly told me that one time when I heard some ladies talking about someone who was cute and smart, I whispered to her, "They're talking about me!"

Even though my brothers and I had been born on a South Dakota farm, our folks wanted "a better life" for us than we could have there. So after World War I, they moved to Long Beach, California, where they could invest the money they had earned in food production during the war. "Wonderful public schools" were available within walking distance in that sunny city, and since I was so smart (!), no one could think of depriving me of kindergarten, which not every public school had in those days. And they let me start when I was still four years old! Fortunately, the cut-off date kept me out of first grade at five, so I was a kindergartener for two years. Later, they had me skip a grade. Because of my efforts to live up to my already established reputation, I was the "Queen of the May," teacher's helper, and all the ego-boosting special things mothers of little girls love to hear about.

I doubled my efforts to deserve that adulation—staying at the head of the class, although at first I was too immature physically to compete well in sports. Later, with extra practice and effort, I made the peewee basketball team in grade school and finally earned my "letter" in high school.

As an eighth grader I brought honor to my school by winning the local and Los Angeles County spelling bee and tying for the California State title. But I had more physical illnesses than my brothers and my robust little sister, including a serious physical breakdown at the end of my eighth-grade year. I had to get out of bed to go to graduation and give my salutatorian speech. I had been beaten for valedictorian by another Dorothy who was also young and smart, but her daddy was a member of the school board! I'm sure that "defeat" hurt my ego considerably and made me even more determined and competitive.

In high school I won the L.A. County shorthand contest, was president and a gold medal member of the Scholarship Society, and valedictorian of my class. Yet peer pressure finally led me to believe that it wasn't popular to be smart and, besides, I was burned out. How I ever understood that I was too young to go to college, I'll never know, but at sixteen I turned down a scholarship to the University of Southern California, got a job, and stayed home a year before going to college. It was the wisest choice I could possibly have made.

Live a Balanced Life

I learned some things as I grew up: first by being too careless, in favor of a good time, and earning only mediocre grades my first year in public junior college. Then I went to a Christian boarding college and, though having gone to church all my life, found God for the first time. I began to find a middle ground, learned to take better care of my health by quality regular meals and sleep, kept a balance between recreation, work, and study, and reached out to help others rather than trying to rival them. This gave me elected leadership opportunities in a different way than I had had before.

My husband has helped me, too, sometimes with considerable initial resistance on my part. For example, if someone happened to drop by, he would occasionally invite them to stay for a meal—without asking me first! This caused arguments, but even after I convinced him to check with me ahead of time, I somehow couldn't refuse, because I eventually found that fellowship and sincere gratitude from students and friends came from just sharing a bowl of soup and bread.

The climax came in Japan when he invited Prince Takamatsu, brother of the Emperor, with his Princess to our campus and dinner in our home. I was panic-stricken, as were all the students and faculty. But he said, "Just feed him like you do me. I'm a son of the King." The prince ate our vegetarian American-style food heartily and came back for more of what he thought were breaded veal cutlets. I, of course, was delighted.

Be Prepared and Keep It Simple

The secret of my first real victory was when I learned, like a good Girl Scout, to "be prepared" with a well-stocked refrigerator and cupboards so that unexpected company did not distress me. I remember one time a crowd of about eight came unexpectedly, and I prepared an acceptable dinner with a great deal less stress. I'm not advocating waiting until guests arrive to start the meal, or never inviting folks ahead of time, but by being prepared and keeping it simple, hospitality can be much more joyous than when trying to do it all so perfectly.

Modify Standards

My second hurdle was to stop being so fussy about trivial things — not standards like health and morals — but looking for *simpler* ways of doing much the same thing and separating what I *must do* from what I *could do* and what would be *nice to do*. Often the last one and sometimes the last two need to be omitted. A helpful friend recently sent me a note about our friend Dr. D. James Kennedy's interview with a physician who gave two rules for handling stress: "(1) Don't sweat the small stuff, and (2) everything is small stuff."

For example, I found that if I wiped up spills on my kitchen floor immediately with a handy cloth or paper towel, I didn't have to mop and wax so often. If I used my leftovers promptly, wrapped things correctly or put them into appropriate containers, and wiped up little spots or spills, a major cleaning was needed much less frequently. We found that the right kind of bedspread greatly simplified bedmaking. I also learned a few things by observation. I remember a neighbor missionary in the Philippines who had a beautiful set of stainless steel copper-bottom cooking utensils hanging in her kitchen "on display." She polished the bottoms *after each use* in order to keep them shining. I had some of the same cookware, but even though I did polish them occasionally, I saw the futility of such a procedure.

I had another neighbor who did spring and fall housecleaning. I learned a lot of *what not to do* from her. In general, I think I'm a good housekeeper, but I've learned not to set unrealistic standards. Clutter still bothers me, but a little dust does not. If you are one who stays up until midnight to get your housework done, please know that there is a better way.

Though I continued to teach and demonstrate a standard to be reached, I found that appreciating my family's and others' *best efforts* in helping is more important than worrying about or redoing each job they do. I also realized that we would all survive very well by eliminating non-essentials.

Set Priorities

After God, human needs should be first, applied in order of importance — your husband, your children, the rest of your family, then others outside the family. Yet *what* the situation is and *when* the needs arise may alter your actions. Your family can often help you serve others in urgent situations (illnesses or accidents). Service is part of a well-rounded life and something you need to help your children understand, but it, too, needs to be monitored closely so as not to get out of hand. Volunteers are always much in demand; yet you can't do everything, so learn to say no when you must. Princess Grace of Monaco once told Raymond, "If only I could do it over, I would give up Red Cross and spend more time with my children."

After five years of professional teaching, I totally turned away from my career when our first baby arrived. At the time, Raymond was a U.S. Army officer in New Guinea, so I gave our baby boy a lot of time. But when Dennis was about eighteen months old, I chose to be involved in "child evangelism," partly because it was the kind of service for which I was best fitted and partly to insure that my own children had the kind of group spiritual life I could approve. I did not have to leave my child with a babysitter nor neglect my husband, because his lay-church involvement took place at the same time. I found this so rewarding that I kept it up for about forty years. But *I often had to resist other requests for my time*. I learned more about priorities the hard way.

Secure Help

After Kathleen, our second child, was two or three months old, I started having dizzy spells, not really serious enough to cause fainting, but enough to wonder what was the matter. When I went to my doctor, she asked me to tell her what I did every day, in and outside of the home. I told her my routine which involved obligations of a college dean's wife.

Her response was, "No wonder!" and her prescription was to hire a high school girl to do my once-a-day stack of dishes (no dishwasher then) and any other chores I could think of so I could take a nap with my children. It was hard for me, because I wasn't sure just *how* she would wash the dishes, but I squelched my doubts and did what I was told. My dizzy spells ceased in short order. *I learned the great value of a short mid-day nap.*

I confess that I didn't teach my children to work soon enough, mostly because I could do it faster and better while they *entertained themselves!* In Japan we had live-in student helpers. Yet our children became unusually good workers in spite of my neglect. Kathie was like my right hand. She often cleaned up after guest meals by herself so that we could visit with our guests. And Dennis earned all his tuition to a Christian high school as a sack boy, then checker in a supermarket.

Because your children need a great deal of your mothering efforts at birth and as long as they are in your home, I suggest that you *don't do anything for your children which they, with proper training, can learn to do for themselves or for you.* This is at least as good for them as for you. Help them know their responsibilities as members of the family team. Encourage them to help others.

Plan Rest and Personal Time

Everyone needs some privacy, including your children. Even when they outgrow naps, they are better off with a quiet time after lunch each day, to give both themselves and you a break — for rest, reading, or nothing. Besides that, you need "Mother's time out," best given by a thoughtful husband, grandmother, or other mother who trades off with you. Raymond always told me, "Name your time."

Accept Your Limitations

If, after applying all the above principles, you still fear failure and are tempted to procrastinate, remember that you need only to do your best *under the circumstances*. It is better to give your house a "lick and a promise" than to leave it in a shambles until you can make it meticulously clean. It is better just to hose the mud and salt off your car than to let it rust out because you never have time to wash and wax it to perfection.

Remember that *you* are the greatest gift you can ever give to your children. And your best for your children *under your circumstances* will likely be far superior to the preschool teacher's best with nineteen other children *under her circumstances*. The very best person you can be is *you*. Eventually, patience will have its perfect work.

Adopt the Serenity Prayer

This has been my panacea. I keep a plaque near my desk: "God grant me the serenity: To accept the things I cannot change. The courage to change the things I can. And the wisdom to know the difference." The "things" you can change are *yourself*, including your emotional blocks, *your negative feelings*, and *your schedule*. I have often heard it said that it's not so much what happens to you as how you react to it. This is *your* choice. Ask God to help you get rid of anger, resentment, a critical spirit, and frustration which devour your energy. Learn to love your "enemies." Develop compassion. Become a forgiver. Do some inner searching to discover what is causing these emotions.

The "things" you cannot change are *others*, *the past*, and *heredity*, You can pray for others, but you must give them the same choice that is yours. I was much relieved when I really accepted that fact. Profit from past mistakes—yours and others—but don't dwell on them or suffer from them. Forgive yourself, and others, as God forgives.

Indeed, knowing which is which will help you most of all. When you are tempted to feel critical, frustrated, resentful of others' actions, breathe a prayer, "God, grant me the serenity . . ."

THE REAL HOMEWORK: FAMILY INDUSTRIES AND SERVICE

BACKDROP: Manual work brings nobility and self-respect no other activity can match. It unites and balances head and hand. Its value is a remarkable verity of history, yet today is commonly disdained. It understands and unites all races and creeds, builds promptness, integrity, and dependability. It thrives on initiative and nurtures creativity. It is far from homework as commonly worshiped—or hated. And it becomes a more effective therapy as students approach and go through the teens.

When united with the heart, the head and hand move out in selfless service to others. There is no discipline formula that can match this experience of work and service. So naturally we are going to be giving it to you often with different stories and in different ways in seminars, on radio and television, and through our articles and books. As most families have moved in from the country to the city, they have left their chores behind and substituted sports and amusements which often build selfishness more than selflessness. And we pay a big price.

There he sits, a noted scholar and teacher who makes his living with his hands so that his classes will survive without having to appeal for funds. He knows his professional field has become an unpopular one, and he just doesn't have the audacity to push himself on others. This quiet, unusual fellow once was one of the most influential and dangerous men in his nation. Now he sits there on a remnant of rumpled "canvas," making and repairing tents while he dictates letters to Timothy, his male secretary, who also is learning the tent-making trade from him.

Our scholar would not be unusual because he has a Ph.D. Being skillful with his hands would not be at all strange in his country. There it is considered almost a crime for a man to come out of school without a manual skill. What makes him different is that he *is* a Ph.D (or its equivalent), and *still* works with his hands, humbly and creatively serving others. He lives and speaks a deep and simple message: "Make it your ambition to lead a quiet life, to mind your own business and to work with your hands . . . so that you will not be dependent on anybody."[1]

This simple man, once a cruel Pharisee, became one of history's most influential teachers. The experiences of many institutions—public, private, parochial, from kindergarten through university—show that the balancing and invigorating effect of developing and using manual skills endows students and adults with unusual mental capacity.[2]

The Benefits of Work

In Japan, the little college that we reorganized after World War II developed from one of that nation's lowest academically to its highest in competitive examinations within four years after starting a work program in which all students worked *with their teachers* at least twenty hours a week. A similar experience in the Philippines was honored by then President Ramon Magsaysay and the Philippine Congress.

In California, where the public high school Regional Occupational Programs (ROPs) work the students half-time without pay, the students' achievement averages *above* California norms. In colleges like Warren Wilson College in North Carolina, Blackburn in Illinois, Hartland in Virginia, and Weimar in California, which have led in such balanced programs, the achievement and behavior of students is exceptional. J. C. Penney so appreciated the work program at Missouri's School of the Ozarks that he reportedly left that institution half the stock he owned in his company.

The one method most likely to help parents avoid burnout in home teaching is to allow at least half the day for activities in which children can work constructively and creatively, usually with you, but with increased responsibility as they mature and can accept commensurate authority. Don't worry if your children are only age six or eight. Make *them* the officers in your family "corporation." Let your oldest or most able be your president; but you had better be chairman of the board. If your name is Smith, call it "Smith Industries," "Smith Associates," "The Smith Corporation," "Smith and Sons," or another name or logo.

Penny Barker offers some unusual insights into this cure for boredom or restlessness which more home schoolers might use to greater advantage, especially if motivation problems are stressing them out.[3] About eight years ago she noticed "that every time the children worked on a constructive project outside, they would spend the next one to three hours involved in some inside activity with intense concentration." It is no accident that her observations are true and she tells why:

> The time outside seems to release an energy that, when bottled up, takes the form of edginess in the more closed environment of the inside. They seem to need the balance of indoor and outdoor activity. Yet it seems to be more than a large-muscle release. I think it is a need for connection with the earth and the air and the spaciousness of the out-of-doors that no amount of running around inside, jumping on beds, or tumbling on the floor can replace.

Of course, she has one great advantage over city dwellers and even suburbanites. She and her husband, Richard, live on a farmstead, and outdoor work for the whole family is not just a choice, but a necessity — a blessed necessity, some would feel.

One day recently they worked an hour and a half pitching bad-smelling manure from their sheep barn. Because of deep snow, they couldn't use their pony-drawn spreader as usual, but had to do it *by hand*. They were so exhausted when they finished and "trudged up the hill through a bitter cold wind," they couldn't even enjoy their "beautiful panoramic view at the top."

After restoking their bodies with brown bread, canned peaches, and sumac tea, the children drifted off to their own chosen activities, their custom after such a "farmstead project." Within fifteen minutes Penny observed:

Dan writing with great concentration on a book he and Ben are writing together. The position of his body and intense look on his face showed me that he was totally involved in his work. From the next room I could hear the typewriter going at a real pace as Britt worked on her weekly newspaper column, "Letters Home," a journal account of a recent fourteen-week trip she took. Ben had earphones on and was listening raptly to someone speaking German as he followed pictures in a book that portrayed what was being said on the tape. Jonah had his wooden barge down on the floor and was carefully balancing model zoo animals on every available space of the boat. Maggie lay near the wood stove on her stomach poring over her book on training sheepdogs.

Penny further notes that being outside makes children more cooperative, calm, and ready for concentration on mental tasks — an almost therapeutic experience. She recommends this *balance* for its very positive effects for both adults and children.

Ginny Greenwood writes from Pennsylvania about her seven-year-old Carol who "initiates an idea and incorporates the neighborhood kids, older and younger, to bring it to fruition," almost always making a profit. Her businesses range from "chip chip" cookies, with or without nuts, to making and selling bird feeders. She sometimes "cons" older children into writing down the orders as she makes house calls, "because they can write faster than she." A brother and sister team, six and eight, recently visited us, reporting a daily profit of twenty dollars making and selling bread, usually one or two days a week.

But work-study programs usually demonstrate their big power when children move into their teens. Heidi Martin of Grants Pass, Oregon, has already been in several businesses, including making and selling bread and muffins. Now, at sixteen, she has her own office equipment business. Her brother Brent, thirteen, packages and sells soy milk locally and across the country, delivering by UPS.

Ideas for Industry
Although we have experimented with work-study programs well over forty years and have read many books on them and written some, we have seen few summaries as well done as this

one which veteran home teacher, Nancy Plent, wrote in No. 25 of her *Unschoolers Network* letter which she entitled "Anything But Nine to Five!" It was written in reply to the demand of a *busy* mother with very young children for an *unstressful* industry "involving very young children . . . to be run ENTIRELY from her home, with no trips out, no need for a sitter, no running around at night selling at 'party plans,' and no big investment":

> The simplest solution is to start a service business based on homemaker skills you already have. If your life is too confined to even think of going out, this is no time to stress yourself by trying something unfamiliar. Sewing, cooking, or ironing services, for example, might fit right in your daily routine.

> We emphasize the service angle, because the big problems arise when you have a finished "product" to sell. Selling products means you have to leave home to show your wares and get orders. Forget about producing adorable baby buntings or clever crafts. Products bring complicated problems that can only be solved by leaving home for extended periods.

> Possible sewing services, for example, include repairing, alterations, decorating (monograms, appliques, etc.), or making up patterns to order. Your customers could do the picking up and dropping off. You might have to go out periodically for thread, but that's about all! Sewing instruction in your home is another possibility.

> It's hard NOT to have a finished product if cooking is your forte. But you wouldn't have to go out to sell baked goods if you planned and advertised carefully. Let people know they can pick up hot, fresh goodies from your home certain evenings as they return from work and see if they don't respond. Or bake birthday cakes to order.

> Producing whole take-out meals once or twice a week for working couples is another idea. You could do that while you cook for your own family. Cooking instructions in your home might be a little disruptive to your family schedule, but perhaps better than going out to teach.

> Working couples who have no time for ironing might appreciate that service. Even in a polyester age, some things like dress shirts need help to look office-neat.

There's a great need for good child care today. This would probably be the most demanding service on your time and energy. Providing a place in the afternoon for latch-key children would be less confining though probably less profitable, too.

Typing isn't exactly a homemaker skill, though it was once considered right up there with cooking as a necessity for women. It still has economic potential. Students with term papers due and businessmen who are understaffed often hire outside typists to do their work.

While you could advertise these services in traditional ways, you might start out just fine by having some cards made up and giving them out to friends and neighbors.

Notice from this list that the very thing you are, a homemaker, is what a two-paycheck family is missing! Aim your at-home services to the families that CAN'T stay at home and you might successfully "find a need and fill it."

We often report at our seminars or in the *Moore Report* about children who sell bread or cookies or muffins. Almost everyone likes muffins. Find out what kind the neighbors, church members, local support group, or people at Dad's office like. Or put up an order pad on a local bulletin board. If local village or city ordinances permit it yet your children are too young to go out alone, let them go from door to door to solicit orders while you remain in the car with the younger children. After they build a muffin or cookie route, they will probably have little more need for door-to-door solicitation. Just be sure you are producing the best around. Good products have a way of selling themselves, once you get started.

When children are old enough to make the products themselves and the growing business is beginning to stress parents, some let their children hire carefully selected friends from the local schools as commission agents. The more nutritious you make these mealtime or snack foods, the better. People are more health-conscious these days, and that's a plus for your market — putting raisins and nuts in those oatmeal cookies and muffins, for example, instead of only chocolate chips and other sweets.

Do your own market research. Find the best thing for you and your children to make or sell, or the best services to provide.

If you are shy, ask a business friend to help you. Better still, encourage your children to do the asking. You may begin with lemonade. So what if they don't make a big profit in money from the start; the profit will be immense in discipline and behavior. One child reported that adults, including their thirsty mailman, were quite willing to pay fifty cents for a large glass of cold lemonade! Some families who make sandwiches, cookies, or bread develop a custom-made operation to avoid strict local restrictions on retail food production—selling to friends, through the church, or simply preparing something out of their home. In any event, it pays to be thoroughly clean in all that we do.

One of the simplest ways to get youngsters started in business management is to get out your past year's utility bills for them to add as an arithmetic exercise. If your bill totals twelve hundred dollars, challenge them with reducing the bills next year by taking shorter showers and otherwise learning frugality; tell them that all they save, the family (or they) can, for example, enjoy next Christmas or for a vacation. This idea of saving can carry over to many things such as car washing and care, food and clothing budgets, and house repair. One of the leading per-hour workers among home schoolers has been Andreas Anderson of New Orleans who was earning up to fifty dollars an hour making computer ROMs when he was fourteen, and now runs his own computer business at nineteen. Another nineteen-year-old, Jeffrey Ryan, started out before he was into his teens and now owns and operates a catalogue mail-order business, computer software business, and is graphics consultant for trial lawyers. He goes to university on the side. The McKim family of Dallas, under the guidance of their mother, Julie, and truck-driver father, earned over twenty thousand dollars last year with work ranging from baby-sitting to catering and arranging weddings.

Such work is not remotely related to child abuse. When you share the planning with your children and they become officers in your family enterprise, manual work becomes a privilege. In almost all cases, those who suggest likelihood of abuse in protesting home schooling lack an understanding of the therapy of work. When we ask parents of honored students how they get their children to study so much, they generally respond, "Study is enough of a change from work that they enjoy it." No abuse here!

The Spirit of Service

Giving without expecting tangible returns is manual labor's character-building buddy. It completes the duo which offers the most for the least effort in bringing out great behavior and selfless maturity in your children. When homes and schools overlook this fact of education, they deprive their students of the most profound understandings and most precious blessings.

Service education should, whenever possible, start in the home with parents sharing the home duties. Notice we say "sharing." Children must realize that if they are to have the security and sustenance of home, they should do their share increasingly as they mature. And usually we expect less than they can readily do. Children are ready to work when they are ready to walk, as we have written time and again in our articles and books. Let them learn how to pick up and put away their own toys and books.

We have enjoyed watching our grandchildren as they have learned to put their things away, with Kathleen teaching Bryon, the oldest, and letting him teach his two younger brothers, Brent and Bradd. We have written of this before, but only recently have we realized the beautiful job by another of several "daughters" who have graced our home. For example, Del Retha Haugen is terrific with her trio: a boy and two girls. Her husband, Perry, is an honored senior in a high-cost medical school, and she works as a nurse on weekends when he can be home with the children. We have never seen her house in disarray, although we have often visited without advance notice. Her oldest, Thor, age eight, teaches the girls. And you quickly observe that whenever they get out a book or two, they put them away before picking out others.

Home is our best base for service to others—in nursing homes, hospitals, and even prisons, or to the aged or handicapped neighbor down the street. Diane Alme and her four sons in Madison, Wisconsin, are a good example. I have watched the Alme boys go on regular weekly or daily missions to aged or infirmed neighbors, setting out their garbage, and running errands without expecting pay. When we stayed with the Sullivan family in Orlando, Florida, we saw their five daughters get up at 5:30 in the morning to get their chores done on certain days so that they could clean house for "a little old lady" before going to church for the religious part of their day's study. Their "Sullivan Sisters Sitting Service", which we have admired for years, has expanded now into a number of "industries" and pays them well as a family both in money and in character.

So we do distinguish "service" here from money-making. Children may weed gardens or mow lawns as unselfish gestures to elderly couples; other times weeding or lawn care will be one of the family industries.

The thoughtfulness of service will enter into the relationships between children both in and out of the home. Janice Dietrich wrote us about her John, six, who visited a little "Sally" with whom he "hit it off well." The next day after the Dietrichs returned home, John worked all morning making her a variety of pretty things. Midway through the morning Janice casually mentioned that Sally's little sister might feel sad if she didn't get anything. He replied, "Well, she's going to have a crown, too," and got right to making the same things for her.

You will note in Parts 4 and 5 that many families combine work and service neatly. The January 1988 *Iowa Home Educators News Letter* tells how Carla Banks and her five teenagers went to Colorado Springs to help the catalog house that was selling the chalkboards, marker boards, cork boards, and easels the Banks were making as a family industry. The catalog company was a month behind in filling orders. So the family went to the Colorado Springs company and helped as volunteers.

The owner and his family were grateful. During that week he had the most business ever. The family returned home delighted with their "apprenticeship" and with what they had learned and the impression they had given for home education. A week later they were startled to find sizeable checks in the mail with thanks.

Another angle comes from Gerald and Pauline Strong in Veyo, Utah, who take in children of tragedy without pay, in addition to the nine of their own thirteen who are still at home.[4]

We have always tried hard to be a close loving family. Since we became a home schooling family a little over two years ago, we have had an easier time of this. Recently through a family tragedy, we have added three more little children to our family. Now we have six little ones between the ages of two and five, plus our nine-, eleven-, twelve-, and fourteen-year-olds who are home schoolers also. Our children are doing well and we believe it is because of your teaching us the proper principles. . . .

I would like to let you know that in spite of our faults and weaknesses which still remain, our family has become well known in the area we live in for our home schooling. The children are well-respected, and the two oldest girls earn about three hundred dollars a month baby-sitting. Our boys help in the garden and are helping Dad add on to the house. Almost every week we receive inquiries on how to begin home schooling.

Working at Home Versus Homework

So, these richest and most available of methods to build great characters and high achievers are there for the asking and the taking, like an open bank vault with an invitation to take all you need. And with a little attention to the principles and experienced methods we suggest, there is very little risk of burnout. Please don't forget that manual work and service are strengtheners of achievement; so don't let anyone tell you that you don't have time. Just do it with your children and have fun as you train them to be good business leaders and great neighbors. Contrast this picture with the average child who already has too many academic pressures and not enough personal teacher attention: He is sent home every day with a lot of books to (1) keep him busy all evening, (2) keep him away from his family whom he needs, (3) prevent him from doing his share of the chores and from learning responsibility, (4) tempt him to have his parents or others do his work for him. And all of this usually with the approval and often the ignorant urging of his busy and indifferent mother and dad.

Even the NEA found that teacher responsiveness and supervised study were superior to homework.[5]

Let your children grow up naturally and spend the evenings *with* you, lest soon they prefer to spend them *away* from you! With *you*, work and services are their greatest learning experiences. Finally, surprisingly, work programs almost automatically provide most of the daily structure and schedule you need for an otherwise natural learning program.

EIGHTEEN

GETTING ORGANIZED *IS* POSSIBLE . . . HERE'S HOW

BACKDROP: The plague of disorganization somehow doesn't pass the doorposts of home schools. Even to those who feel they are *organized*, it is more deceptive than they think, and to those who are sure they are *disorganized*, it is simpler than they think. Here we will try to point out a few common pitfalls, scuttle a little ego, and show how any homemaker can be organized *enough*— but not too much.

The only person I have ever known who was perfectly and consistently organized every moment I ever saw him was one of my college roommates. In order to be so clean and manicured, he got up every morning *at least* an hour before I did to do his ablutions at the one lavatory-and-mirror we had in our dorm room. He made his bed perfectly before he left the room *every* day. Shoes were polished and clothes immaculately clean and pressed. Never a hair was out of place. Comparatively speaking, I was disheveled and disorganized, yet he treated me with a respect bordering on reverence. Although eventually he became a highly skilled professional, he seldom seemed really happy.

Which leads us to ask, "Organized for what?" For ego's sake? For superefficiency? Or for an uncluttered, relatively orderly life? The last is the one we recommend to home teachers.

What do we mean? In the first place, one of the most frequent cries of despair is, "You just don't know what a battle I have. I have no idea how to get organized." Yet you chance into their homes, and one will be beautiful, another a wreck. On the other hand, some have no worries and no compunctions about organization or order, yet do a fairly good job at teaching.

Where is our midpoint? Our optimum operation? After having successfully run a few labor crews in partnership with Dad, and later school systems, colleges, and universities, one would expect that I would be organized. And corporately, I was. I could plan and delegate duties and follow through to be sure they were carried out. Yet personal organization was a problem to me until Dorothy *by example* showed me how. You don't live happily with an organized person for fifty years and not learn something about personal order! Today I am almost more organized than she.

But she has taught me that there are such things as priorities. Sometimes Monday's washing may have to wait until Wednesday, and *very* occasionally, dirty dishes may have to pout in the sink or dust particles may have to remain on the coffee table. Hardly ever, but we've even been known to leave the bed unmade in an emergency. When we are writing books, our writing room—just now our bedroom—remains in orderly disarray. Yet there is no excuse for sloppy, disheveled rooms with clothes scattered all over the floor, children who eternally look as if they never had a bath, and flies, roaches, or mice running all over the place retrieving crumbs carelessly strewn around.

This kind of home gives me the shivers when I'm called to witness in court, or even to claim the family as one of home schooling's own. Yet some of these dear people are among the most creative we have ever seen, with emotionally stable and mentally thriving youngsters who are often more courteous than many from refined families we've seen in elegant mansions. Is there any reason why we can't find some compromise in all this? To avoid either extreme? We think we can.

Our daughter, Kathie, taught several years before her first son was born. Now she has three little boys and is blossoming in her organization as a home school leader-teacher-mother-wife. When Bryon was almost a year old, Dorothy wrote her a letter, which evidently encouraged her, because she kept it and recently sent us a copy to excerpt for this book:

I have been thinking of your plea to help you get a little better organized — that you sometimes feel you don't get much done. I sense your feeling of frustration.

In the first place, don't try to be like me. Remember, you're the duckling and I'm the Mother Hen who was surprised to hatch a duck's egg. We're just different in personality, though I am gratified and sometimes surprised to see how many of my ways have rubbed off on you. Besides I have thirty-three years head-start on you in which I have learned a lot — one part of which is that I will *never* catch up. My favorite saying is, "The hurrier I go, the behinder I get."

I doubt that I am actually as organized as I seem to be — perhaps in contrast to some, but never as much as I would like. . . . *A creative, reasonably ambitious person never has enough time to do all he thinks up to do.* And homemaking has a lot of creative possibilities. Besides, giving Bryon proper nurturing is the most important work in the world — more important than making granola or even cleaning the house. Just be sure not to *indulge* him — thinking always of his *best* good now and in the future.

Of course, it's always good to plan your day — usually the night before — making a list and marking things in order of priority. It is also good to make weekly and monthly lists. This gives you direction. But if you don't finish a day's list on that day, put it on the next day's list. Mark off your items as they are done. If you keep your dated lists around for a while and look at them later, you will be surprised how many things you have actually accomplished.

Charts and Forms

Possibly the worst hazard on this path to organizational moderacy is what I call "The Daytimer Syndrome." This is no sneer at *Daytimers*. It is publishers' *misuse* of such ideas that leads inexperienced mothers to *over organization* — an evil likely to burn them out even faster than disorganization. Some people think they must record every thought and act of the day to be orderly. They end up frustrated because they haven't enough time even to jot down recordable tasks, much less carry them out!

A tearful, if not appalling, example was an obedient, fearful, but meticulous mother for whom we witnessed recently in an east coast court. She was an excellent teacher, though almost burned out from a combination of formal curricula, official pressures, and—her family "organizer." She bought it from a speaker-exhibitor at a home school meeting and had *tried* to use it, but just "couldn't do it all." This is the very kind of educational litter that keeps classroom teachers so preoccupied with minutiae that they don't have time to exercise the most valuable teaching tool of all—the warm personal response. Such litter becomes garbage with a psychological stench, stifling creativity, destroying freedom, burning out parent and child.

If it had been a little Daytimer-type notebook, with pages of mostly the same kind of forms, I might have justified it, at least with some modification. But when some of us asked to see how she was organized, she showed us *fifty-one* pages of *different kinds* of forms, many of which were masters which she was to duplicate for daily or other repeated use, plus fourteen large, mostly two-columned, fine-print pages of instructions on how to use the organizer. Then she apologized: Because of pre-trial confusion, she couldn't find *dozens more* of the "organizers" other forms!

I didn't have time to look them over at the time, but heard the groaning of mothers as they looked over those sixty-five pages during court recess. *Four or five forms would have been plenty.*

What forms do we suggest?

First, make up your mind whether you are willing to plan your work and work your plan. If not, don't read any further.

Second, if you do want to be organized and are willing to plan and work it, obtain or make for yourself and your children these simple methods and use them approximately as we suggest. At least try before you burn out. Otherwise, home schooling becomes an endurance contest to your breaking point. Most of the veterans testify that being organized is the only way to cope.

1. Note Pad with Tear-Off Sheets. These will be throw-away lists, once the item is purchased or the errand done. Keep your pad in a handy place such as on your kitchen bulletin board or secured with a magnet on your refrigerator. The sheets should be small enough to be handy and big enough not to lose when you need them most. Jot down the grocery items when you see your supply getting low to avoid extra trips to the store.

Consolidate and jot down here other necessary errands — the bank, dry cleaners. Think through your routing so that you will not have to retrace your travel. Unnecessary trips burn you!

2. Calendar. Monthly calendars are available which have a block of space for each day of the month. We often get them free from supermarkets, funeral homes, and other sources. Or you or your children can make your master copy on an 8½ × 11″ sheet of paper or old file folder, five squares high and seven wide (without the dates). Then duplicate it twelve times and let your children put on the dates! Write in family appointments, birthdays, or anniversaries you want to remember and field trips, workshops, or other home school meetings. This can be on your bulletin board, or if it is better for you to have everything together, punch holes in the edges and put it in a three-ring binder with a divider for each of the types of records you need. Some parents make their lesson plans on one of these and their journal in another with *larger* spaces.

3. Menu Plan. Anticipating meals for a week or more saves both time and money and helps you to know that you are giving your family the proper nourishment. Add to your shopping list while you jot down your menus and keep them flexible enough to take advantage of the produce specials. Put down "green or yellow vegetable" instead of "carrots" or "broccoli," or "raw salad" instead of "lettuce and tomato." Use simple, fresh, unrefined foods, and don't forget those leftovers!

Shop on those days when the freshest produce shipments come to your market as well as the weekly specials. Buy only when fresh and the price is right. Don't be afraid to substitute.

You may want to include this menu plan in one division in your notebook. The chart simply has the days of the week listed down the side and "Breakfast, Dinner, and Supper" across the top with another column for little jobs which need to be done the day before to plan for the meal, such as "Soak beans tonight," "Make up waffle batter," or "Take out frozen fruit."

4. Lesson Plans and Journal or Diary. These documents, *especially the journal*, are not only mandatory in many states but are vital if you are ever investigated for any reason. There is no guarantee that you won't be, whether you are up front with the school officials or operating "underground." If you don't have the "qualifications" required by the state, they are even more essential to demonstrate your competence.

Good records are the best protection you can have and officials are usually impressed. They are even more impressed if your children also have their own faithfully kept journals. If too young to write, let them dictate a few words to you in reviewing each day. These provide nostalgic reminders for later years and reminiscences when you become grandparents.

If you make the kind of flexible, skeletal lesson plans we suggest—with large blocks of time—and then flesh them out at the end of the day with the activities accomplished, you will have the best record you can keep. The usual two-page spread with a block for every subject is more than most people could—or anyone should—have to fill in. You can keep separate records for each child or combine them. At the end of the week or the month, review your plans to see what you've covered. Then after checking your objectives fill in the chinks, if needed, for the next week.

5. *Grade and Attendance Book.* We think such records are unnecessary, but if your state requires this separate record, you can usually pick up a folder or booklet from almost any school or school supply house if you don't make your own. Otherwise your dated daily log may be adequate. After all, if you had "school," your children had to be present. We don't believe in grades either, but grade as you wish or the state demands. The easiest system is usually S for satisfactory and U for unsatisfactory. School officials are generally most impressed by what they are used to seeing—attendance and grades "at a glance." This record can fit your own formal, semi-formal, or informal program. But don't over-record as the workshop promoter urged our court mother to do or you will be exhausted as she was and may burn out!

Order in the Court!

Finally, there is a matter of organization which too many home teachers overlook. In some respects it is the most crucial of all: cleanliness and order. If a sloppy, filthy, disordered home doesn't stress you at least a little, you — and your children — are to be pitied. There is no earthly — or heavenly — reason for a littered car, a smelly refrigerator, an all-fall-down closet, a cluttered back porch (or any room), or cupboards that look like a tornado went by.

This problem is not limited to "uneducated" people. Two of the worst we've seen were homes of highly respected and successful home teaching families. In both families parents had master's degrees and were Christians. If order is the first law of heaven, God must have been disappointed.

Our concern is the children and what they are being taught by example. We must repeat what we've suggested earlier: We have held our breath a few times when we knew that a social worker or school official might visit one of these homes. Would this confirm their worst theories on home education? It takes only a few blots on an otherwise white wall to give an impression of collective stupidity and filth among home schoolers. So all of us have a stake in this. We've had to urge some parents, in the face of possible court investigation, to clean up their acts.

What we oftentimes face is a chronic habituation to filth, so that parents really don't have a decent standard. If you have any idea that you may be one of these, invite a friend in confidence to your home to help you elevate your standards and to straighten you out. Make it a total family project. Some take before-and-after pictures, like those of the weight-losers' ads.

Have a place for everything, and everything in its place, even if you have cardboard boxes for certain sized toys or muddy shoes or kindling wood. Be sure that *all* clothes are either hung up or folded and put away — again in cardboard boxes if you have no other containers. Hang your shirts, suits, and dresses all in one direction. Line up your shoes on the floor or on a shelf and keep them polished if they are "for best." Have a plan for your kitchen pans; keep your silverware separated by wood, plastic, or cardboard divisions.

Organization is not time-expensive; it is time-saving! It is not keeping fancy, exhaustive records; it is eliminating them by using simple devices and common sense. Organization, in the final analysis, is your mind-set. With the few suggestions we have given you here and a little determination, a lot of your burnout stress will disappear. We know. We've tried it! And you will be doing some of the greatest teaching of all — giving your children by your example the character base of healthy bodies and orderly minds.

PART FOUR

BURNOUTS WHO BECAME HEROINES . . . AND HEROES

One Little Boy, by Helen E. Buckley

Once a little boy went to school.
He was quite a little boy.
And it was quite a big school.
But when the little boy
Found that he could go to his room
By walking right in from the door outside,
He was happy.
And the school did not seem quite so big
Anymore.
One morning
When the little boy had been in school awhile
The teacher said:
"Today we are going to make a picture."
"Good!" thought the little boy.
He liked to make pictures.
He could make all kinds:
Lions and tigers,
Chickens and cows,
Trains and boats—
And he took out his box of crayons
And began to draw.

But the teacher said: "Wait!
It is not time to begin!"
And she waited until everyone looked ready.
"Now," said the teacher,
"We are going to make flowers."
"Good!" thought the little boy.
He liked to make flowers.
And he began to make beautiful ones
With his pink and orange and blue crayons.
But the teacher said "Wait!
And I will show you how."
And it was red, with a green stem.
"There," said the teacher,
"Now you may begin."
The little boy looked at the teacher's flower.
Then he looked at his own flower.
He liked his flower better than the teacher's.
But he did not say this.
He just turned his paper over
And made a flower like the teacher's.
It was red, with a green stem.
On another day
When the little boy had opened
The door from the outside all by himself,
The teacher said:
"Today we are going to make something with clay."
"Good!" thought the little boy.
He liked clay.
He could make all kinds of things with clay:
Snakes and snowmen,
Elephants and mice,
Cars and trucks —
And he began to pull and pinch
His ball of clay.
But the teacher said: "Wait!
It is not time to begin!"
And she waited until everyone looked ready.
"Now," said the teacher.
"We are going to make a dish."
"Good!" thought the little boy.
He liked to make dishes.
And he began to make some
That were all shapes and sizes.

But the teacher said "Wait!
And I will show you how."
And she showed everyone how to make
One deep dish.
"There," said the teacher.
"Now you may begin."
The little boy looked at the teacher's dish.
Then he looked at his own.
He liked his dishes better than the teacher's.
But he did not say this.
He just rolled his clay into a big ball again.
And made a dish like the teacher's.
It was a deep dish.
And pretty soon
The little boy learned to wait,
And to watch,
And to make things just like the teacher.
And pretty soon he didn't make things
Of his own anymore.
Then it happened
That the little boy and his family
Moved to another house
In another city,
And the little boy
Had to go to another school. This school was even bigger
Than the other one,
And there was no door from the outside
Into his room.
He had to go up some big steps
And walk down a long hall
To get to his room.
And the very first day
He was there,
The teacher said:
"Today we are going to make a picture."
"Good!" thought the little boy,
And he waited for the teacher
To tell him what to do.
But the teacher didn't say anything.
She just walked around the room.
When she came to the little boy,
She said, "Don't you want to make a picture?"
"Yes," said the little boy.

"What are we going to make?"
"I don't know until you make it," the teacher said.
"How shall I make it?" asked the little boy.
"Why, any way you like," said the teacher.
"And any color?" asked the little boy.
"Any color," said the teacher.
"If everyone made the same picture,
And used the same colors,
How would I know who made what,
And which was which?"
"I don't know," said the little boy.
And he began to make a red flower,
With a green stem.

NINETEEN

WARNINGS FROM DISAPPOINTED MOTHERS

BACKDROP: Here are a few of the many letters which stimulated and guided the writing of this book. Some authors were burned out and have recovered. We have not been able to reach any who did not recover. Some never burned out at all, and they have told us why. We pass these on because they remind us of the hundreds of you who have said to us, some with anguish, some with latent anger, "Can you?" or "won't you?" or "why don't you do something about it?" Here they are, generally unedited.

From Washington State

My daughter has been heartbroken as one after another of her friends have returned to school—five families at the beginning of this school year and three more since. In *every* case they were using the same format curriculum. They were so structured they couldn't take a day off to go on a field trip.

It was the parents who burned out, not the kids. The kids wanted to stay home but the mothers couldn't handle being the teacher, pushing all the time with no time to enjoy their kids and be their mother. Instead of giving up the rigid curriculum and school-at-home concept, they have sacrificed their kids to the public schools.

I have learned quickly from fellow home schoolers to relax and balance structure with learning experiences. When we began home schooling one and a half years ago, my daughter, who had been in a K-3 Christian school, was lost without the formal structure. We did use more structure the first six months, but got away from it by the end of last school year.

This year has been even more fun than last year. We do use some curriculum, including workbooks, but we skim through, using only a few problems per page, mostly in math and Bible. We are really enjoying science as we have gotten into the unit method or block-learning method. One way we are learning history is by reading good books (biographies). I dropped structured penmanship and spelling in favor of creative writing. It's amazing how she loves creative writing this year and hated it last year. Yet her penmanship is very nice and her spelling is excellent, without the weekly spelling test.[1]

From Texas

We have not experienced the burnout so many seem to have, because as the years pass we find ourselves *living* the education our daughters, ages ten and six, are receiving. I think many parents in doubt about their own capabilities as *learners with their children* turn to the structured curriculum first. That's okay as long as they can remain open-minded and make adjustments down the line before the burnout hits.

I think it would be helpful to identify not only causes of burnout, but also early warning signals in their young children. (Sounds like preparation for a nuclear blast, doesn't it?) The easiest detectable signal for us is when *we've initiated* a learning process instead of picking up on child-initiated learning. When we as parents push potty-training, we get wet beds. When we push independence, we get more extremes of dependence. We can't *force a rose to bloom* before its time or we get a stunted or distorted flower. The blossoming has to be God-directed from within the rose (the child) so that "patience may have its perfect work."

I have also learned through this kind of thought that I have the freedom to take my child off the grade/age-level expectations put on us by the school system. (I used to teach in the public schools before family arrived.) I feel that my husband and I have cut through many of society's ideas about school, about formal education, but I know we have a long way to go. I expect it to be a *process* that is *revealed* to us as we continue in home schooling.

We are probably a little on the side of too much unstructured learning which I do struggle with from time to time. That little voice sneaks up and says maybe we need to "do school." Well, I've found that *doing school* is what initiates the problems.

We make the most progress in life, in our growing, in our learning, when our *education* comes from daily experiences. I keep thinking there will be more formal lessons as the children get older, but I keep getting shown repeatedly that God is in control of what we need for the moment and He has put us in touch with many resources and experiences for our blossoming.[2]

Another From Washington State

[Burnout is] real — *very* real. Here [in Seattle] *many* parents are putting their kids back in [school], or in for the first time. *Many.* Because of my various leadership roles, I see and counsel many home schoolers. I see some kids being put back in school at age six — some at ten or eleven. Many home school until first grade. But by that time, the parents are so burned out by fast-paced curriculum methods, that it's a relief to dump the kids at school.

Others homeschool until the children are ten or eleven and when they run head on into pre-puberty personality conflicts, they give up. I've seen three families using the same highly formal classroom materials quit in the last six months. . . . There is nothing better than one-to-one homeschool friendships to keep families inspired and on track![3]

TWENTY

A PLACE OF
THEIR OWN

Linda Winkelried-Dobson

BACKDROP: Helen Hegener publishes one of the most fascinating state newsletters in the home education business. We found this story in her *Home Education Magazine* and could hardly put it down. Linda Dobson is a home schooling mother and free lance writer from Rainbow Lake, New York.

Luckily, I made a lot of mistakes when I started to home school. Yes, luckily. For in discovering what home school isn't, I uncovered the inherent potential of our Rainbow Holistic School. My first and nearly fatal mistake was attempting to duplicate the classrooms of my own childhood—a specific time for this, a certain way to accomplish that. And heaven forbid I didn't squeeze in at least a few math problems every day! Then one fateful afternoon, I actually fell asleep while preparing the following day's lesson plan. I vowed never to impose such drudgery on Charles, my only student, again.

But the following year when Erika, student number two, entered kindergarten, I watched helplessly as history repeated itself. Her initial enthusiasm deteriorated into quiet resignation, an acceptance of school as one of life's inevitable chores. In my struggle to reach the stars, I didn't realize that navigating with a public school curriculum was akin to traveling there by way of Cleveland—in a Chevy!

A curriculum does not a school make, but I stubbornly continued, attempting to "spice up" the curriculum in an ever-failing attempt to make school more "fun." The self-imposed stress of outrageous expectations, coupled with that of abject failure, forced me into a subconscious hiatus. And the less I worried and planned, the more Charles and Erika responsibly assumed control of their day. They had inadvertently discovered a more direct route to my lofty goal.

Tailored to Fit

The school had to be a place of their own. There existed a fundamental difference between their route and mine. Typical schooling is imposed from without, while proper schooling should emerge from within. A home school is not created for the children, but of the children. Although obliged to follow some sort of curriculum, it is a place tailored to fit the children it serves, not vice versa. It's a place where young minds may inquire freely, where individual interests flourish, where children learn at their own pace. One night's simple realization for me; a new dawn for Rainbow Holistic School.

I spent that wonderful evening assessing our dining room turned schoolroom. It appeared to have been transferred directly from the local school: neat rows of books, a shiny globe, and a world map reflected the room's purpose. The green chalkboard stared back blankly, awaiting my interpretation of the following day's lessons. Too bad: there would be no lessons tomorrow.

Charles and Erika whooped and cheered at the announcement the next morning, then seriously pondered the question, "How can we change this room to make it a nicer place?"

We commenced a remodeling project immediately. Although we kept all the basics, their places of honor were usurped by more personal belongings. Charles wanted our parakeet in the room; we moved the globe. Erika disliked trudging to the attic for the scrap box each time she desired to undertake a much-loved art project, so the corner bookcase found a new home in the front room. The scrap box is now as accessible as her creative ideas.

"What else don't you like about the room, gang?" I asked, eager to please.

"What I'd really like," Erika answered, "is to be able to reach the shelves myself."

By relocating the shelves lower on the walls, even Adam, the preschooler, can easily help himself to anything he wants. We gained precious wall space, quickly filled with Charles' favorite planet poster and hanging skeleton model. Erika contributed her recent, painstakingly completed needlepoint project, and suggested we hang a few special photographs from our recent trip to Montreal. Adam returned from the kitchen with a favorite doggy mug to hold pens and pencils on the work table.

Although tired and hungry by noon, we delighted in the results of our work. After a lunch devoured in record time, all three children hurried back into their room to touch, explore, and independently settle down to paint. Each completed a couple of pages of math, to boot!

A relaxed attitude and a new sense of space contributed greatly to work completed, both in quantity and quality. But I sensed that the school was still merely a place in the house. A physical place may be special, but it's the emotional ties that bind. Our school needed to occupy a place in the heart. After a democratic vote, blue and white became our school colors. Art class yielded a newly designed and colorful school flag. And our school song, like other contents of the hearts, is readily available everywhere. Written to the tune of "You're a Grand Old Flag," the song echoes loudly whether we're taking a trip to town or hiking through the woods.

As a celebration of our emancipation from a school calendar, we now create our own holidays. Whether celebrating "Kitty Cat Day" upon adopting an abandoned kitten or "Jack Frost Holiday" when we wake to find the lawn sparkling in the fall . . . the anticipation of a day integrating personal interests and scholastic pursuits awakens sleepy minds.

Living in Their World

However, my children's minds are rarely sleepy anymore. They are, instead, filled with anticipation and wonder. After two years of trial and error, the true light of home schooling shines through, for I have learned to live in their world, and what a wonderful world it is!

Unfortunately, it is hard to understand, and harder to accept that, under normal circumstances, society forces adults to live in a world far removed from our children. We become comfortable with pattern and habits; children thrive on novelty. Our day overflows with obligations; theirs with delight. While we worry about tomorrow, our children are busy living today. Yet it is our *knowledge* of a better way that allows the seed . . . to grow . . . our *action* that transforms the idea into reality . . . the *reflection* of all that is our children that causes it to be what it naturally should be: a place of their own.

TWENTY-ONE

FATHER TO
THE RESCUE

Kirstin Harrington

BACKDROP: The Harringtons were living near Boise, Idaho, where the family was making and selling tofu and sprouts, when an unfortunate experience suddenly took their chief sponsor out of state, and left them abruptly without capital. They then came to Hewitt Research Foundation where Kevin joined the master teaching staff and Kirstin helped the Moores as an editor, working at home and bringing up their five youngest children, ages one to eleven. They were forced to leave their business in the hands of five of their six older children, ages fourteen to eighteen. Kristina, twenty-two, is on a full scholarship in medical school. Their middle child, Joe, fourteen, is a consultant to Idaho's largest chemical corporation, assisted by his seventeen-year-old brother, James.

Kevin is Harvard educated, with an economics master's degree from a Texas school. Kirstin has a Harvard B.A. and a master's degree in art history from Tulane. Yet they found their classical education of little help in meeting their children's needs. After a few years of disappointments with public and church schools, they opted for teaching at home. Why not? Since they both had excellent educations. At least that is what they thought. Here's the rest of the story!

"But you *do* know the answer!" I slapped my poor son Johnny, certain that he clearly understood my "brilliant" lecture. I just knew he was stubbornly refusing to answer my question.

Nothing was going to stop my new adventure — into home education.

But after only a little reflection on this disgraceful scene, I knew I was all wrong. My home school, only a few months old, was collapsing around my ears. I'd been reading about burnout, but that was for kids. And here I was "Exhibit No. 1."

From Distress to Success

That September of 1979 we had begun with four of the older children of our large brood. We had purchased a rigid curriculum which specified that each pupil memorize a long list of Bible verses *perfectly* before proceeding to the next material. Our kids had good memories, but after a month of doggedly trying to finish this list "word perfect," we gave up. There was nothing wrong with memorization, but *something* was wrong, terribly wrong!

Next, we substituted Mama, a former college teacher, as instructor instead of the "canned curriculum." We followed a strict schedule, "teaching" all subjects every day. Then I came face to face with John in the infamous debacle above. I knew better than ever to slap in anger. Home school was a disaster. I told Kevin I resigned. Where on earth were we headed?

Surely God wasn't frowning on us, for after my mother had reported us to the school authorities, we had miraculously been granted permission to go ahead. This had never happened before in our area for anyone! Considering our public or church school options, we had gone too far to retreat. We knew what we wanted for our kids academically, behaviorally, and socially.

Kevin had the clearest head on this at the time and offered to step in. Though extremely busy starting a greenhouse business, he rearranged his schedule to include the home school, making the business one of our chief educational vehicles.

We all pitched in so he would have time for school, too. I knew from living with him over the years how vital the father's involvement is, especially for his sons. We found that working together with our hands as well as our heads was most educational of all, and far less stressful than pure book learning. Kevin had tutored extensively during his college days. Now we found that one-on-one also worked best in the home school. We did have classes, yet one child with one teacher produced breakthroughs in learning, sometimes with children teaching.

When our twins, Katharine and Kevin, Jr. reached high school age, we briefly gave in to conventional wisdom and sent them to a church school for half a year. But they soon complained that the younger kids at home were getting ahead of them, so we taught them all at home again.

Finally my husband and I could no longer stand to submit the youngsters to the school process. We were learning that our formal education could be more of a handicap than a help, if we let it be. It turned out to be a wise choice. With his practical, on-the-job applications, Kevin taught them well. All now excel in math, including a good bit of calculus. John, who once hated math, now delights in it most of all. He plans to become a mathematician. Face aglow, he regales us with the latest math "proof" he has learned, and habitually picks up a bit of math from his books and mulls over it as he goes about his work. I am amazed by how little time produced this dramatic turnaround in this boy I stupidly slapped, and in me, his teacher. No parent or child burnout around here anymore!

Katy represents other principles we learned. Although only two years older than John, she cared for him in his younger days like a little mother. Much of her gentle, obedient spirit rubbed off on him. Responsibility for the safety and happiness of others taught her valuable lessons rarely learned from books, so we strongly support the idea of cross-age teaching — using the older to teach the younger and the stronger to help the weaker — for real efficiency in home or school.

Katy, once a socially reticent child, has turned out to be a skilled teacher through her home school experiences. At twelve she delivered a self-composed, competent English lecture at the blackboard for the school authorities' visit. Now eighteen, she delivers our sprouts and tofu to supermarkets and produce companies and regularly handles a salesperson's duties. She showed how a load can be lifted off a parent's shoulders by one child caring for another, *and was blessed herself.*

The teacher always learns the most, so we often let the youngsters teach, and I sit there only to make my interest known. Control comes easily, and the kids develop social poise. For instance, Jim, a creative chef, assists me in tofu cookery classes for community education. He does much of the cooking and speaking to the all-adult groups—drawing from his speaking experience from home teaching.

In addition to letting the children teach the group, we let them tutor one-on-one. Eight-year-old Sylvia's reading to six-year-old David has tremendously motivated him to read. Now for the sake of his eyes, we have to limit his time with books. Teaching reading has never been a big problem. Kevin and I are both avid readers. Mama's bedtime story hour, often patronized by the whole family, helps spread the reading "bug." At mealtime we exchange ideas or stories we learn from our reading.

Yet we have learned other, more important, lessons about reading. Joe, one of our later readers, learned to read from the Bible and another very spiritual book. The positive results in his very fruitful young life—as you will note in a few minutes—demonstrate the vital importance of providing truly *great* books for children to read. I must emphasize as one who grew up reading large *quantities* of books that now I know from experience with our children that *quality* is more important.

I am convinced that trying to do too much is a common problem for most parents: too much reading, too many subjects at one time, too many field trips, too much social interaction outside the family in the name of socializing our children. Exhausted from keeping such a three-ring circus going, we wonder in bewilderment why the results aren't better. Our motto now is "Less is better." The children have our *guidance*, but we support their *initiative*.

Intellectual education—where most schooling points today—delivers hollow victories unless based on character development. Most discouragement comes from neglecting character defects in our children while we are preoccupied with academics. Day-to-day relationships suffer while "schooling" reigns. Argumentative and rebellious or self-centered children dishearten and burn out parents far faster than the mechanics of teaching. We found it a good tradeoff to work more on character building and less on academic education: Our children are giants in both!

I realize that not all home teaching parents claim to be praying people and some may think that a Harvard man or woman doesn't pray. I'll confess I didn't—but I do now! One day my son Kevin, Jr. and I clashed. I tried to reason with him; I tried to get him just to go along with me whether he agreed or not. Nothing worked, and finally he stomped off in a rage. Baffled, I didn't know what to do next. I had tried everything—everything but prayer.

After he left, I prayed for us both and our troubled relationship. To my amazement (for my faith is weak) he returned within thirty minutes to apologize, and we were ready to start over. I am convinced that prayer changes things (me as well as the kids).

Catching Our Children's Motivation

Why struggle with and push our children to learn something when they don't want to? "To everything there is a season," wrote King Solomon. The wise parent, we have discovered, patiently waits for "springtime" and "harvest" rather than forcing something prematurely. When we find ourselves pushing, we back off and try a new tack.

Perhaps our greatest lesson in learning to tap natural motivation came from an experience with our son Joe. Dad bought each older child a chemistry book and included thirteen-year-old Joe as an afterthought. From the start Joe *seemed* uninterested and uncooperative. But at closer look we noticed that rather than start at the beginning of the book as his dad had suggested, Joe kept turning to the back to study the advanced subjects. Next we found him making frequent calls to the research department of a large U.S. chemical company. We gently advised that he mind his own business and get started on the first chapter of the chemistry book if he ever expected to make a real contribution in chemistry.

Then one day we learned that Joe, now fourteen, had made an appointment with Idaho's largest chemical corporation *to show them how to improve their chemical processes*. Since the plant manager was aware of Joe's age, we decided to stop dragging our heels and learn a little more how real learning happens at home. So we started giving our blessing to what we came to realize was a monumental educational project entirely at his own initiative.

His first demonstration succeeded and the company signed him along with his brother, Jim, seventeen, for a three-month consulting contract. Shortly the company raised the contract from five hundred dollars to six thousand dollars and then to ten thousand dollars. The boys were successfully demonstrating how Simplot could make remarkable savings in making ethanol out of potatoes and corn, and getting several times as much gold out of ore.

Joe and Jim have also been honing their writing skills as they busily make out company progress reports and apply for grants. A well-motivated student who digs deeply into his subject can't help learning many other things as he pursues his own interests.

This is the learning process at its best—inspired from the inside, rather than applied from without. As Jim recently observed, "We are valuable to the company more for our ability to learn than for what we already know."

Daniel, now eleven, has been our Mr. Fix-it the past few years. He had little interest in reading and writing, though he was basically competent in both. Recently he began reading for pleasure, and guess what? Harvard Classics? No, the Bible. He wrote a Bible research paper entirely on his own initiative.

In our home we have found studying one subject for a period of time to be the most effective and least stressful way. While there is often some overlapping, one subject area usually dominates the scene. Math, history, science, religion, and English have all been covered intensively for a year or more.

Some ask us how parent-teachers keep *their* motivation going. We say, decide on your priorities and stick with them. My personal projects often have to be put away for the time being. Adult-only socializing is a thing of the past for Kevin and me until our children are grown. We now value doing things as a family far more than we ever enjoyed our old social lives. On the other hand, I don't dare neglect my personal health, spiritual life, or our own marriage relationship.

So Dad and I have revised our cast-in-concrete formal teaching in more than one way. It hasn't been easy, for we tend to teach as we were taught, and the more education we have, the harder it is to change. We are rather careful disciplinarians, yet we are certain that without freedom to learn, and often to learn in their own ways, that discipline is worthless. We now are sure that discipleship—being examples—is discipline at its happiest and best.

Now we also understand better what Dr. Moore tries so hard to tell parents and teachers: "Wherever and whenever your children are ready to learn, don't let your ideas dampen them. Give them your best guidance, but don't get in their way!" That's what we're *trying* to do.

TWENTY - TWO

THE PENNSYLVANIA ABSURDITY

Peggy Smeltzer

BACKDROP: It couldn't have happened to a more worthy state group of home schoolers. But in a state known for its brotherly love it was an inconceivable absurdity. A girl was found to be doing poorly in her school work, despite a better than average mental ability. She had a poor self-concept and was not adjusting to school life even though she felt secure at home. She was given permission to be schooled at home. Three years later she was examined by local public school officials and found to be gifted. The officials decided that she was too talented to be educated by a high school graduate mother who had brought her from the educational doldrums into the gifted realms. So they ordered her into school and threatened to prosecute if her parents didn't comply. The parents, backed by their state home education leaders, refused to acknowledge this absurd reasoning, and a court case was in the making.

Why all the excitement? We are simply the fortunate parents of two lovely daughters, Lora, now twenty-two, married and a hospital receptionist, and Maggie, just turned fifteen. By the time Maggie was near school age, our church was considering a school. Lora somehow survived public school quite well, but for Maggie things were quite different, to say the least.

The day of reckoning passed its first hint to us in the spring of 1978 when we were notified to register her for kindergarten. Although Pennsylvania law requires enrollment at eight, the school system assumed all children should be in kindergarten two or three years earlier. But we didn't know the law!

The Public School Trial

We didn't want Maggie to attend public school, but the Christian school would not open until the fall of '79, so we were feeling the pressure, as so many parents do these days who don't know any better. If I had known then what I know now about child development, we could have averted many problems simply by giving Maggie more time at home to mature. But, we trotted little Maggie off to kindergarten to be with thirty other five-year-olds.

I feel so sad now at my ignorance when at a teacher-parent conference I was told that Maggie just wouldn't pay attention. They assumed she hadn't "been read to enough" and so didn't know how to sit still. They said she didn't join in group play— probably because we were from the country and she hadn't had the "advantage" of playing in the town park and being "properly socialized." I was more than a little uneasy about all this, for we read to her a lot, and she played well in the country.

The Christian School Trial

Needless to say, my husband and I were anxious for her to begin first grade in the Christian school where she would have just fourteen classmates. It seemed to be the perfect answer: small class size with opportunity for the individual attention Maggie obviously needed.

Our optimism began to crumble when the new teacher reported that Maggie was doing well only because *she already knew the material being taught*. This sounded strange. She said we could expect problems when subjects became more difficult because Maggie just didn't pay attention. She was, in their opinion, very immature, yet no one ever suggested taking her out of school for a while.

For two years she suffered through that Christian school. The pressure to achieve was unbelievable. They seemed to be trying to outdo the public schools and drove the children much harder than necessary. Some children were able to cope fairly well, but we saw our happy, light-hearted little girl becoming morose, even depressed. Her self-concept was being destroyed. Academically she was close to failing and didn't even care. This is what we were paying more than a thousand dollars a year for? We were convinced that neither Christian nor public school was ideal for Maggie.

In the fall of 1982 Maggie entered the fourth grade and the nadir of her young life. Academically, she was lost. She felt stupid and was sure the other children agreed; so she avoided them. Her teacher seemed extremely overbearing, and we were frustrated about what to do. I tried to help her by working evenings with her, but only succeeded in further burning her out.

Maggie never said that she hated school. Maybe she was afraid that such a remark would be sinful. One evening as I was straightening up I found a little picture that Maggie had drawn: a very sad looking little girl with the words, "School, school, school, what shall I do?" I cried out to God all night for an answer.

The next week we attended the Institute in Basic Youth Conflicts in Cleveland. Bill Gothard was there on Friday and through him God answered my prayer: Teach her yourself! It seemed so simple, so perfect and, as Bill said, so scriptural. I began to research the subject as soon as I got home.

I wrote the Gothard office. They recommended several books, and I "accidentally" found John Holt's book, *Teach Your Own*. It contained a list of professionals who would help people interested in home education. So we contacted Andy Peterson, a psychologist who also turned out to be a valuable ally and friend in the adventure which followed.

I was sold on home education from the start, but my husband was concerned about socialization and the expense if a legal battle were to ensue. I researched the issue and prayed constantly. Meanwhile, at school the situation worsened for Maggie. The pressure was destroying her, and she began to manifest a variety of symptoms which doctors attributed to stress. Finally we mustered the courage to talk with the school superintendent.

As expected, he was totally opposed to home teaching. But since Maggie was in a Christian school, he didn't act defensively. He suggested that she be put in one of *his* special education classes which could deal with her "special needs." He said she obviously had some learning disability which I would never be able to handle at home. He added that he would never approve our teaching Maggie and that the only way we would get permission would be in court.

We told him we weren't surprised at his answer; we would initiate legal action to get Maggie released from school. (We didn't know what we were talking about, hadn't even intended to say it. But saying it kept me from crying. And we did mean it; our daughter meant that much to us!)

"Well, I didn't really say 'No,'" he offered as we were about to leave. "I'd like to have some testing done on your daughter to determine the extent of her problem. If it isn't too severe, I might allow her to stay home for a year." Being a bit suspicious by nature, I was concerned that he might interpret test results to serve his purposes. So we asked Andy Peterson also to test Maggie. He agreed. So I let the word drop to the school district's psychologist that in view of a possible court battle, we had employed another psychologist as well. I also wrote the superintendent to ask for official papers of the district's Long Range Development Plan—anything that had legal overtones. He said it would be expensive to duplicate and that would likely not be necessary since he would probably approve us, which, to make a long story short, he did.

Trying Home School

We enrolled in the Weimar College Child Development Center course started by the Moores. I began to teach as I had been taught, and soon understood with some remorse what the teachers meant by Maggie's "inattention." Also, I began to realize what the classroom had done to her: I'd explain things and ask her a question. When she realized that a response was expected, she would look from side to side as if waiting for someone else to answer. Then, realizing that *she* was the only one to answer me she showed consternation and could neither repeat the question nor answer it. Before long, reading, exploring, and responsiveness replaced my lectures and questions.

When the superintendent visited us, he was impressed with our curriculum and materials and approved us for the next year. We were ecstatic! Yet, lacking boldness then, we maintained a low profile. I had to give up some church and social activities, simply for lack of time. At the time there seemed to be little human support. But I always had my wonderful husband and God.

That year, despite my bumbling, and many painful reminiscences for Maggie, her depression turned to optimism. Here is one of her many short stories (which were usually accompanied by her drawings) exactly as she typed it, even to the capital letters, copyright note, and two misspelled words:

> Once upon a time there lived a magnificent unicorn named VW. The Silver Unicorn and the Yellow Monster are enemies. The Silver Unicorn rescues 1 child her name is Maggie. She loves the Silver Unicorn. The Yellow Monster and the silver unicorn are nothing but a silver car and a school bus! Copyright AllRights Reserverrd 1983

The next year (1984-85) when Weimar College discontinued its curriculum, we shifted to Hewitt, which in 1983 had established its Child Development Center and curricula by popular demand. The Hewitt teachers tailored the program to Maggie, and allowed us much more freedom in our academic approach. We could call on them any time, and they did not demand reports every month. That year the school principal, our regular visitor, was not rehired. So we had further relief.

We were doing great until we were called in for a conference with top school officials to discuss Maggie's plans for seventh grade. They put on the pressure, reminding us that they had no less than nine teachers who could do the job better than I, that we were depriving Maggie socially, and would not likely obtain approval after grade seven. Yet they did approve us for the seventh.

They knew I was only a high school graduate (never mind how much common sense or experience), so I felt the pressure as a non-professional preparing Maggie for tests. I still had those urges to teach as I had been taught instead of less formally. Our home school would have been much more a delight if these state-mandated tests [had never been] a threat. But the Hewitt teachers were always there to encourage us.

During the 1985-86 school year, Maggie's seventh grade, we had no school district contact until year's end when we again faced achievement tests and an eighth grade approval conference. This time they greeted us with enthusiasm over Maggie's achievement scores. "Talented, gifted," that's how you spell "relief."

But not for long! The meeting was totally negative. We were told we didn't understand about credits (no, I probably didn't; does anyone?). Maggie was being deprived socially as she was learning only *our* values! Then came the real shocker: She was so high in her tests that *we* could no longer meet her needs. Only *they* could meet them. When they realized that we would not comply, they proposed a compromise — just bring her in for half-days. This might have worked several years earlier, but now with an exciting curriculum, much freedom, some experience, and a taste of real home teaching success, our answer was, "Thank you, but no."

Avoiding a Court Trial

Soon we received Superintendent John G. Buchovecky's letter denying our request. He suggested a gradual move into his schools, insisting that Maggie "should be placed in the academic track in order to reach her full potential and maximize *her God-given abilities* . . . [for] the full educational and social development of Maggie Smeltzer can no longer be delivered in the home-tutorial program as provided by Mr. and Mrs. Smeltzer" [emphasis ours]. Three times he offered this kind of line.

We wrote Dr. Buchovecky that we intended "to go beyond what you can do." We notified the Home School Legal Defense Association, and now with more confidence than ever, ordered our eighth grade program from Hewitt's CDC.

The first day of the 1986-87 school year, the principal called to advise us that Maggie wasn't in school. No surprise. But within three days we were charged as *criminals*. Quite a surprise! All kinds of scares seared our minds — publicity, jail, huge fines, possibly having Maggie taken from us. What a week!

HSLDA president, attorney Michael Farris, went right to work. He notified the superintendent that he was filing a complaint against him in federal court for violation of our civil rights. When his legal counsel was informed of this intent, his response came like a stroke of lightning. Dr. Buchovecky promptly had a change of heart and approved us for another year.

The rest of our story may be anticlimactic to you, but it has been a real challenge to us: loss of our low profile, publicity on Maggie's high achievement at home after having been pronounced learning disabled at school, and her invitation from Parent Educators of Pennsylvania to speak at a legislative breakfast in Harrisburg. This was crowned with her witness at the state capitol where she joined our state home education president, Tom Eldridge and others before the House Education Committee. We are grateful for our home teaching friends throughout our state and nation.

Thank God, Maggie is happy and settled now, not so much because school officials declared her gifted, but because she faced many threats and conquered. She's glad to be a home schooler. Last year we finally relaxed. We have now what we wanted all along—home school instead of school at home. And it was well worth the battle!

TWENTY-THREE

THE PLUMFIELD SCHOOL

Amy Jo Roland

BACKDROP: Warren and Amy Jo Roland home teach their covey of six, ages three to fifteen, in the Southwest Iowa town of Atlantic where he is a funeral director, involved in real estate, and a totally committed home school dad. Amy Jo, a "retired" beautician is a great home educating mom.

Four years ago after our family became acquainted with some very impressive home schooling families, read the Moores' books, and listened to Dr. James Dobson on Focus on the Family, we unanimously decided to take the plunge into the wonderful world of home education. As of this year, the children are in grades nine, seven, four, two, kindergarten, and preschool, all at home. It has been a thrill-packed educational experience, to say the least.

To get off to a great start, we named our new way of life after Louisa May Alcott's school, "Plumfield," from her book *Little Men*. At Plumfield the students observed and recorded according to their own interests and abilities. Instead of the regimentation and authoritarianism of the nineteenth-century schools, with emphasis upon strict discipline and the "cram method" of learning, each child at Plumfield was a separate variety of flower with its own special beauty, cared for according to its individual needs.

So ours is the Plumfield philosophy. Our children like the relaxed, shorter, flexible school day of a few hours in the morning. This session is combined with chores and music lessons, and lots of free time after lunch for putting their ideas to work.

The Plumfield Program

During our first three years of home schooling we covered several subjects a day, but this year we're experimenting with one or two subjects daily. We've shortened our study time from four or five hours to two or three hours (less for the elementary grades). With six, changing becomes bothersome. We get more accomplished by keeping with one subject longer. We touch on the few skills that need more repetition more often.

For variety, some days we read in the living room, lounging in bean bags by the fire; on others, we let all choose their own "secret places"—to do deep thinking for story writing. They also exercise in the attic, do art on the back porch, chemistry, mechanics, and woodwork in the basement, and of course science out-of-doors. Yet they all still like their colorful classroom seated around tables for most of their book work.

Handwriting class is a most practical one for us. The children write daily. They keep personal journals, write thank-you notes to people who have given us tours, correspond with foreign-country pen pals, write reports, and fill out their own orders for gadgets or books they want. They feel good about all that they accomplish during penmanship practice.

Heidi helps Jim in seventh grade math by her own choice. This frees me to work one-on-one with the four younger ones, and they gain confidence by helping one another.

Dad gets into the act, too, passing a little football to one of the children while calling out a problem (addition, multiplication, etc.), and the child, in turn, responds with the answer, hopefully, before the ball is received. If incorrect, Dad gives the answer and the child repeats the problem and correct answer as he returns the ball to Dad. It's a great way for the whole family to enjoy math.

Our history class includes Heidi (ninth grade), Jim (seventh), and Burdette (fourth) sharing an Old World history book for oral reading. They may answer questions at the end of a chapter or discuss what they are reading, but are seldom tested until the end of the year at which time they take Iowa Basic Skills. In spite of the unthinkable way we operate, they all score well, averaging near the 85th percentile. Heidi is scoring near the 95th percentile on Iowa's state scale (higher nationally).

Our local public school board requires that a certified teacher visit us an hour a week. She sees where each child is on a subject or two, checks my scheduling to see if I'm keeping track of where everyone is, and brings a fun storybook, activity sheet, or perhaps a suggestion of a research assignment for them. She is a super teacher of the Mary Poppins variety who is very supportive of home schooling and develops good rapport between us and our public school.

Our children learn *wherever* the action is. We turn them loose to observe and even assist when plumbers, electricians, carpenters, and various repairmen work in our home. Our older two take classes such as stenciling and making jointed teddy bears at our local community college. They make videos of school-related meetings, attend legislative coffees, lobby for better home school laws, and feel at home at our state capitol. They use our public library, and computer education excites them.

And they love the cottage industry idea. The children are always inspired with the challenge to create a product that interests the general public and makes a profit.

They've named their cottage industry "Plumfield Plum Good Products," and have experimented with selling cookies and popcorn to the paper carriers at the newspaper office entrance when hungry boys and girls pass by after school. They are also into "Plum Good Productions," dubbing videos. They tape choice television clips on home schooling news and interest shows that "peddle" well within the home school community. Presently they are thinking of renting a table at a bazaar for selling crafts that they make.

The children especially like to help with our funeral home business where they are paid by the hour for working as receptionists, answering the telephone, running errands, and helping with the lawn and snow removal. They occasionally help on funerals, and we find that they are well accepted and a comfort to grieving families who bring their children to the funeral home.

We also encourage our children to serve and to glean ideas from grandparents, relatives, elderly friends, and neighbors. Our youngsters dearly love their grandmothers with all of their very special wisdom and creativity that comes wondrously with long years. One grandma restores antique dolls, and is a regular on their visiting list. She reminds them of Mrs. Santa Claus working and living in her cozy little dollhouse. The other grandma is a "Cookie Grandma," with great things always happening in her kitchen that excite little noses and hearts. If the grandkids have ingenuity and cooking talents, we'll be able to trace them with no trouble!

Among our Plumfield extracurricular activities have been Boy Scouts, AWANA, YMCA, swim lessons, tennis, gun safety, piano, guitar, singing lessons, and attending various church activities. They are especially fond of singing for church parties, programs, and nursing homes. Our children are comfortable with all age groups. They have no age-segregation problems or peer dependency and have plenty of after-school friends and neighborhood pals.

"Plum Good" Speller

Heidi likes spelling, so last year when she heard that the state spelling bee would be coming up, she eagerly looked into it. With much confusion about getting a home schooled student entered, we quickly agreed to the terms that if she would happen to win, she should give the credit to the public junior high school here. Even after three years of being away from the school, she gladly accepted the challenge. For weeks she studied thousands of words from a dictionary so large we could hardly lift it; and we had to learn to pronounce many of the words in order to be able to quiz her.

At last, Heidi arrived at Schuler Junior High for their local level contest of the state bee. She wandered a bit nervously to the room where students were to meet for the big moment. Upon her entrance she was delighted to find several of her old fifth grade friends who had gotten word that she was coming and gathered there to cheer for her. It would have been fun enough to just participate; but, to our great joy, she took first place out of the fifty competing that afternoon. Thus, Plumfield has its first trophy gracing our bookshelves.

And Schuler Junior High got its credit!

TWENTY-FOUR

THE ALMOST
ASTRONAUT

Helen Jackson

BACKDROP: In 1987 when I was asked to be key witness at a
Fort Worth, Texas class action suit against the State of Texas and
some of its school districts, some people suggested that I would
be the star witness. Not so. A number of black, Hispanic, and
white families had retained Fort Worth attorney Shelby Sharpe
to institute suit for damages because of school officials' harassment of home teaching parents. Among these families — the real
stars — were John and Helen Jackson, a black couple who, with
their five children, had lived in Houston.

When Helen was called to the witness stand, four state attorneys, male and female, zeroed in on her, one of them an assistant attorney general.

They wondered if she believed in women working. Yes. Had
she worked? Yes. Where? Houston, at NASA.

They were curious about what she had done there. Some in
the courtroom assumed perhaps she had been on the custodial
crew. She made no effort to impress, but questioning brought
out some unusual facts which made the prosecutors' mouths
drop: Helen (1) was an astronautic electronics engineer from
Johns Hopkins University (where her husband also graduated as
an engineer); (2) had worked at NASA for six years as an
engineer in her field; (3) had been recently upgraded two years
on the coveted rosters of astronauts-to-be; (4) had discovered
serious behavior problems developing with one of her sons; (5)
quit her job to teach him at home; (6) in a few weeks had him

settled; and (7) decided that motherhood was a *higher* professional calling than being an astronaut at NASA.

I'm sure you've heard the saying: That which is not worth dying for is not worth living for. So a frontline defense for anything is the depth of conviction. That conviction entails not just the drive and purpose to stick with something, but the vision and resilience to change a program of action when things aren't working, rather than quit.

Running the Race with Endurance

As much as I glorify home school, I've very often been frustrated and wished for a virtuous way out. I do believe, however, that having formerly been a marathon runner has helped me to be mindful of the fact that the satisfaction is glorious at the end of a long grueling run. Unlike some marathon runners, I ran not to win but for the sheer satisfaction of completing twenty-six-and-a-quarter miles. The first race I ran I learned that unless a runner is well trained (and even sometimes then), pain was to be expected and overlooked. Somehow, though, every time a race was over, the pain soon left. So why quit at twenty-two miles? I also learned, when the pain seemed unbearable, not to quit, but to slow down and keep moving.

When I began home schooling, I had a perfectly laid out plan for how it was supposed to be: how well behaved my two- and five-year-olds were going to be as I taught the others, how enthusiastic the children were going to be with every new project I assigned, how orderly the house and household chores would be, how pleased family and friends would be.

Well, how many of us know the demand of undivided attention that toddlers and small children require? So I have learned to structure my teaching schedule for the older children around the time I spend with the younger two. That has turned out to be a much wiser course. As far as the children's accepting every project that I propose, I have to make some concessions. I have a scientific background but I realize I cannot force them, via home school, to follow in my footsteps. So as long as some type of project is done regularly within a listed range of areas that exercise creativity as well as demand effort, I've learned to call a truce.

Trying to keep house has been a frustration. There is always that sublime worry that an unexpected and picky guest may arrive and condemn us, despite our lengthy explanations. I manage to rest at ease behind the fact that both God and my husband understand.

And as for my family, God bless them. They've seen the incredible results. Yet the constant subtle as well as outright insinuations that we are denying the poor little darlings a chance to experience life as other children do eventually seep into their circle and causes confusion—sometimes serious conflict. Then there's the unsupportive church circle: "How dare you imply that our church school can't offer the best possible education available?" *Some even report you to authorities, attempting to have you locked up.* We faced this possibility in Texas, Pennsylvania, and Alabama.

So why persist against the odds? What kind of person are you? If your marriage is troubled, do you leave or try to work it out? If you're running a race, do you quit when the cramps start shooting or just keep on moving at a slower stride? How deep is your conviction, how ephemeral is your purpose in the midst of difficulty?

Who are life's winners? In my opinion, those who hang in there through good and bad times. Total burnout does not occur because there is no terminal verdict for those who understand that boredom, frustration, exhaustion, and mini-failures are but facets, not an end within themselves, to so many of life's ventures. School, marriage, sports, and careers all have their low points in which many are tempted to quit. I cannot overemphasize the need to be flexible, to regroup if necessary, or to change speed *while keeping your goal.*

Most fundamentally, who or what is your motivator? Why do you home school your children? God is my motivator, my lamp, the One who convicted me with this mandate for change. Of course, I home school because it is better spiritually, socially, and academically. But when God guides our convictions then only He tells us to quit. Better academics and socialization are just by-products of a very critical task He has endowed us with. I personally cannot separate my home school stand from the Source of my strength. God makes a way for me to continue on if my endeavors have His blessing.

Seeking Results, Not Perfection

What about the quality of our home school? Can we expect a perfect school in an imperfect home? I'm sure all those who pursue home schooling see a certain level of excellence above and beyond alternative schooling available for our children. But suppose my child really has organic brain damage? Or is seriously emotionally disturbed? Suppose our home/family life is troubled or broken? Suppose I can afford very little teaching material? Suppose it seems that I, their teacher, am just too inadequate?

Many families I have talked to about the option of a home school have brushed away its feasibility, claiming my family's success was due to ideal learning situations and educational background. How wrong they were, in my mind anyway. Being well educated in many areas is nice, but that's all. The amount of education is not the key. Insurmountable statistics accrue to verify that.

There's a certain very special something that makes a good teacher. That special something is a spiritual quality, a firmness of character, and lies latently available to be used by any and all parents if they so choose. Love is basic in all this. What patience, an understanding heart, compassionate acknowledgments, and, yes, that very necessary discipline can do. It cannot be surpassed by degrees and certificates.

Whenever I'm troubled, I remember: If there's difficulty, even tough difficulty, the God who made and knows every star by name and purpose is capable of assisting me. I don't expect perfection—I don't know what it is anyway. I seek results and am flexible with that. When I think home school is just too frustrating, I am reminded of our family's first graduate. I marvel at the happiness, hope, and balance now in my daughter's life. I am amazed at the direction she's choosing. She feels it is largely due to her home school background, and so do I. To appreciate my amazement, you must understand that *much of the time in our early years she had put up a big fight against home school*, and was only minimally cooperative.

We are now in our second year of living in a cramped pioneer-style cabin in a remote area of Tennessee where we live while building a larger home. Fugitive but not criminal, we came here exhausted and somewhat disoriented. We expected to reap optimum benefits from home school in this setting. But, it was here that things had to change drastically from an intense hi-tech-inspired curriculum to a survival-oriented one.

Building a house from rough cut lumber, living without running water, doing constant emergency patchwork, bailing hay, defending oneself against poisonous plants, snakes, and insects on a daily basis suggest just some of the ways our educational goals had to change. And we're learning that even if you follow all the rules of the book, whatever book, you're still not exempt from trauma that can shake your very foundation. Sometimes, perhaps devoid of proper spiritual armor, I am tempted to feel that a conviction such as home school is a mistake. But I seek discernment, look toward the glory at the end of the run, and prayerfully remember Who can fight a good fight for us. And friends are always there, delighted at the gifted children God — and home teaching — have given us.

THE TEACHING BOY WHO "LEARNS DIFFERENTLY"

Brenda Lewis

BACKDROP: Chapter 2 of our book *Homestyle Teaching* is an introduction to this story. Brenda Lewis wrote angrily to Dr. James Dobson for having a male chauvinist like that Dr. Moore on his program. We answered tenderly, of course, when Dr. Dobson forwarded her letter to us. Several months later she called frantically for help. Her son, Matthew, was seriously withdrawn and under treatment by a psychiatrist at seventy dollars an hour.

We advised her to take him out of school where, as a late developer, he was failing anyway. High-school educated, she feared trying to teach her children at home. Yet she gave up her job, stayed close to her son, and three months later was told by her psychiatrist that she didn't need his services any more. Two years later her young son, Matthew, was helping her tutor learning disabled children. And her older son, Daniel, elected to study Greek at a local college—which he did with alacrity. And both of the boys are thriving on experiences with their dad and older scholars.

Yes, I'm the one who wrote to Dr. Dobson protesting his interview with Dr. Moore, who begins our story in his book *Homestyle Teaching*. I had bought the liberal line that fulfillment could only be found in my management consultant career outside of the home. But now with a son diagnosed as learning disabled, and regressing socially, my reluctant but only hope was Dr. Raymond Moore's advice to home school.

My husband, Ward, read the Moores' book *Better Late Than Early*. He was immediately convinced this made far more sense than the PET (Parent Effectiveness Training), psychiatrist, and special education the school recommended. What a shock to this career mom! Now Ward was giving me this new message about teaching Matthew at home. On the Sunday before school started, I finally agreed. What a decision! I could hardly face giving up my job. I tried to work part-time, but soon knew I had to choose between my family and an out-of-home career. So home teaching became my full-time school-year profession. And there's no more exciting career anywhere. I still do a little consulting work on the side, especially in the summer, but when fall comes it takes a back seat.

Desperate, certain I would fail as a teacher, we organized a few books for minimal seatwork, with a focus on communication skills. Each day Matthew and I selected a new word from Ward's college dictionary. We discussed the word, used it, and played phonics games with it. I read to him up to two hours every day. His favorite story was Thomas Edison's early "learning failure." I was inspired by the thought that when the teacher gave up on Tom, his mother still believed in him. I secretly wondered what my son would become. Both Matthew and Thomas Edison were burned out on learning methods that created frustration.

"Learns Differently" was the title Matthew himself gave his way of learning. He disdained the term "learning disabled" as meaning "defective." He knew his problem was not insurmountable.

By age eleven Matthew was helping other "learning differently" youngsters. He took over my literacy tutoring job with a learning-failed boy his age from the class for the emotionally disabled in our local school. Together they enjoyed books and talked about things Matthew had learned. At year's end, our young friend was "released" from the class (a "prison" to him) he had been in since kindergarten.

By the spring of sixth grade, Matthew's vocabulary score ranked PHS (post high school) on the Peabody Picture Vocabulary and Stanford Achievement test. We are still working with low areas, but we see continuous progress. We found that children who learn differently often have large discrepancies in the skills and may need special tutors for specific problems from time to time. A certified speech pathologist has been working with Matthew recently. Public schools often provide such help. The Association for Children with Learning Disabilities asked Matthew and me to present a workshop on home education at their Indiana State Convention. Matthew was the workshop hit of the day, receiving excellent reviews on the conference evaluation sheets. This underscored our beliefs that educators and parents are curious about how children perceive their learning experiences.

We have no illusions about learning problems, and realize they aren't easily overcome. We've intended to give our son the opportunity to live free of the stigma and the "dumbing down" that sometimes happens when children are placed with slow-learning peers more than adults. I am thankful that Indiana no longer restricts parents from the option of home education.

Gifted Program at Home

Our oldest son, Daniel, joined us in home schooling the second year. I was a little afraid of handling two students, so we tried a "pace" (workbook) program in conjunction with a nearby private school. But we dropped the program like a hot potato when we saw the boys' reaction to its repetition and stale routine. For our boys, the less structured, integrated, tailored approach made a world of difference.

Textbooks now have become resources more than texts. *The less time spent on workbook material, the brighter they seem to get.* Daniel didn't have learning failures. Our early program consisted of one-on-one tutoring in basic skills as needed for an hour or so per day, lots of discussion, plenty of quality magazines, reference books, community resources such as the library, individuals with special expertise, tutors, and — no television. Although we didn't throw out all textbooks, our boys, at their ages, do better with reference books.

Daniel earned eight college credit hours when he was 13. He was accepted at Fort Wayne Bible College, Fort Wayne, Indiana, to study New Testament Greek. Reporters called and came to our door to meet this home-schooled boy enrolled in one of the toughest courses on campus. He competed with Bible college students and completed both semesters, though 50 percent of the students dropped the class at midterm.

And we believe in using older, wiser folks! Dr. Walter Wente, a ninety-three-year-old retired Concordia Seminary professor of languages, has been a mentor to our sons, who became interested in Greek and Latin. This wonderful gentleman taught for fifty years and now delights in sharing his knowledge and wisdom with our sons. His world travels and love for God have impacted Daniel and Matthew for a lifetime. Dr. Wente eagerly awaits the boys' visit each week as his opportunity to share a part of himself with the next generation. This is a great exchange for impressionable young minds and older folks—wonderful resources that they are. Another unique master is retired attorney Joe Lesh who practiced in all levels of court from Justice of the Peace to the United States Supreme Court. He has been prosecuting attorney, public defender, U.S. district attorney, and special assistant to the attorney general of the United States in charge of all the U.S. district attorneys. Attorney Lesh read a letter to the editor I had written and called to get acquainted with our family. Daniel has been very interested in law for the past year, and eagerly accepted Mr. Lesh's offer to tutor him! So he now learns under this fine expert, plans to become an attorney, and is making his college plans while working on paralegal skills with his tutor.

Work has become an important part of education with us—a real character builder. Earlier, when I was burning out from the structured programs we used, we began renovating rental properties and selling Home Grown Kids products as family ventures. Integrating skills is fun as we learn in our family businesses. It led Daniel into his first independent job at fifteen and Matthew into his first job at thirteen as landscaping assistant at a factory.

I am not a college graduate, but have gained most of my skills through on-the-job training in public relations and office management. My high school counselor didn't think I had "what it takes to go to college." Ward, on the other hand, earned a Bachelor of Science degree from Ball State University and is my teaching partner. He has graded math papers, taught science material, assisted me with lesson planning, led family devotions, and kept me going when I lacked confidence. The boys and I agree that "one father is worth more than a hundred schoolmasters."

Ward's mother, a school teacher, originally questioned our plan. I shouldn't blame her, considering my first anger at the home schooling idea. But as she saw the results she became one of our strongest supporters. *Now all her grandchildren are home educated.*

Worth the Effort

Our near tragedy has turned into near ecstasy. We now praise Dr. Dobson instead of deriding him. And those times when I've been distracted by other demands, Daniel Webster has helped me keep my direction:

> If we work on Marble,
>   it will perish.
> If we work on Brass,
>   time will efface it.
> If we rear Temples,
>   they will crumble into dust.
> But if we work on Immortal Minds;
>   as we embue them with principles,
>   with the just fear of God
>   and love of our fellow men,
>   we engrave on those tablets
>   something that will brighten all Eternity.

Was home schooling worth putting my career on the back burner? I'll say! And living on one income? Yes! And it can be done without a college degree? Absolutely! Would I do it again? Without question!

THE NAVY WIFE

Mary S. Kauffman

BACKDROP: The Kauffmans are a San Diego-based Navy family now finishing their fourth year of home teaching. We include their piece for its unique, imaginative, and in some respect, *new* approaches to education. Mary has discovered some happiness keys to get through the doors of home education's maze. They may relax you a bit.

I talk a lot to people deeply discouraged with themselves, their children, and home schooling. I also note with dismay a growing number of families who never give home school a chance after witnessing a friend or fellow church member "fail" at it. I remember doubting my ability when we first decided to home school. I wasn't sure I could teach formally six hours a day, 180 days a year for ten years. I wasn't sure I could get through even *one* year. So, in the beginning we had as our goal a flexible, enjoyable, challenging school year—and we succeeded!

Our Activities and Achievements

Our children were born in many places and have varied backgrounds. Vinh, our tenth grader, escaped from Vietnam about eight years ago and has lived with us for five years. He does well in his studies, despite having to learn English along with everything else. He takes piano lessons, plays on our men's softball team, raises and sells hamsters, and is a Trainman for the Railroad Museum. He is also a reliable newspaper carrier.

Anne, our aspiring author, is an eighth grader. She is a piano student, an excellent cook, and a budding seamstress. She works on child care and development in 4-H, and is president of her youth group. She, like Vinh, is an outstanding newspaper carrier and works for the Railroad Museum.

Our sixth grader, Earl, is a history buff. He works for Vinh on his newspaper route daily. He is an amateur astronomer, a qualified Trainman, and Assistant Patrol Leader in Royal Rangers.

Angela, a fifth grader, came to us two years ago, an abused child who thought she was a "failure" in everything. She couldn't read and HATED school. No wonder! She was about to be placed in a class for the mentally and emotionally disabled. *We bolstered her confidence by having her work at short, easily accomplished tasks at her skill level.* For a while much of her work was at the first and second grade levels. Large subjects were broken down into small pieces—what I call the "How-to-eat-an-elephant" approach. She loathed history, with the question/answer approach her teachers had always used. We stopped using the text entirely, and had her read instead short, *simple* biographies of early American heroes. She liked that approach and used the books for her book reports, too, thus finishing two requirements at once and filling her notebook with "good" reports she enjoyed rereading. She is learning to cook, earns money washing cars, helps Vinh with his hamsters, and is active in the Missionettes. She recently scored at the "average" level for language and math and "low average" in reading. We couldn't be prouder of our daughter.

And we had our first experience with an exchange program this year and loved it! We will definitely participate again. Our student was from Japan, so we learned a lot about Japanese geography, history, and culture. She brought many materials to share with us, and we did some research, too. She taught the children to write their names and sing a song in Japanese. We learned how her house differed from ours, what she normally ate, what her daily schedule was, and so on. Again, nobody thought of this as "school."

Some Different Approaches
Here are a few things we don't often see people doing, but which have really excited us and made learning fun.

Feast Days
Americans normally celebrate days like Christmas and Easter; at least Christians do. Understanding Thanksgiving and the Fourth of July is important to us. But a great book called *Celebrate the Feasts*, by Martha Zimmerman, has brought to life all the Old Testament history concerning Passover, Sabbath, Yom Kippur, etc. By observing these (once, anyway) and preparing and eating the traditional foods, we have richly increased our understanding of Jewish history. *Nobody* thinks of this as "schoolwork."[1]

Field Trips
We get mileage out of our trips, not just as a reward or final part of a unit. I prefer to use the trip *at the beginning* to arouse interest and enthusiasm. My children are always more motivated to study and do research to answer their own questions about a place or subject they've visited or experienced. This makes my job a lot easier — helping them "find out," rather than "teaching." One trip often leads naturally in several directions, and the children share discoveries.

Teachable Moments
Everyone probably notices these moments with their kids, but too often I see or hear parents squelching curiosity rather than exploiting it. My children are normal, and they often get interested in something at an inconvenient time. As I see it, the trick here is to defer the subject without killing it. Of course, if possible, I address it immediately! If it is not possible to pursue it then, I try to make a note of it and ask a few related "I wonder" questions of my own to show interest. *Their curiosity* is a rocket boost to learning!

We had a lively discussion recently when the kids objected to the way a newscaster reported a story. They felt that he had presented a person they admired in a very negative and untruthful way. In this case, I asked, "How did he do that?" We proceeded to talk about the purpose of news programs versus editorials. We identified some of the language used to slant the reporting. We suggested ways the facts could have been conveyed with less prejudice. They found it harder than they expected to be really objective in their reporting. I was pleased by their observations and comments, and it was NOT "school" to them.

In addition to these informal activities, we have other ideas for avoiding burnout:

1. I write down my goals and read them often. We use them, not the comments of neighbors, to evaluate our progress.

2. We make a plan to meet these goals, and seek advice if we're unsure. But we stay flexible. Each of our children is unique.

3. We deliberately vary activities and seek out and use resources around us, including unexpected talent among friends.

4. We try to be consistent, keep a brief daily journal, and have the kids keep one, too. When things are difficult, I read back in my notebook and review successes — those with "gummed stars."

5. We try to relax and remember that everything doesn't have to be mastered today!

TWENTY-SEVEN

A SINGLE MOTHER
AND HER
WASHINGTON WINNER

Corinne Kern

BACKDROP: This single mom, after deciding on a less formal home school, added to her young son's education by traveling. When Sunny eventually decided to take the General Educational Development Test, he scored highest out of the 192 tested in his Washington State region. He was invited to go overseas and teach English in a mission school.

My interest in home schooling began when my son, Sunny, was five. I felt cheated in my education and the education my daughter was receiving as a senior in a private school. She was always asking *why* about this or that, and I remembered having asked myself these same questions. I have found that most of what I needed to know for my adult life I learned because of a "need to know."

Although a single parent, I began to face the reality that I might have to teach my son if I wanted him to have the kind of education he needed—one of a harmonious balance between head, heart, and hand. Never having attended college, I was unsure; but I soon decided I would do my best to build my son's character and teach him the right attitudes and how to serve with joy.

As my son approached his seventh year he began to talk about *real* school. Although I felt that we shouldn't be in any hurry, he was adamant about it. So he and I went to work fixing up a room with our desks and calendars, maps, and all the things I had remembered from my school days.

Having seen only one other home school — in which the children nagged and complained at Mom — I decided to do something different. So at five minutes before nine, I had my son run out the door saying, "Bye Mom," then run around the house four or five times (fresh air and exercise), and come back in saying "Hi, Mrs. Kern, I'm here ready to start school." So it was not Mom in the classroom, but a teacher. Teachers usually get more respect.

Thus, we started: teacher at her desk and student at his. We were only "having school" for two hours, but even that was a lot for me. I had a hundred other things I wanted to do, but couldn't. Sunny was frustrated with my being there to supervise his every move. We were at loggerheads; neither of us was happy with our situation.

A Change of Course

About that time I heard about a seminar in California by a Dr. and Mrs. Moore — whoever they were. So off I went, hoping for some help with my problems. Two things I remember well from that seminar changed the whole course of school for us.

During one of the talks, Dr. Moore said something like this: "Children who are given their lessons, shown how to do them, and left to do them, with Mom popping back in now and then asking if they need any help or have any questions, do much better in their studies than those who have someone standing over them."

Wow! My mind went into high gear. I didn't hear anything that was said for the next five minutes as my mind processed all the ramifications of that statement. How I could use that freedom to do other things while he was studying! All I had to do was pop in and out "to be available if needed."

Dr. Moore's other story was about famed psychiatrist J. T. Fisher whose father insisted that Jimmy, then eight, must go out west on a ranch before beginning formal schooling.[1] Despite the protests of his socialite mother, he went west to herd cattle. At thirteen he returned to the big city, bowlegged but unable to read or write; yet *he finished twelve grades in three years.* When I got back home, I put the new plan into action. Knowing now that everything we did was learning of some kind, our "school" took on a new style. *Formal education gradually took a back seat to the character, attitude, and service ideals I wanted for my son.*

Learning from Life Experiences

The joy of home school was that we were free to drop formal learning and make the most of life experiences—a type of learning which I felt was of supreme importance. For example, we sold our acre, bought a van, fixed it up, and took off on a four-month trip through the south and east, visiting friends and relatives. Here was my chance to teach Sunny the joy of service. I impressed him with the need to do whatever he saw that needed doing—like washing dishes. I counseled him to be a *partner in the household* wherever he found himself, and not to be fussing or complaining all the time, but to be content with whatever our lot was.

And there were other learning times—long stretches of time when other things got in the way such as new babies in my daughter's house which required grandma's help, and the near fatal accident of my daughter. During that time Sunny took complete charge of his three- and six-year-old nephews while I took care of my daughter.

As a single parent, I was worried about getting through the teen years and the communication gap. So when Sunny was eight, I started having little chats after he went to bed to discuss the day's events and find out if anything was bothering him. This paid off 100 percent in learning opportunities for me and counsel for him. We still talk as friends; he still seeks my counsel. I always told him just to listen carefully to see if what I was saying made sense, then he could make his own choice. He usually chose wisely. Soon after his eighteenth birthday he was invited to go to the tropical isle of Palau, near Guam, to teach English as a second language. This triggered his taking the GED which we had long been talking about. So we quickly went to the local community college where he took the pre-test. Since he did so well, and time was important, he was allowed to go ahead and take the test rather than wait the usual month. Officials thought his final score might be the highest for that year. And sure enough, in April 1987 he received an award for scoring the highest out of the 192 tested in his Washington State region.

PART FIVE

HEROINES WHO ESCAPED THE FLAMES

Tied Down?

"They tie you down," a woman said,
Whose cheeks should have been flaming red
With shame to speak of children so.
"When babies come you cannot go
In search of pleasure with your friends,
And all your happy wandering ends.
The things you like you cannot do,
For babies make a slave of you."

I looked at her and said: " 'Tis true
That children make a slave of you,
And tie you down with many a knot,
But have you never thought to what
It is of happiness and pride
That little babies have you tied?
Do you not miss the greater joys
That come with little girls and boys?

"They tie you down to laughter rare,
To hours of smiles and hours of care,
To nights of watching and to fears;

Sometimes they tie you down to tears
And then repay you with a smile,
And make your trouble all worth while.
They tie you fast to chubby feet
And cheeks of pink and kisses sweet.

"They fasten you with cords of love
To God divine, who reigns above.
They tie you, whereso'er you roam,
Unto the little place called home;
And over sea or railroad track
They tug at you to bring you back.
The happiest people in the town
Are those the babies have tied down.

"Oh, go your selfish way and free
But hampered I would rather be,
Yes rather than a kingly crown
I would be, what you term, tied down;
Tied down to dancing eyes and charms,
Held fast by chubby, dimpled arms,
The fettered slave of girl and boy,
And win from them earth's finest joy."

—by Edgar A. Guest.[1]

TWENTY-EIGHT

THE FORMER ASSISTANT ATTORNEY GENERAL

Evelyn Hill

BACKDROP: Assistant Attorney General Evelyn Hill was one of Iowa's most popular legal figures until five years ago when she decided that mothering was her most important profession—at least as long as her children were at home. Although she now lives in Arkansas, she still finds time occasionally to touch the political scene—as long as it doesn't interfere with home. Recently she managed a congressional campaign in Iowa, and she practices a little law out of her home. But family comes first!

Over these past five years as we've all come closer and closer to understanding what home education really is, we're getting over the notion that unless you spend a certain number of hours each day going through textbooks, you're not home schooling.

In the beginning, I gave assignments for each day, kept daily records, gave tests, etc. In other words, we had classroom school —at home. Kelly was in fifth grade when we started home educating, and Daniel was five. It took no more than ten days to discover what I had vaguely suspected in Kelly; she had learned to get good grades via her innate intelligence, but she had lost her motivation to learn. She wanted me to spoon-feed her. I wouldn't succumb to her ideas of how teaching ought to be, so we were at a stand-off from about October through February.

In February, she visited "real school" for one day with a friend, and came home horrified that she wasn't learning anything and was going to fail (in what, I don't know). At any rate she immediately found her motivation again, albeit fear.

Since then, we've been more and more laid back, trying to flow with our lives, including education, rather than rigidly imposing school in such a way as to interfere with God's plan for our family. We're learning more and more that if we live life exuberantly and consistently, exulting in learning and emphasizing the learner more than the teacher, education happens!

Learning to Wait

One of the most difficult areas I've had to deal with relates to the truth of the IML.[2] The Moores talk about the "integrated maturity level" as the time when a child's senses, reasoning ability, and brain development seem to come together and provide readiness for school learning. We wholeheartedly embraced the concept when we first learned of it, and have expounded on it whenever and wherever we've had a chance. But sticking to our guns has at times been especially difficult for me. The last time I faltered and wanted to teach Daniel, now nine, to read regardless of his IML, Kelly, now fifteen, gave me a lecture on why I couldn't do that—and strangely enough it sounded very familiar!

I see Daniel developing, and his potential unfolding according to his particular built-in IML, but I guess I still have a little ingrown peer pressure of my own to contend with!

Relationships and Responsibility

Emerson said, "The years teach much which the days never know." How true that is! We've been through struggles and readjustments as we've worked out home education for our family, which can get quite frustrating. But what we're seeing in our children and in our family relationships is so much more than we ever dreamed or hoped at the beginning that I praise God without ceasing for all He has done through this decision we made almost six years ago.

In Kelly, we see a strength and depth of character that is awesome. She doesn't give even a fraction of an inch on any of her moral and spiritual convictions, yet is gracious in dealing with others, no matter what their age, no matter how weak or strong. She also has developed judgment—an ability to put the important ahead of the urgent—something I need to learn from her!

And, oh yes, there is now no lack of motivation to learn. Kelly has basically been on her own in learning for most of the last two years. She has currently taken over all our cooking and food purchasing, and following her mission trip to Mexico last month, prepared a complete Mexican meal for us and another family. I was in court that day so she had no assistance, and everything was done just so, including a welcome poster on the wall (in Spanish, of course!) and the hand-embroidered Mexican dress she was wearing.

Another satisfying outcome of our decision to home school is that the results in Kelly have silenced the opposition. The proof is in the pudding, right? Our adult friends love to have her over and to visit with her. She is not age-segregated. People we counsel or otherwise help tell her all their adult problems and she counsels in a mature way.

At first I was floored at the conversations Kelly would relate to me. But when she told me how she counseled these people, I was thrilled at her understanding of Scripture and her blossoming wisdom. What's really sad, though, is that we find a child like Kelly so outstanding. She is the way children ought to be.

The home teaching years have developed an unbreakable bond between Kelly and Daniel. They do have squabbles, but their commitment to each other shines through. Kelly stands firm on the IML concept and has never doubted her brother's progress, even though as a boy he seemed to develop slowly.

On the spiritual side, Daniel has always been deeply compassionate and empathetic, a quality I've noticed in other home taught children. His thoughtfulness proves a real ministry of encouragement both within and without the family. He makes friends easily; and his interest in the welfare of others is constant.

Daniel often goes with me to visit judges, other attorneys, clients (some in jail!), and also to court proceedings. I know from his questions that he's learning a lot!

What's More Important?

Over the years I have made two observations which may help those reading this book. The *first is that those considering home education must first answer whether they are willing to give up the rewards promised by traditional schools — honors, sports stars, and other things that make you look good to others.* This observation is seldom a topic of conversation, but I know parents whose decisions are made primarily to feed their egos rather than to rear children strong in character. And they pay!

My second observation concerns the lure of programs for the talented and gifted which have been swallowed hook, line, and sinker by many parents of all creeds. They are deceived about the purposes of these programs and appear blind to the sad results in their children. Many of these parents are not open to home teaching, for they have already chosen to place their egos above their children's better interests.

Recently we met a couple who began home schooling because the public school had tried to place their son in a talented and gifted second-grade program. In checking out the program, the father was told by its state director that its goal was to "disabuse children of the out-dated notion of moral absolutes"!

Thus two observations offer two questions: To home school or not to home school? Which is more important, my ego trip or my children's best interests? These questions are serious, sobering to me.

TWENTY-NINE

THE PHYSICIAN ON LEAVE

Betty Deloach, M.D.

BACKDROP: Betty Rhea Deloach is a physician who recently took leave from her pediatrics practice when she discovered that she might be her sons' best teacher. She has been married twenty-five years to her husband, Donald, an American Board-certified surgeon at the Minden Medical Center. Their boys are sixteen and nearly fifteen. Last year Eagle Forum chose her Louisiana Homemaker of the Year. She has been a member of the State Textbook Adoption Committee and has witnessed before the Louisiana Legislature. Recently the Deloaches have moved near Atlanta, Georgia.

I have enjoyed just about all the "perks" a modern professional woman hopes for. I took a degree in medical technology in 1961, and a master's in microbiology at Louisiana State University in 1967. In quick succession I was granted my M.D. in 1971 and a residency in pediatrics. There is no point in going into offices and honors here, but I have had more than any woman needs. Yet six years ago I took a twenty-year maternity leave and discovered a far greater happiness than all those boards and societies and honors. It is the larger and deeper ideal of being a teaching mother to my two fine sons, not before and after school, but time without end. And they seem to like it!

Doing Our Duty
I have a profound love for all home educators. And I have a special respect for those who have come into the home schooling

circle without benefit of Scripture as I know it. But, my guide in this educational endeavor is the Bible.

For instance, King Solomon's admonition to "train up a child in the way he should go, and when he is old he will not depart from it" means to me, "Train up Steve and David in the way *they* should go, and when they are old, *they* will not depart from it."[1] When anyone wonders why I should want to give up my practice for my sons, that isn't at all hard to explain. My husband, Don, and I are simply doing our kingly and queenly duty. And that is at least as great as being physicians.

I am learning more every day — at least as much as Steve and David. The Golden Rule — doing to others as we would have them do to us — has taken over my life more than ever.[2] I'm sure that selfless people of all creeds understand what I am saying in doing my full-time best to inspire these two young men God has given me. Time passes rapidly, and I now realize that I won't have that influence much longer.

When people ask me, "When do you educate?" I point to the words of Moses: Teach them as you walk, when you rise, when you sit down and when you lie down to sleep.[3] And I am constantly asked, "How do you educate boys of that age?" That is a fun question to answer, for we genuinely enjoy our Deloach's Academy of American Christian Education. We started out quite formally, but have moved to an informal relationship with a great deal of togetherness, of mutual responsiveness. As Steve and David have moved into high school subjects, they work more and more on their own. This is perfectly logical for youth of their maturity. This is a freedom to learn that their peers in conventional schools neither know nor understand.

Learning On the Go

That freedom includes going places and doing things whenever we want. Not long ago we accepted an invitation to give medical help to the Mesquite Indians in Central America. While Don did surgery and I helped the children, Steve and David were building houses for these poor people. Opportunities like this, we have discovered, are available for almost any youth these days all over the world.

If Don heads to a professional meeting, we not only tag along, we do *our* professional thing, too. And these field trips are not limited to professional meetings. Last fall we drove down the East Coast from Plymouth Rock to Philadelphia to relive the Colonial Period, 1620-1787. We lobbied our senator in Washington, D.C., visited the White House and the Supreme Court, then went on to George Washington's home at Mount Vernon. On other trips we have seen memorials to George Washington Carver at Tuskegee, Alabama; Robert E. Lee at Stone Mountain, Georgia; and Stephen Foster, one of our favorite songwriters.

Using the Principle Approach

We are not modern slaves to textbooks. We read into the lives of men and women like Lincoln, Lee, Columbus, Webster, Abigail Adams, and Susanna Wesley. We take the principle approach to these people to find out what they really stood for, what really made them "tick." We research them, reason with them, relate our lives to theirs, and then record what we have learned.

Learning how to think has been central in our educational plan. The boys have learned to reason from cause to effect. The simple use of why and how as the boys have matured has developed searching and creative minds.

We do many kinds of experiments, but we always apply three scientific tests to our projects: Be sure they are observable, reproducible, and non-falsifiable. The boys usually diagram their experiments and often put these on boards or otherwise prepare displays which they present at science fairs. Steve gets a lot of his ideas from medical students, and David from engineering students.

Well-Rounded Experience

Among other central ideas which we have come to emphasize, we teach the boys to be debt-free and to build healthy bodies; these are serious matters with us. We also insist on a church which reinforces what we are doing in education, and choose a summer camp for the boys that does the same. We see that they have more time with adults than with peers, and help them find adult help for anything we cannot provide.

Our boys are high achievers by any standard, yet achievement is not so important to us as character. If the character qualities we have mentioned are good enough for Moses, Sir Isaac Newton, Lincoln, and Carver, they are good enough for us. And we see no signs of Steve and David departing from them.

THIRTY

WORDS OF WISDOM
FROM A PIONEER

Virginia Birt Baker

BACKDROP: Among many veterans of the home education movement, "Ginny" Baker is one of the most respected. She began teaching her four children at home in 1972 in Texas after reviewing public school textbooks for years and noting the behavioral manipulation underlying the supposed teaching content of the books. And when she discovered the schools were not teaching her older children how to read, she took it upon herself to give them a "crash" summer phonics program, thereby raising their reading scores five grade levels! She knew the time had come to take things into her own hands.

Husband Chet's business required the family to live in other states while they were bringing up the children, and when the State of Montana was hostile to those of her kind, she dug in, along with other home schooling parents, to bring success out of diversity in what appeared to some of us to be almost total chaos. Montana passed a bill very favorable to home education, which Ginny had a hand in writing.

Meanwhile Ginny has graduated to "Grandma Ginny." For fifteen years she had been busy rearing and teaching her brood of four who then, as now, distinguished her as a great home schooling mom. And she gives much of the credit to her husband, Chet; without his full support "the whole thing would have been nigh impossible." When his work returned the family to Texas, there was plenty of room for the Bakers to extend their tents and strengthen their stakes. Although part of her story is told in her book, *Teaching Your Children at Home,* she brings us up to date here.

In all those fifteen years, I don't remember ever experiencing burnout. Teaching our four children was my ministry, and I wasn't going to let it get the best of me. Our program was organized, in the sense that I had clearly understood goals with purposeful activities. I knew that teaching was more than imparting knowledge; it included my being the motivating force in their educational lives, molding their philosophy of living and goals. Our attitudes and general conduct had a greater bearing on our children's development than their knowledge of subject matter. I instructed the children; I disciplined them, keeping them on the task at hand; I helped them evaluate and judge their own progress. And although our school had a framework of planned academic instruction, which evidently was successful, I tried to keep a relaxed atmosphere in our home.

Baker's Burnout Prevention

I think there are several ways to avoid burnout: First, a mother must learn to say "No." She must put her children ahead of everything else. She must say "No" even to some church activities: social gatherings, quilt-making, and non-Sunday meetings. She must say "No" to club memberships, teas, and much volunteer work outside her home. I think it is vital to train your children from the early years to participate in all household chores. Not only is it excellent training for them, it relieves Mom of an unnecessary burden. When friends asked how I could run a farm, teach the kids, read so many books, correspond with friends, entertain, and still keep house, I explained (and the children beamed with pride): "I haven't done housework in years! The children have done this beautiful job!"

Second, I do not recommend organized, sequential correspondence courses or highly formal courses. Our home school was never on an umbrella school's time schedule, and we had a great deal of freedom to respond to each other and to explore our own interests separately and together. We more or less followed textbook outlines, but we often ended a semester in the middle of a book, only to pick it up again the following September — and sometimes not. We were not tied down to a daily lesson plan, since often tomorrow's lesson depended on the evaluation of today's homework. I do believe in having a written, organized curriculum, but of the parents' own choice. Home education is individualistic and each family should remain independent to build upon its own values and goals. My point is that if you are on your own time schedule and not that of an umbrella school, you will have less stress by not having to meet someone else's time schedules. If you're tired, take a day off. The kids will love it! (Take two!)

In our school we spent a lot of time "dialoguing" — conversing with one another. We always had plenty of stories to tell, anecdotes which illustrated our lessons. If a mother is comfortable with her brood and they with her, that comes naturally. A lively imagination is a treasure both in parent and child. I often seized on their momentary curiosities and their long-term interests, even if not immediately germane to the day's lesson. It was crucial to maintain motivation. And speaking of motivation, may I digress for a moment? I think the use of too many workbooks, although great timesavers and necessary sometimes, especially with very young children, can be the death of a home school. In order to improve thinking and writing skills, the young student needs a blank paper, a pencil, and lots of creative imagination. Yes, it takes time. Yes, it means more work for Mom. But it will prevent boredom in your child, make school more interesting for you all, and in the long run your child will be able to express the thoughts of his own mind and not limit himself to the multiple choice of others.

Bountiful Harvest

Although the fruits of our labors have not always been easy to cultivate, at the harvest they have been very sweet. And our home-cultivated fruit? Four kinds: a Julie, a Chris, a Nancy, and a Matthew.

Julie lives with her husband, Lou, on their ranch, cradled in the eastern slopes of the Rocky Mountains in Montana, where Lou raises hay and grain on the largest sprinkler-irrigated system in Montana. There she designs and sews their own clothes, including Lou's shirts, preserves their own meat that Lou provides from hunting, makes stained glass gift items, sells her own dried flower arrangements, has a hobby of photography, and she even holds a United States patent on one of her own inventions. And, she teaches Heidi, eight, and Jonathan, seven, and Rachel, six, and Gracie, three, and Laura, one. What a heritage; what a life home education has given twenty-seven-year-old Julie!

Chris completed his master's degree at Texas A & M University, where the president, Frank Vandiver, has a background of studying at home during his high school and college years, entering formal schooling at the graduate level. While at A & M, Chris worked in the dean's office and was prominent in extracurricular affairs. He has been a volunteer fire captain with sixteen men under him, a Christian camp counselor many times, and has represented his school at various functions. From A & M he went to Virginia Tech to begin his doctorate in animal and human nutrition. Twenty-six-year-old Chris has spoken at several home school conferences contrasting his seven years of home schooling through the high school years with the average college freshman's background relative to entering and staying in college.

Nancy lives not far from us in Lindale where she manages The Travel Shoppe. She takes night classes at the University of Texas at Tyler, completing her degree in business management, marketing, and business law. In between work and studies she has traveled to London, Hawaii, France, and Switzerland. An avid skier, twenty-four-year-old Nancy is considering entering law school full time. Socialization, of course, is not and has never been a problem; she has friends plentiful.

Matt is currently an A & M freshman with scholarship aid— thanks to his SAT score—in the College of Agricultural Engineering. He is also not plagued with any socialization dilemma, either with his steady girlfriend or his athletic bent in tennis and skiing. He has a regular job near College Station, balancing his studies as Dr. Moore and others so often suggest. He will continue his studies at A & M with still another scholarship.

All the children are active, participating Christians, well liked by their peers and persons of all ages. They are natural leaders, and they have so many socializing skills, I can't keep up with them! If we sound proud of our children, we are. It's not because we are unusual people. We just had an "unusual" system: home education. Does it work? You bet it does!

THIRTY-ONE

THE UNIVERSITY KIDS

Diane K. Alme

BACKDROP: Diane and Michael Alme of Madison are among the top home education leaders in Wisconsin. She attended the University of Wisconsin and works closely with the legislature and State Department of Education. Michael is a skilled mason who was educated at the University of Wisconsin, Platteville, and the Madison Area Technical College.

We had fears about home schooling, just as everyone else we knew. But we are grateful that we could investigate long before jumping in with both feet. We explored philosophies, methods, and curricula so we could select the best to fit our children's interests and ability levels. The Moores' books and the counsel from the Hewitt-Moore Child Development Center were invaluable in helping us to lay the foundation for the development of our program. Our homework in this area was burnout prevention for us.

As a home school mom, I'm committed to many responsibilities. I have found two keys: B-A-L-A-N-C-E and F-L-E-X-I-B-I-L-I-T-Y in a program of work/study/service. This has had a positive effect on our four sons during the four years that we have home schooled.

We know that different families have different reasons for teaching at home. As Christians, we believe the Creator holds us responsible for educating the whole child—head, hand, heart, and health as in Christ's own childhood, best described in Luke 2:52, "And Jesus increased in wisdom and stature, and in favor with God and man." We have a semi-structured program. After morning chores are completed, we begin our school day at 8:30

A.M. All formal studies are out of the way by around noon, leaving the rest of the afternoon for involvement in community service, work projects, or support group activities. Yet we aren't tied down to this, nor are we imprisoned by our textbooks. We insist on freedom to explore.

Community Opportunities

We live in metropolitan Madison, the capital and home of the University of Wisconsin. This affords us the advantage of many activities relating to government, education, and commerce. As often as possible, I involve the children firsthand in these community opportunities. To see our government at work makes social studies and history alive and exciting! Going to university classes and exhibits stimulates our curiosity, broadens our interest areas, and helps us understand that learning is an ongoing process involving various ages and cultures. Many places of business and industry open their doors to us and help us see the importance of learning concepts and skills valuable to the community.

We have found, as Dr. Moore has said for years, that if we respond to our children warmly and give them "extravagant opportunity to work out their own fantasies, their own creative ideas, they will develop very bright minds." We see this happening with our boys and others around them. Shane, now fourteen, was getting ahead of my education by the time he was eleven. Since no quality elementary or high school classes are provided for gifted children in Madison, the University offers enrichment programs. They are college-level classes, but cater to bright younger children.

Shane has taken a year or more of astronomy, biology, chemistry, and this year is enjoying a course on the stock market. His home school friend, David, also started taking biology and chemistry at about age eleven. Another, Andrew Groth, began studying aeronautical engineering at the same age. These experiences have widened the horizons of these boys without interfering with normal home life.

Often in our textbooks we come across a place we've visited or an experiment we've conducted, and the children's eyes are wide with excitement as they relate to me the joy of that experience. This is one of the benefits I see in remaining flexible. Instead of chaining myself and my children to textbooks, I allow us the freedom to be creative and stimulate our program with exciting hands-on opportunities. So there are "teachable moments" throughout the day and year as opportunities arise for learning. *I want our children to know that learning does not just take place between the hours of eight to three, Monday through Friday, 180 days out of the year, as most conventional school calendars dictate.* Each day is new and exciting!

We occasionally use TV and radio when they tie in with a topic we are studying. And we find educational and inspirational tapes as well. Some of the most exciting concepts we've learned have come from our community experiences. This helps to prevent burnout as I schedule activities away from home and take advantage of community instructors.

Constructive Play

Usually on Fridays we work into our program what the kids call "Game Day." It gives me a break from teaching as the weekend approaches. The educational games cover every subject area. We use board games, educational computer games, videos, and homemade games. The children look forward to it and actually learn faster and enjoy themselves at the same time — another bit of burnout prevention for us. If you don't own a computer, try using a friend's as we do or go to the library as soon as your youngsters can use a computer constructively — for more than silly games.

I came across this anonymous poem that expresses the game — the constructive play — philosophy:

> I tried to teach my child with books.
> He gave me only puzzled looks.
> I tried to teach my child with words —
> They often passed him by unheard.
> Despairingly I turned aside, "How shall I teach this child?"
>   I cried.
> Into my hand he put the KEY,
> "COME," he said, "AND PLAY WITH ME."

Many games can be made from materials on hand or with little expense. You can check for ideas from games in stores and make your own at home adapted to your curriculum needs. An example is "Go Fish," using math problems and answers, states and capitals for geography, and phonics blends for language arts. Teaching with games is guaranteed to delight both you and your child![1]

Develop math skills while you teach your child how to place an order from a catalog. We call this game "Shopping Spree." I give each of the kids a specific amount of pretend money to work with, depending upon their ability, and a copy of a Christmas catalog and let them go on an imaginary shopping spree until they have exhausted their money supply. We all have fun with our "wish lists." Let your imagination go and find time to be creative. Such ideas I call my "Plan A" strategy. I use my "Plan B" strategy for those times when things aren't going smoothly — the days when the phone keeps ringing, the laundry has piled up, company is coming for supper, and the children seem to drop off *your* team to join the other side, and they are winning!

Living Skills

My "Plan B" strategy is what I call living skills. We don't neglect basic skills, but living skills are important, too. I gained valuable insight in this area from *401 Ways To Get Your Kids To Work At Home*, by Bonnie Runyan McCullough and Susan Walker Monson.[2] It gives techniques and strategies to ensure that our children know all the basic living skills by the time they leave home.

We use the "Home Progress Chart" from this book, incorporating living skills into our academic instruction. The chart helps me to know when to introduce a skill, the age it should be mastered, and has a record of accomplishments, including personal care, clothing care, household skills, cooking, money, navigation, auto, and other miscellaneous skills. My boys learned fractions helping me fold laundry into halves, quarters, and thirds, and measuring *double* batches of their favorite cookies — and they had fun eating their product!

This balance helps prevent burnout by giving us a break from routine and the monotony of a strictly academic program while building valuable skills my children will need someday to make it on their own. Your librarian will help you find books and exercises to develop a sense of responsibility and time management skills. The key here is consistency from both you and your child.

Home School Support Groups

An interesting curriculum offering a variety of alternatives; a flexible program allowing free exploration to work out initiative, creativity, and motivation; game incentives; and building living skills—all help to avoid burnout. But one of the most helpful suggestions I have is to join a local support group. Join whether you teach your children all day or when they come home from school. We have the greatest gifted people in our group that I've ever met. They come from every conceivable color, race, and creed. If you don't have a support group, start one!

A burning coal left by itself soon grows cold and dies out. We need each other. The advantage of being able to pick up a phone or write a note and have a sympathetic, understanding listener is immeasurable. We learn from one another. Burdens shared are always lighter. We find new friends, exchange ideas, and share encouragement.

Among things that make our home school program exciting are the support group activities for parents as well as children. We meet once a month and have legislative updates, curriculum nights, kickoff picnics, potluck suppers, seminars, workshops, Christmas parties and caroling, special speakers, etc. The children's activities begin with an arts and crafts day the first Tuesday of each month with an opportunity for the moms to learn a craft. Our nursing home visitation is the second Thursday of each month and offers our students the opportunities of volunteer service and interaction with the elderly. We have a variety of exciting field trips the third Monday of each month and they are a valuable part of our program. We've arranged with a local library to have programs the fourth Friday of each month, featuring an educational movie or filmstrip with an emphasis on nature, science, social studies, and the classics.

We have organized a 4-H Club for home schoolers with many interesting and educational experiences. This gives dads a chance to get involved in instructing the children, too. We also began a YMCA program that meets for classes while other kids are still in school. We have a music program for band and choir and plan to perform at nursing homes and community events. We have a nature club, a home school newspaper by the children called the "Kid's Report," and a project to help the mentally retarded. We believe every responsible group and state should have its own newsletter to get news on time.

Our activities allow plenty of interaction and refute rumors that home school children lack social opportunities. Public educators comment that we offer our children more opportunities than they could! We are so grateful for our support group members and the time they take to share their talents. Last, but most important to me, is dependence upon God's strength to keep me from coming apart and to keep my program honorable. I am convinced of the deep spiritual commitment in one way or another of virtually all dedicated home educators. Our purpose should be to encourage and strengthen one another regardless of our philosophies or race. This, I believe, is the spirit of true home educators!

THIRTY-TWO

THE EDITOR'S WIFE
Jaime Adams Ryskind

BACKDROP: Jaime Adams is a city mom, home teaching in the middle of the nation's capital. She is a writer and wife of the Washington, D.C., editor of *Human Events*. You'll find she has a different approach to home schooling.

Many home schooling advocates might not consider me a "pure" home schooler in that home schooling for me has really evolved into an old-fashioned, one-room school in the large attic of my house in Washington, D.C. There my good friend and partner, Mrs. Julie Treichler, and I have taught several children in addition to our own for the past eight years. The atmosphere is informal, non-threatening, and familial. In the winter, I sometimes have a pot of cocoa in the classroom, and a couple of the children who come early are very comfortable with making their own breakfasts in my kitchen. It is not at all unusual for our old setter to plop himself under someone's desk for a scholarly snooze.

However, beyond the very homey circumstances, in no way is our school "child directed." From the beginning we have had specific, long-range goals as well as a regular daily routine. We meet every weekday from nine to one, and we give report cards and administer achievement tests at year's end. I have always felt that one of the best parts of the home schooling movement is that it allows freedom for many different types of educational styles.

Having taught in a Christian school for eight years, I am sorry to say that I had become very disillusioned with what seemed to be a lack of thought about what constitutes a good

Christian education. It is true that our school taught the Bible, but in every other way it rushed to emulate the public school system, never questioning any of the county's textbooks, curricula, or teaching methods.

I wanted very much to see if it were possible to have a strong academic program and at the same time instill in children a deep love of Christ and his teaching. So when my youngest child was ready for first grade, I knew I wanted to teach her at home. At the same time, my partner had a boy ready for the second grade and she was thinking along the same lines. We decided that we would both retire from classroom teaching and would work together in a quiet way with our two children at my home.

Attic Additions

From LD to TAG. Somehow another woman who had a little girl — I'll call her Sondra — called us. She told us Sondra was having difficulty in first grade, could not read very well, had been tagged learning disabled, and that so far as she could determine, the LD classes had done nothing to help her. She begged us to take her child. Stepping out into the unknown with your own child is one thing, but taking someone else's child is a heavier responsibility. We told the mother that our program was experimental, that we were not at all certain of its legalities, that we couldn't say how long we would continue, and that we didn't know how easy it would be to get back into a regular school. If we took Sondra, we told her, the only promise we could make was that we would teach her as one of our own. The mother said that was all she asked. So we started that first year with three children. Sondra learned to read well that year and now, eight years later, is in a talented and gifted (TAG) program in a Maryland public high school.

The following year a D.C. public school teacher came to us. She had seen one of our student's work and was impressed. She practically insisted that we take her girl. The child was bright but overweight, and her life was being made miserable in school. Her mother felt our situation was just right for her child's needs. Although we were sometimes uncertain ourselves, the public school teacher never faltered in her fierce support and encouragement for what we were doing. That year we added two other students as well.

Attic Activities

Reading for Content. From the very beginning, as I stated earlier, my partner and I never had any doubts about the kind of program we wanted for the children. Early on, I received a very valuable piece of advice from a retired school teacher who had advanced degrees in both chemistry and Russian and was a fine scholar. She said that after a child reads on a fairly solid second- or third-grade level, there is no reason to keep him in the graded readers with their controlled vocabularies; rather the child should be encouraged to read real books on real subjects. *He should be allowed to read for content.* This advice fitted exactly into our plans for we knew that we wanted history to be the core of our reading program. We also wanted the children to write every day, and we wanted them to have a solid mastery of arithmetic when they left us.

By the third grade, after we were certain that the children were reading well, we started a systematic study of history: in the third and fourth grade, we studied American history; fifth grade, ancient history; sixth, seventh, and eighth grade, world history starting at the Dark Ages. We included many biographies of persons from the periods being studied. (There are many of these written for children.)

Also, we always attempted to interweave literature relevant to the period we were studying. For example, we read selections from the *Arabian Nights* after studying the spread of the Muslim empire, *Beowulf* after studying the Vikings, and *A Tale of Two Cities* after studying the French Revolution.

It is an indescribable pleasure to teach history to children in this way. Literally every subject from the history of art to the history of zoology can be sensibly woven into a history curriculum. The horrible mockery of history, social studies, which is being foisted on our children, is nothing more than the most tedious, materialistic *almanackery.* Our children are being robbed of the knowledge of mankind's sufferings, struggles, sins, victories, and redemptions. To the Christian parent particularly, let me say that there is no greater vehicle for showing children the joyous practicality and efficaciousness of Jesus' teachings than a detailed study of history. In fact, I think this is the real reason history is not taught today. We have some very militant, anti-religious forces shaping our school curricula and endeavoring to wipe out every vestige of Christianity from American life; if history is taught, it is almost impossible to avoid talking about ethics, and ethics leads inevitably to religion.

Writing
Our writing instruction always related to what we read. Every day the students answered questions, and I went over what they wrote for accuracy, logic, grammar, and mechanics of capitalization and punctuation. There were frequent re-writes, obviously, and the questions got more difficult as the reading level became more sophisticated.

Workbooks
We used no workbooks. The massive use of workbooks where all the punctuation and capitalization and thinking are done for the child is one of the central reasons children write so poorly. I despise workbooks in which children only circle the correct answer, choose A, B, or C, and never have to formulate an answer from their own brains.

Math Facts
Concerning arithmetic, I would like to make a point which I cannot overemphasize to parents who may be thinking of home schooling. Your child's attitude towards math is shaped early on by how well he knows his addition, subtraction, multiplication, and division tables. The child must have an *instant* recall of the answers. He does not know them well enough if he hems and haws before coming up with the correct answer. The sooner your child acquires this ability, the better. When our children were in the first, second, and third grades, my colleague started every math class with speed drills. We used papers that had 100 multiplication facts on them, for example, and would have daily drills to see how many the children could do in a specific time. We had one child who could write sixty answers in one minute, but some children just can't write that fast. Any child who can answer

forty-to-sixty math facts in a minute knows his facts. The entire world of fractions and percentages, so difficult for many children, opens up effortlessly to a child who knows his facts well. I am familiar with the Stanford, the California, and the Iowa elementary achievement tests, and I can promise you that if your child knows his tables well, you need have no fear of his scoring poorly on the math sections of any of these commonly used achievement tests, grades one through six.

Outgoing Achievers

Socialization. We have been asked if we were not afraid that home-taught children were being overprotected. Though I was not very interested in the socialization issue when we started, I must state that now, much to my surprise, all our students are extremely gregarious and poised. They are all leaders in clubs, sports, and church activities.

This is a happy year for us. *Our original five students are ready for high school. Every one has been accepted in an Honors program at either public or private high schools in the area.*

Not long ago a woman called me to ask about home schooling. She said she was rather drawn to the idea but didn't know that she wanted to be "tied down." There is no question that for the past eight years I have been "tied down" every day from nine to one, but I feel that what I have done has been vastly more important for my children and more stimulating for me than any office job could ever have been.

THIRTY-THREE

AN ARTIST'S PERSPECTIVE

Gordon Wetmore

BACKDROP: Gordon Wetmore, a former public school teacher, is a portrait artist, known for his paintings of world leaders and royalty such as Prince Ranier, Princess Grace, and their son, and such books as *Promised Land* (which he did with Abba Eban, Israel's former foreign minister, and with author Leon Uris— *Exodus*), and his recent children's prayer book for Ideals Publishing Company. He is in demand as a teacher at leading art seminars and conferences. He lives with his wife, Connie, and three daughters high on Signal Mountain north of Chattanooga, where Connie is a teacher and homemaker. In their travels, they are widely applauded as devoted home education ambassadors.

The first time my wife, Connie, suggested that she teach our seven-year-old daughter, Amy, at home, I thought she was outlandish. The year was 1981, and I knew zero about home education. It seemed bohemian, or worse, downright odd. Years before, I prevailed against Connie's wish to withdraw Amy from a strict Catholic school, where, at the age of four, she was having difficulty adjusting. Connie instinctively knew that our daughter was being called upon to tackle situations beyond her maturity. Hindsight is often clearer than foresight! I'd never send *any* young child into a formal classroom again! Years of marriage have taught me to appreciate a woman's instincts. Connie seems to have a vision, unrestricted by the prevailing norm.

The very week we had to make a decision about Amy's schooling, Dr. Raymond Moore came to Chattanooga at the invitation of a group of businessmen and educators. We had read his books, *Better Late Than Early* and *Home Grown Kids*, and knew of his wide-ranging research in education. A luncheon was held in the dining room of the Provident Insurance Company, whose chairman was a sponsor of the visit. We went to the luncheon and later offered to take Dr. Moore to his next stop in Nashville, and he accepted. We took Amy, and on that ride, he recommended emphatically that we teach her at home. Her principal, a dedicated educator who attended the luncheon, agreed. We considered the timing of Dr. Moore's visit providential, and teaching Amy at home has turned out to be an inspired decision.

In watching her progress through Catholic, public, Protestant, and finally home school, we have had an excellent chance to compare educational experiments. Our nine-year-old daughter, Alexandra, on the other hand, gives us an example of a child who has never attended a formal class.

Considering the fact that, historically, excellent educations have been attained both at home and in the classroom, it is inaccurate to say that a child is automatically placed at a disadvantage by not receiving instruction in a school. Yet our home school experience has led us to believe that a loosely structured, flexible program yields results far superior to that of rigid curricula.

Even so, following a relatively unstructured home school is so different from the way most of us were taught that its very newness scares us. We fear failure, and have an uneasy foreboding, for it is unconventional and might ruin our children's lives. At first, we can barely make it from one testing period to the next. We need to be reassured. This is where support groups shine.

When Connie became pregnant with our third child, she didn't have the energy to keep up her normal schedule. She worried that the girls might lose a year because they had to do so much on their own. It turned out to be a blessing in disguise! To our amazement, when they took standardized tests in the spring, they scored as well or better, than before. As Buckminster Fuller said, "The only true learning is self learning."

Over the years, we have approached home education in several different ways. Connie has often tutored other children also. We have obtained help in algebra, language, and music, and we cooperate with other parents to teach our children together.

Often the talent we need is in our support group or among willing retirees who like to work with the younger generation.

One of the most enjoyable home school meetings we remember took place when the families in our support group all got very honest as we took turns describing an average day. Everything was confessed, from oversleeping to having the family dog eat a science project. That day we learned that there is an enormous amount of leeway in individual teaching compared to classroom situations. No two families were much alike, yet all were performing above schoolroom average.

Our Daily Schedule

Our school day usually consists of about three hours of not-too-formal study in the morning, with projects reserved for the afternoon. The morning session consists of such activities as instruction from Connie and reading aloud. We have some drilling in such things as rules of grammar, spelling, phonics, and multiplication tables. These lessons are often said out loud, often in unison. A project for the afternoon might be to make a salt and flour relief map or to write or memorize poetry. It could also include raking the yard, work at the local nature center, or a trip to the gym. Amy regularly grooms and rides her horse in the afternoons. Our short morning schedule is misleading when one realizes that learning goes on all day long. Both girls love to relate to us the plot of a story they have read. One day I was trying to concentrate at my desk when Alexandra excitedly began to tell me about a book she had just completed. I started to snap at her that I was busy, when I realized how foolish that would be. I thought to myself, "I remember how I hated giving book reports. I would read a comic book version or a synopsis, see the movie, or just skim over it and bluff to keep from actually reading the book. Then getting up in front of people to recount the story was like having teeth pulled. Now here was my daughter giving me one of many 'book reports' with no prompting." So I listened.

With the theory that learning never stops, we don't observe the usual full summer break and we take advantage of unique opportunities for "field trips" related to my work. The girls have been to Israel, England, and Canada during school terms. Every day we are conscious of educating our girls, not for two or three hours, but for every waking moment. We carefully explain anything in which they are interested. We often let them operate machinery and help us with things when it would be easier for us to do it alone.

I apprentice Amy who has unusual artistic talent, and I pay her. She has her own checkbook, which she balances better than we do ours, and she pays her horse boarding bill and other expenses from her earnings. She breeds rabbits and thus studies genetics while gaining insights about life cycles. Her veterinarian allows her to observe surgery and has let her work off her own bills by helping. She doesn't like history, so Connie plans, at the suggestion of a friend who is a retired principal, to devise a unit or project tied in with the history of the horse. Since the history of horses is interwoven with the history of countries, we think she'll learn about both.

Admittedly, there are times when no one seems to want to work, but things eventually get back to normal. On the other hand, there are times when the children are up early in the morning, or late into the evening, doing pages of math, reading a book, or working on a project without prompting.

The Value of Waiting for Maturation

Alexandra exhibits less resistance to study, perhaps because she never endured long, boring days which her older sister remembers as "having to get dressed up to go sit." Alexandra was taken to school as a five-year-old when Connie was a substitute teacher for the Christian school. She took toys and was allowed to play on the floor while her mother drilled the children in phonics. Even though she seemed not to be paying attention, she learned all the sounds. She now tends to get perfect scores in her lessons because she has the ability to concentrate totally when she works. We subscribe to the theory that children are natural learning machines if they are unhampered. Amy and Alexandra were both offered piano lessons. When Alexandra wanted to quit, we allowed her to do so even though we believe that she is musically talented, because we expect her to make up for lost time when she is older. That has been the case with Amy. Even though she started later than many of her friends, she now is swiftly moving through each level.

With Alexandra we used the same theory with sports. She is highly coordinated and participates in an active athletic program in our community of Signal Mountain near Chattanooga. Although she is new among veteran athletes, coaches already applaud her.

An interesting thing happened with Amy's math instruction when she turned fourteen. We found a tutor to cover first year algebra during the summer of her freshman year. A hindrance to learning, which we feel resulted from her having entered school too early, reasserted itself, and she began to have difficulty concentrating and keeping up with the homework. Toward the end of the summer, her teacher told us that Amy was just going through the motions and that we were wasting our money.

One would think that the worst thing that could happen would be for us to interrupt her studies at that time; but, we did, allowing her to attend a camp in Canada, where she swam, rode horses, and went on canoe trips during the month of August. When she returned, her teacher gave her a test with the forlorn purpose of seeing how much, if any, information she had retained. To her astonishment, Amy had apparently remembered essentially everything and could recall it after the month's break. That gave her a second wind. She is now more diligent about finishing her homework soon after her lessons. As a result, she is progressing very well.

Sharing Talents

We believe home teaching parents can be of great help to one another by cooperating in various ways. Connie has on several occasions been able to help by tutoring children having unusual difficulty. One boy who was two years behind his grade level caught up after spending a year under Connie's loosely structured tutelage. Similarly, his sister is now blossoming.

Other successful joint ventures have included a weekly Bible class, an art class, a manners class, a Spanish class, and a number of social and school gatherings, although we never schedule these in a rush or create any pressure with them. As the children's interests arrive, we move on with them.

Our minister, Harry Erwin, comes weekly to our house to teach a number of Signal Mountain's home school children, and

I'm amazed at how much they enjoy it. I'm sure those sessions will be very beneficial to them throughout life.

One of the mothers, Jane Watson, held an art class at her home to make papier-maché masks. They were imaginative and beautiful, and the Mountain Pizza Parlor displayed them in their rotating art exhibit. I was always proud to go in there and see that impressive display with its prominent sign, "By Signal Mountain home school children."

Another mother, Sally Daugherty, conducted a manners class which lasted several weeks and concluded with two formal dinners, one for the older children, another for a younger group. The children dressed and conducted themselves beautifully for their "commencement." Now all the children are improving in manners. I was startled at the dinner table recently when a neighborhood child who had attended the class struck up a conversation with me in a very mature way. It finally dawned on me that she had learned to do that at the manners class. And manners are values seldom learned in *any* school any more! We wish all parents could know that home schooling is a gold mine.

THIRTY-FOUR

AN OVERSEAS MOTHER

Deborah Taube

BACKDROP: We tell this story because it is replete with ideas for teaching young children. Deborah Taube was a young married woman in her early years of her university course when we first met. She scored high on secretarial tests at the university placement office and shortly demonstrated her skill to our delight as Hewitt Research Foundation's lead secretary. Her husband was also on top of his profession as a young CPA and senior auditor for Clark Equipment Company at nearby Buchanan, Michigan. Too soon for us, Debbie and Jeff decided to have a baby. That was now about seven years ago. Meanwhile Jeff was called to head a Clark Equipment project in Belgium where they are home teaching their children. Debbie suggests many things a creative mother can do in giving her children a start.

Nathan, our oldest, is just six, so our curriculum to date emphasizes values and life experiences without formal education. Among the first of these values, we feel, is a correct understanding and appreciation of work. We have attempted with success to keep the children involved *with us* in home duties to the extent that they can accept responsibility. Most of us underestimate this ability in our youngsters, and push them into mental exercises where we *overestimate* them. Nathan feels a sense of accomplishment in caring for his clothes, preparing simple meals, setting the table, doing laundry, sewing on buttons, and sundry other chores.

Audrey, who is three and a half, is learning to make her bed, dress herself, care for her clothes, tidy the living room, and run errands. We are convinced that such work experiences, combined with service in the home and to others, build real nobility.

And, speaking of service, another value we have stressed is that of helpfulness, first learning to help the other members of the family, then gradually making them aware of the needs of others in the church and neighborhood.

Through their daily experiences we want our children to develop such positive characteristics as promptness, precision, cheerfulness, honesty, courtesy, and persistence. One particular characteristic we are taking pains to mold is that of following instructions carefully *without the need of repeating directions*. We make sure we have Nathan's attention, then slowly and very clearly explain our directions. Next, we ask him to repeat them. This seems to help us avoid having to request him twice, or more often, to perform the same task. Practicing courtesy and manners ourselves is the only way, we believe, to teach our children unaffected courtesy and thoughtful manners. They are encouraged to speak pleasantly to one another, and lovingly and respectfully to us. We also allow them to greet our guests, help one another and guests with wraps, bring water, and sometimes serve dessert.

God-Centered Approach

We have found our faith in God an invaluable aid in helping our children to develop desirable character traits, for we believe and so instruct our children, that our heavenly Father loves us and blesses us every day, and we ought to do our best in all of life's transactions to please Him. Accordingly, much of their preschool program is God-centered, helping them to realize their relationship to Him through day-to-day experiences.

In our morning and evening family worship a portion of Scripture is read, and the children take part in the singing and praying. They also, in their own time, are memorizing Bible verses. We invested in a set of the Holy Bible on cassettes, which certainly made the people of the book come alive for Nathan. Certainly these stories are among the great all-time classics, and they unmistakably build sound character. In our children's play, they often personify episodes and individuals from the many thrilling accounts.

Not long ago, we realized in a larger way the importance of consistency in teaching values and being role models in the home. One evening on the way to the hospital for the birth of our third child, we left our two older children with another family. Later our friends told us that as soon as Nathan had his coat off, he stated, "Well, it's time for worship! Let's start singing!" Our friends were somewhat taken aback, but soon joined in their little charge's enthusiasm for his bedtime prelude.

European Adventures in Learning

Two years ago my husband accepted an assignment in Europe, which was to last two or three years. At first I was apprehensive, wondering about possible conflicts with our home schooling plans. But, living in Europe has turned out to be a wonderful experience for us all.

We are child-centered, so naturally wherever we go in the surrounding countries, we always take in some sites of especial interest to the children. We visit zoos and safari parks (animal study); walk in scenic places (nature study), pointing out differences in sea, mountain, forest, desert, etc. (geography); and encourage them in their collections of rocks (geology), flowers (botany), and other treasures from each of the places we have visited. One morning in England, we spent an enjoyable hour studying the crustaceans along the seashore of Beachy Head with the magnificent chalky White Cliffs of Dover in the background. In the Netherlands, we discovered what it was like to live and work inside a windmill. In Wales, Nathan had the opportunity to spend some time with a real blacksmith, helping him to pump the bellows on his old-fashioned forge. In the Ardennes, we explored underground caverns with the odd formations of stalagmites and stalactites. In Luxembourg, we hiked through a wild rocky gorge, and in Spain we wandered through the ruins of an old Greek and Roman settlement, pointing out the different ways in which they had lived.

On one trip we made to the beautiful Alsace region of France, we took the occasion to visit Kayersburg, the village where Albert Schweitzer was born. There a small museum is dedicated to him and his work with the suffering African people. Nathan was already familiar with his life through a biography on cassette. Later during the trip we viewed an immense palace built by another man who was not motivated by the same principles as those of Albert Schweitzer. We saw it as an opportunity for an object lesson. We asked Nathan which was the greater man, Albert Schweitzer who sacrificed his brilliant career in Europe to help others, or the other man before whose palatial home we stood, built (according to the guidebook) to show that his home could rival those of the kings? Nathan considered a moment, than asserted that Albert Schweitzer was the greater. The point was obviously clear in his young mind.

Everyday Learning

Aside from such simple tasks as learning to tell time, recognize the alphabet, write his name, count to 100, and read road signs, we have not attempted to teach Nathan formal skills. He has shown a remarkable aptitude in engineering and mechanics, which reveals itself in hundreds of different things he creates from a construction set we bought him. After watching a local Flemish farmer cut and combine his hayfield, Nathan reproduced an exact replica in miniature with his set. He studies many different machines and copies them with all the details intact.

He and Audrey both enjoy art and spend quite some time coloring, drawing, cutting, pasting, and painting. She is fortunate to have him as a teacher. His math is yet limited to simple arithmetic he has learned from ordinary events—counting the seeds from olives and the whole ones remaining on his plate to see how many he began with. To help teach the numerical value of numbers, we ask him to locate the hymn selections in church. For instance, if he's on page 55, and the selected hymn is on page 83, he knows he must go forward to the correct page. Sometimes when he becomes restless, we turn to Psalm 119 and have him count the number of each verse.

Something the children very much enjoy learning about is physiology and health. During meal preparation we often talk about different foods, with the children usually asking why a certain food is good for them. We also tell them about the way their body works through stories. Sometimes we look at our home medical books together, and that always stimulates questions. When Nathan was five we began talking about teeth in preparation for the eventual loss of his baby teeth. We looked up information in our home medical guide and discovered some very interesting things about teeth (some of which were new to us!). When he turned six, he showed a strong desire to read. I tried to put him off since I had hoped to wait another year or so. But he would not let the matter rest. So very cautiously we began a reading program of my own devising, based on word recognition. He learns one word a day, with a test for retention at the end of the week, until he has progressed to four-word sentences. He is very enthusiastic and is always waiting with his books for me to join him for his lesson (a fifteen-minute affair). But the initiative is always his; there are no formal schedules or "musts" in this!

Our educational aids consist simply of a lot of interesting books, cassettes, and felts. We find this sufficient, allowing us to use our imaginations and follow our own interests, unhampered by textbooks and class schedules. We encourage their grandparents to be involved also. There was some resistance to our plans at first, but as they witness the lovely budding of the children's characters, and compare them with the results of child-rearing methods practiced around them, they now thank us for being good parents! Often their gifts to the children are in the form of educational accessories for our home program.

We have noticed that home-schooled children are calmer, happier, and more sociable with all age groups. They are cheerful, optimistic. Many people comment on how peaceful and friendly our children are, contrasting them with the hyperactive children around them. Jeff and I agree that it is great to be parents and to share as these little ones grow naturally.

WAITING WORKS

Solveig Swanson

BACKDROP: Solveig Swanson is a home schooling mother of five years who offered this article to her master teacher at the Hewitt-Moore Child Development Center.

In 1981 our first child, Andy, was one year away from kindergarten. I felt uncomfortable sending this flesh of my flesh off to a place where he would waste precious hours daily in lunch lines, bathroom lines, and buses. I taught fourth and fifth grades in public schools. I knew how time was spent there.

We visited two good church schools, but were not impressed. I was depressed to see that sitting still carried more weight than joy, creativity, and excitement about learning. Yet I knew no other alternatives. It would be public school. The door closed.

The day I accidentally ran across a new book on display in our public library, that closed door popped right off its hinges. *Teach Your Own*, the book's cover suggested. Since its author was John Holt, whose earlier books had been required reading in my college education classes, I grabbed it. I assumed the happy family on the cover was working together on homework given in the children's public school. I was wrong.

"Bruce," I said to my husband. "This book is about having school at home. People actually do that."

Soon I knew deep in my knowing place that I had my answer. Never mind that there was no reason in my head. Never mind that my husband, father of this same child, had not one drop of desire to support this idea. I knew, so I began a year of research. One year later we had not found much written research. But we had watched our child and spent hours in discussion. So we did it — we kept Andy home from kindergarten. We had only one reason: We believe one-on-one is the most effective way to teach.

Jumping the Gun

Three months later, in December 1982, I was introduced to Raymond and Dorothy Moore's research. We had already stopped the phonics and handwriting practice that frustrated us in September. Now, reading their books, I quit feeling guilty. They said to wait until age eight or later before trotting out those practices.

However, I did not wait well. Consistently, every September — 1982, 1983, 1984, 1985 — I felt driven to hours of planning: what times we'd have school, what books we'd use, and which pages we'd finish each day. After all, I was certified! Faithfully we'd live "school" for about two weeks each fall before I'd come to my senses and realize that Andy wasn't ready. How did I know? He reversed letters and numbers (although fewer each year), and he could not grasp the concepts behind memorized phonics rules or math processes. Therefore, he forgot memorized rules quickly. Daily drill brought dread. From my reading and my child, I knew it was not yet time. Consistently, every September, we put the homemade worksheets away and relaxed.

I knew he was not dyslexic. On his own, Andy learned to read at the age of seven years and three months. He had four weeks of phonics instruction, two in 1981 and two in 1983, five months before he picked up a book and read it to my mother in January 1984. By the fall of 1986 he had progressed on his own to the *Saturday Evening Post.*

All in Good Time

Eighteen months later, January 1988, I can say absolutely that waiting works.

Today our son is eleven years old; he would be a fifth grader if he were in a public school. I taught fifth grade; I know fifth graders. This one can read, write, talk, think, sing, play Cribbage, and ninety or so of the games on the Carom board. He can measure, sort, follow written directions, run a copy machine and a movie projector. He has replaced locks on four doors. He can change the oil in our car. (He also knows how to start the car, but we think he's had enough practice on that for a few more years.)

He is beginning to understand phonics this year, so his spelling is progressing by leaps and bounds. He learned the entire cursive alphabet in two weeks. He can diagram a simple sentence. He has progressed through three and a half years of math in one and a half years. (To be totally clear, we were able to begin with the second-grade book, thus skipping much busywork.)

Our child can look up words in any dictionary, use encyclopedias, draw maps and floor plans from his head, and ride a skateboard (although he has much room for improvement there).

He has his own savings account and keeps a notebook with several accounts within his one bank account. He counted the home school support group money last week and balanced the account book to the penny—but only after an interesting discussion about why that last, missing penny was also important.

We don't say this is a wonder child, although by some comparisons these days he is brilliant. Yet he can easily use a table of contents or an index to find information in a book. He likes looking up the copyright date on the back of a title page to see how current each book's information is. He has learned to locate books on library shelves by their numbers.

For three hours yesterday he typed a letter to be sent to seven addresses in Alaska for information to use in his social studies booklet. I'll have to buy a new bottle of correction fluid, but *I* think the letter is beautiful. Today he dictated a two-page story for *Highlights* Magazine. It is clever, precise, orderly.

He's teaching himself and his sister to play recorders. He bought himself a harmonica and learned "Oh, Susannah" within an hour. It took us four years to get through the first piano lesson book, but four weeks for the first twenty pages of Book Two.

Dr. and Mrs. Moore are right. Trying to teach children before their minds and bodies are ready wastes priceless time.

Yes, I'm curious—even nervous—about how our son will score on his first-ever state-required achievement tests this spring. But I remind myself that tests can also be learning tools. I will learn what I have left to teach.

I even dislike school some days. The worst are those times a newsletter arrives with glowing reports about superchildren winning science fairs or spelling bees. Did we make a mistake?

But we haven't. We've simply waited. We continue to wait. Good things have come. Wonderful things. Waiting works.

[A few weeks later we talked with Andy. His Stanford Achievement Test scores were 99 percent on listening skills, 96 percent on reading and an overall average of 85 percent. He thinks he'll do better next time when he "won't be so scared." Nor will his mother, anymore!]

PART SIX

SOME ENCOURAGING INFORMATION

GETTING INTO COLLEGE

BACKDROP: One of the most stressful worries of home educators, especially those who have foresight, is, "Will our children have their choices of colleges?" Or even, "After we get through with them, considering all the prejudices out there in higher education, will our children get into any college at all?" We show here that such a worry is unnecessary.

Pioneer home teacher Mary Bergman asked admissions officers of Idaho State University if they would accept her home-taught daughter, Cathy. The answer was a resounding *No.* So she made up a diploma and transcript of grades with the name of the Bergman school printed nicely, and applied from that *private* school. (After all, how private can you get?) Cathy was accepted immediately. Five years later at age twenty-one, she took her master's degree at ISU and began teaching there.

Cathy's success in getting into college is not out of the ordinary for home schooled kids. We have shown you in this book how average parents can teach their children well. But, let's not be presumptuous: you need to be sure you are teaching your children how to reason *why* and *how.* If you are using that analytical approach, if your children are reasonably devoted to their studies, and if they read a lot of stories from history, good literature, Scripture, science, and life in general, then they should be able to pass a major college entrance exam.

Be Prepared

Let's face facts. These days if you want to score high on the Scholastic Aptitude Test (SAT), American College Test (ACT),

General Education Development Test (GED), or any other of these monsters, it is better to put the beasts to sleep with a shot of pretest manuals than to face them off coldly in unfamiliar academic jungles on test day. We don't like to tell you this, for this is teaching to a test, and we don't think that's good education. It is a cram experience, or learning for the moment, instead of for life.

We don't even think these tests are ultimately ethical, for they do not really test the overall person. Such tests are the currency of education, one of the principal means admissions officers have of keeping people out or bragging about those they take in. The currency in most countries today, like the dollar, is not altogether honest either, for while we think there is something backing it, economists tell us it is not as solid as we would like to think.

So what do we do, assuming we have followed the other suggestions in this book and have operated a reasonably sound and balanced program?

Go down to your nearest public, university, or other library and pick up a copy of the latest test manual for the test of your choice — GED, SAT, ACT, or specialized tests for law school, dental school, medical school, etc. Practice on the tests until you know them backwards, forwards, and upside down. You might do this a year or two before college time to familiarize yourself with the questions and approach of a given test and to avoid surprises or a sense of urgency at the last minute. It's better to meet an old friend in daylight than an enemy on a dark night.

Dr. Frank Vandiver, currently president of Texas A & M University, quit school at the beginning of junior high, skipped junior and senior high and undergraduate college. He studied to take the Graduate Record Examination with the help of tutors, passed easily, was accepted into a University of Texas master's degree program, and before long completed his doctorate.

Don't be afraid to ask tips on test taking — from a librarian, college or university professor, high school or junior college counselor, or any likely person in the profession. Many of them have been through the testing scene and know its pitfalls and secrets.

When you do take the test, find out if there is any penalty for guessing and arrange your strategy accordingly. Remember that the first questions in any given section are usually the easiest. Do the easiest first throughout the test if the test is timed, then come back and do those which require more thought. If there is more than one way to answer, take the simplest way out. Don't worry if someone appears to finish ahead of you; he may be quitting because he didn't plan ahead. Don't try to cheat in any way. It doesn't pay. You had your day ahead of time with those practice manuals. Now you are their master.

Be Professional

When you apply to a college, put your best foot forward: Be neat, businesslike, and to the point, and let them know of your specific and broad interests. Some home educators have their own cumulative records printed with their school name on them, or use a standard form and type the name on it. In other words, be as professional as possible. Talk with others in your support group or among your state leaders. Counsel is valuable but not costly if taken ahead of time.

Pick out references which are likely to have the most impact: your physician, lawyer, business people, teachers. Some universities are skeptical of pastors, thinking that they will be Pollyannas for you—knowing only good about you. If yours is to be a religious school, that is another matter. Prepare a simple but complete resume. You can get books on resumes from your library or coaching from a personnel officer of a bank or other business.

Be Positive

Linda Callaway of Marshalltown, Iowa, wrote us the other day of her happy experiences with her son Huston who is preparing to enter college next year.[1] The admissions officers they have met have been complimentary about home-educated students. "More well rounded" is a compliment they often hear, and when on occasion the students are found behind in any subject, "they quickly catch up."

We probably know more home educators than most folks today, simply by virtue of our longer experience and diversity of contacts, but we know of no family to date whose child has made plans to go to college and who has been *ultimately* denied. The record across the nation and overseas finds home schoolers averaging high in achievement in every state and country. Take courage. Any college or university worth its salt will likely feel fortunate to have you (unless you feel personally unworthy — an unlikely event among home schoolers). *And those who are rigidly biased against home education don't deserve you!*

THIRTY - SEVEN

WHAT IS A "WORKING MOTHER"?

BACKDROP: There is no reason here to get into a feminist flap. We men must realize that we have brought a lot of this ire on ourselves, demanding as we often do barrels of authority while accepting thimble-fulls of responsibility in our homes. Our failures accentuate motherhood's glory! Our main concern in this chapter is to examine assumptions which reign today in a great deal of policy making—local, state, and national—and even intrude into churches and our private lives. They include family economics, mothers' professional dignity, personal ambitions, and the unmeasurable service of love.

Mothering is more than a profession. It is a calling. Who else among mankind actually creates life? With this act of creation (in which man has only a momentary contribution, and sometimes involuntary at that) goes what some would call a Brobdingnagian responsibility—meaning enormous, colossal, titanic, herculean, gargantuan. There is nothing to compare with motherhood on this earth in height or depth, length or breadth, mentally, physically, emotionally, or spiritually. The quickest way to play the fool would be to deny this.

Then what is our problem? *First,* some of us haven't bothered to stop, look, listen, or think. *Second,* we are slaves of conventional wisdom. *Third,* we are victims of *groupthink*—slaves of pressure people around us, totally unwilling to face up to vested interests or power-hungry activists. *Fourth,* we are a selfish people, and this is the antithesis of motherhood in its finest hours.

Professional Dignity

Motherhood is in no sense unprofessional, nor does it deny the work ethic, as any mother and loving father knows. It is simply the highest calling on earth. Mother is, in one South Carolina daughter's words, "a friend, a comforter, an encourager, and an adviser." She has the most of the greatest character principle of all: Love — seasoned with a dash of patience, a cup full of humor, and bushels of forgiveness.

Many young women of the sixties who delayed motherhood in favor of executive offices are finding that there is a larger fulfillment even than Wall Street and corporate board rooms. They are becoming creators as only they in the human race can create. Mary Cunningham Agee, once one of America's most noted female executives, revels so winsomely in motherhood that she organized a national *Nurturing Network* to support the mothering instincts in girls and professional women who are pregnant out of wedlock.[1]

We in no way depreciate those women who must work out of the home for financial or other reasons. We simply want to make it clear that a professional job in no way dignifies women above men. For women who need distinction, there is motherhood. Mothers have discovered this in new dimensions and have given up lucrative and prestigious full-time careers to shape surely their children's lives, as you have read in this book.

Personal Ambitions

Let's put our prejudices to one side and admit that some women have a large contribution to make in business. Our concern is for those of them who haven't thought the matter through and have had less thought for their children's welfare than for a dog or cat or a market report. A couple of months ago, popular columnist Ann Landers published this letter:[2]

> Dear Ann: I have been reading with interest the letters from women who left their very young children in day care centers while they pursued high-powered careers in business and industry. My daughter was another one who was sure she could "have it all." "Eleanor" was always an academic star and a superachiever. She had a wonderful husband and two children.

But her career came first. She traveled a great deal and worked crazy hours, leaving the children with incompetent help.

Within twelve years her marriage was a shambles and her children were in therapy. Today she has a big job and lots of money, but no marriage and she is trying to establish a relationship with her children. The worst part is that she is full of guilt and far from happy.

— Tears in Ohio

Ann answered: "Thanks for supporting my position. My head is bloodied, but unbowed."

We are grateful for Mary Agee and our Part 4 and Part 5 authors. They are heroines to us, operating the most noble of all callings. We could add others such as Sheryl Eberly who enjoyed one of the most prestigious women's jobs in the nation as a White House secretary to Nancy Reagan until she fully grasped the meaning of the once-in-a-lifetime privilege of rearing her little ones. Today she is a home teacher, with belt tightened a little, living on one salary, out of the Washington whirl.

Family Economics

And while we are talking about money, let's remember that most women, particularly married women, don't make that much extra after they pay for more clothes, child care, transportation, meals out, and a dozen—or hundred—incidentals which otherwise would not be necessary, not the least of which are income taxes. The April 10, 1988 *USA Today* reported that working couples were hit hardest of all in current income tax levies. For many mothers it doesn't pay to work, especially considering their value at home.

But beyond this there is a devilish assumption passed as truth across the land that offers little or no truth: It insists that it is harder for a family to earn a living today than "in the old days." If you share this conviction, read what *Fortune* Magazine recently found:[3]

It is said to be no longer economically feasible for Mommy to stay home with the kids as she routinely did a generation ago. Proportion of married women with children under six who worked in 1956: only 16 percent. Proportion today: 54 percent.

Government aid is needed, the argument goes, because families today are in a cruel bind. They need Mom's paycheck but also need somebody to take care of the kids. . . .

Are American families today really under more economic pressure to generate two incomes than they were in, say, the fifties? No way. Women today may be under new social pressures to get out there and work: they are also looking at job opportunities not available to their counterparts thirty years ago. But America's daddies today are on average more able to support the mommies than they were in the fifties. In 1956 the average male head of household with a nonworking wife earned $4833. Adjusting for thirty years of inflation that's $22,000. The equivalent figure for 1986 was $25,803.

Some mothers, of course, become stressed because their close friends are providing "so many more nice things" for their families. They would do well to do some deeper thinking. And one way to do this is to look deep into the faces of their sleeping babes or the fond, upturned eyes of their little ones, and ask, "Who do they need more than me?"

Unmeasurable Service

There are much deeper needs than money. Children need adult figures, most important of whom is their mother, with whom they can identify hour after hour, day after day, year after year.[4] Much or all of this need is unmet when the mother is not there to comfort and bless when she is needed. *Quality time is worthy only as it is available when children need it; quality time without quantity time is largely meaningless.*

The child left day after day in the care of an aide or babysitter — a person who is hired and may not be around six weeks or months down the road — is a child in limbo. Such children are far more prone to disease, emotional distress, and eventual maladjustment, delinquency, and irretrievable loss. We like Erma Bombeck even if eight or ten years ago she used up a column joking about us.[5] A couple of years ago she rolled over in bed to take a day off from the typewriter and spend it homemaking. At day's end she concluded she hadn't earned a dime nor done much for posterity. But she had a peace like she used to have when she bedded down three kids in clean sheets after making sure their feet were clean and their noses weren't running.

Those mothers who prefer to teach their offspring at home or to supplement their school when they get home, to give them counsel, companionship, and love, rank pretty high on professions' ladder, even on Erma's. Even on Donahue's and Oprah Winfrey's! They have all given home schooling time or space. Let's not deny mothers this grace in the mistaken impression that it's not popular to be a mom and to take care of their own. Asks one of our newsletters, *Why should mothers play the outfield when they do best at home plate?*

THIRTY-EIGHT

WHERE DOES THAT LEAVE DAD?

BACKDROP: It is commonly assumed that mothers do almost all the teaching in the home. Is this really true? If so, why? And if not, why do we think so? What is a father's place in home schools? Where in all the achievement, behavior, and social records credited to home education in recent years, has dad been?

Home education is awash with impressions that dads do little or none of the teaching. And for some that's true. But if your definition of teaching is not narrow, most dads do a lot more than they get credit for. How about washing the car, doing the garden, leading at story time or worship? Yet few children know anything about what Dad does all day long. Ask a few five- even eight- or ten-year-olds what their fathers do and wait for the puzzlement or indifference to your question. Isn't it about time the youngsters found out? Erma Bombeck reportedly said, "When I was a kid, a father was like the light in a refrigerator. Every house had one, but no one really knew what either of them did once the door was shut."

Patsy Redden writes in the *Newsletter of Kansans For Alternative Education*, of one dad's leadership in *field trips*.[1] After describing how he took the three youngsters "on a tour of our small-town bank" in Gypsum, Kansas, and all the interest that ensued, she tells how she got over another "daddy" hurdle:

We had a bit of a problem as they had been wanting to see what Dad does at work, but he works at a battery factory, building equipment, and for safety reasons we couldn't tour while it was in operation. However, we did find a time when everything was shut down to have a tour of the factory, and to see what Dad's new machine looked like.

Few of us parents ponder sufficiently what this knowledge means to most children in terms of family closeness, particularly father-closeness. And when mothers do their best to generate this, there is even deeper meaning in terms of mutual respect which the children see in you. And family togetherness flowers!

Your Definition Makes a Difference

What is *your* definition of teaching? If it is didactic, confrontational, look-and-say, point-and-answer, under-the-rod, dogmatic pedagogy, then someone will burn out — more likely Mom than Dad. And unfortunately we think of teachers more as pedagogues than as friendly, responsive examples.

But if you embrace the three-point formula laid down repeatedly in this book — warm responsiveness, close family life, and freedom to explore — Daddy's portion becomes much larger than four tenths of one percent! If you think of education as example, as many good dictionaries do; if part of your program calls for Dad's reading during morning and evening story or worship hour; if you give him teaching credit for washing the car together with the kids or sharing with them in the family industry, or playing together in the back yard or on picnics or on camping trips, then his percentage multiplies mightily.

If you are interested first in character development as we are, this kind of teaching *by both parents* through association and example is the most powerful education of all! So when reporters ask, "How about dads?" we seldom have to apologize.

In a very few families, the father stays home as house-husband and the mother earns the money on the job. This is not always bad. For example, a father we know is a skilled carpenter and the mother is a nurse. During cold winters his work slows almost to a stop, but nurses are needed more than ever. So they change off as "homemakers."

Yet we are old-fashioned enough to see the mother as the prime mover within the home. Our chapter on motherhood and working mothers gives some of our reasons. As fathers soon find out, there is no more demanding work on earth than skilled homemaking. One fact that underscores the mother's intrinsic advantage in home teaching is the certainty that a home school may survive without a father's strong support, unfortunate as that may be. But without a *mother's* initiative and willingness, home teaching is almost sure to stall, if it ever gets on track at all.

Crucial Value of Fathers

We have watched fathers from Larry Fenzel in Roanoke, Virginia, to Don Broesamle near Stanford University in California, and from Lloyd Bellamy in Alaska to Jack Goodchild in Fort Lauderdale, Florida, and we are convinced that they serve as backbone to much of the home education movement. They do things with their own children and/or are constantly helping others. In reviewing our lists of state and regional home school leaders, I find that they are split roughly three ways: *about* one third women, one third men, and one third couples. And within the movement we have seen no inter-gender strife whatever.

We find fathers more often leading in outdoor activities, math, astronomy, and the sciences. But some of our most skillful bakers and cooks are men. And of course family industry is a father's natural opportunity, whether in the kitchen or in the garage or shop.

Mothers need fathers' support in almost all things, but especially in making use of a boy's motivation. When a mom asks, "How can I get him going?" the father can help. Mothers also can do much to bring kids and dads together. One successful and articulate midwestern home teaching mother double-underscores the crucial value of fathers in home education. First, she notes that it is the women who are "in the trenches," who read the books. She wishes more fathers would read. Then she adds, "Burnout just naturally follows when there is never any relief from a supportive, encouraging husband."

Walt and Jolene Catlett share the ownership of a Nebraska drive-in restaurant. They have taken Cara, thirteen, and Jana, twelve, into their business some evenings and weekends. Even Joshua, eight, and Joel, six, often help by cleaning up the parking lot and doing chores as they are able. They agree with their mother that, "We can better understand Daddy's job now, and why he can't always be at home just when we expected him." Stephanie Whitson says that working with their father as well as their mother has not only taught the children responsibility, but has made them feel they now have common goals with their dad and are important as a part of his work.[2] Such family unity is difficult to explain unless you experience it, and is most difficult to achieve without making good use of a helping dad.

THE GRANDPARENT TRADEOFF

Robert and Shirley Strom

BACKDROP: Among the greatest reservoirs of help for home teachers are older folks, whether related to you or not. They are also one of our greatest opportunities for service! Yet we have largely ignored them. Many, unrelated to us, will help just for the asking. Others tutor for minimum pay. Yet they frequently bring a heritage of old-fashioned values which we should cherish. They often can reduce our stress while we help reduce theirs! Here are ways we can encourage them while profiting ourselves.

Bringing grandparents into the home education scene is a two-way street. It enriches children and makes grandparents younger! And they don't have to be related to one another. In most of the organized programs they are not! For example, Foster Grandparents nationwide are paid to ease the caretaking burden for one-parent families, parents of retarded children, and school-attending teenage mothers.[1] The University of Florida has an adopted grandparent program in which primary-grade children rotate as daily visitors to a nearby nursing home. This has served as a model for public schools and long-term care partnerships throughout the country.[2] The Grandpersons Program in Michigan matches retired mentors with interested elementary school children.[3]

In all these programs older folks experience a sense of purpose and self-satisfaction. For children, the benefits include help, establishing friendships, and recognizing older people as people who care about the welfare of others.

We wish we could report that similar gains have been made in grandparent-grandchild relationships. But, without family-oriented education programs for grandparents, we can't. For more than twenty years, descriptive studies have tried to place grandparents into categories based on their behavior styles. During the 1960s, grandparents were identified as *formal* (occasionally helping out but expecting parents to raise their own children), *funseeking* (maintaining a playful and informal relationship with grandchildren), *surrogate* (grandmothers who assume regular caretaking responsibility), and *distant* (the benevolent figure who emerges on holidays and special occasions).[4]

Recent research says grandparents now qualify for new categories such as *companionette* (affectionate but somewhat passive), *remote* (geographically distant but not necessarily emotionally so), and *involved* (ready to enforce discipline and family rules).[5] Other studies relate grandparent styles to divorce, family separation, etc., and conclude that more help is needed to counteract alienation and build mutual respect within the family.[6]

Family-Oriented Education

Education has proven to be an effective way for young adults to improve their unique family relationships. Grandparents need this too. Although nearly fifty million Americans are grandparents, little has been done for them. We don't even know whether grandparents can be favorably influenced by instruction relating to their role.[7] So we are working on this.

We began with a group of four hundred self-selected collaborators from metropolitan Phoenix, Arizona, who shared personal accounts of satisfactions, successes, teaching opportunities, difficulties, frustrations, and needs for more information. We identified perceptions grandparents have about relationships with adult children and grandchildren; existing strengths of grandparents, and their need to acquire certain attitudes and skills *they* were never taught; acceptable methods for providing them with instruction and evaluation; and curriculum elements that match their aspirations and concerns. These outcomes provided useful information for the program we are developing. We intend to determine whether grandparents can benefit from family-oriented education. We have made several assumptions:

Assumption 1: The grandparent role is becoming ambiguous. There is general agreement that the grandparent role is no longer clearly defined.[8] Parents can take courses to remain competent in their changing role, but such opportunities are unavailable for the approximately 75 percent of older people who are grandparents.[9] Instead they are left to wonder: What are my rights and responsibilities as a grandparent? In what ways can this role be more influential and satisfying? How can I know how well I am doing as a grandparent?[10]

Assumption 2: Grandparents can learn to improve their influence. Parent education has enabled many mothers and fathers to increase their effectiveness.[11] Similarly, grandparents can enrich the lives of grandchildren *when they are prepared to fulfill their guidance function.*[12]

Assumption 3: Programs for grandparents ought to be developed. As people continue to age, they should also continue to grow — and not just in leisure terms. As things stand now, senior citizens are the least educated population and, ironically, the only one without any defined educational needs or programs. Since the size of this age group is expected to grow faster than any other age segment, it would be a mistake not to do something for them.[13]

Sharing Feelings and Ideas

We find among our grandparents and young parents that sharing feelings is the basis of intimacy. It helps both to unload emotions for the sake of mental health. Grandmothers and grandfathers also have much to gain by sharing anxieties, hopes, satisfactions, and observations with other grandparents. It can become a highly profitable activity for you and your children to promote such relationships — getting them together to get acquainted and consider questions. For example:

1. How do you suppose raising children now is different from your own experience as a parent?

2. How does your performance as a grandparent compare with how well you did as a parent?

3. What should parents teach children to expect of their grandparents?

4. What obligations do you expect of your grandchildren?

Listening to Young People

After sharing their viewpoints, the grandparents can listen to young parents and children for insights into their feelings and ideas. Each of us could be more effective in our relationships by considering the way other age groups see things. Unfortunately, grandparents seldom have a chance to be observers when grandchildren carry on discussions with their friends because our age-segregated lifestyles prevent it. There should be a better way to acquaint older people with the perceptions of children and teenagers. It would reduce stresses and become healing for all.

One approach we are exploring is to videorecord discussions within one age group for viewing by another. Teenagers, for example, are asked to discuss questions like these:

1. Who are your heroes and why do you look up to them?

2. What are some of the fears you presently experience?

3. How important do you think extracurricular activities are in high school?

4. How do you suppose growing up today differs from when grandparents were your age?

In our ASU program, elementary and high school students in these groups are not related to the grandparents who see them on tape, so there is little defensiveness. The young people live in another part of the city, and an immediate response to their comments is unnecessary. So grandparents are less likely to be offended. This kind of experience also helps them understand how their grandchildren resemble and differ from agemates.

Grandparent development also requires learning what it is like to rear children today. The satisfactions and difficulties of people like you in the middle generation are often misunderstood both by aging parents and dependent children.

Encouraging Mutual Storytelling

Grandparents need to learn from their peers who have family roles similar to their own and from understanding the perceptions of teenagers and parents. Long-term memory does not decline much with age, so older persons can recall events and emotions that occurred many years ago. This is why grandparents have always been a firsthand source of information about the past. The way they tell stories depends on their personalities and individual styles. What matters more than their method is their story content. Like all historians, grandparents must identify the experiences that most deserve to be shared. If grandparents are to convey certain lessons, they must go beyond spontaneous storytelling to include some planned sharing as well. You can help them get to the point, the points you and your children (or support group) need.

Because boys and girls properly consider events in their lives to be as important as the events grown-ups report, we encourage mutual storytelling. This uncommon practice helps both generations to understand and respect each other. Themes such as dating, sports, schooling, health, and careers are accompanied by questions grandparents and grandchildren use as the focus for mutual sharing. Here are questions you can use for grandparents (which can be slightly reworded when directed to grandchildren):

1. What things had an influence on your choice of a career?

2. Did you ever change careers or wish you could have later on?

3. How did your parents affect your decision about a career?

4. When you were growing up, what was the reaction to women who wanted a career?

5. As a child, what careers were most appealing?

Developing Questioning Skills

Boys and girls today encounter circumstances unique in history to their age groups. Therefore, grandparents can learn directly from grandchildren what growing up is like now. Otherwise, they increase the risk of being ignored as a course of guidance, for in our age-stratified society children are turning more and more to each other for advice. Parents and grandparents can change this if they establish a respectful dialogue with youngsters.

Most grandparents we work with admit that they sometimes have difficulty getting boys and girls to talk with them (although this is less of a problem among homeschoolers). Asking good questions is one of the most important skills parents and grand-parents need. For example, listening together to any story in books, the Bible, or on radio or television can be an excellent way to learn about the impressions, understandings, and values of grandchildren. The following purposes and matching questions can be used with almost any story or program.

Purposes	Questions
Recognizing motivation	What do you think caused this person to act that way?
Influence on others	How will that person's behavior affect other people?
Perception of potential	What did you like most about each of the main characters?
Scaling consequences	How do you think that person should be punished?
Recognizing similarities	Has anything like this ever happened to you?

Focusing Self-Evaluation

Grandparents, like parents and children, want to think well of themselves. Yet often they don't know how to evaluate themselves. Our method for focusing self-evaluation begins with grandparent groups brainstorming a list of the rights they feel are appropriate for persons in their role. The important outcome is to help individuals define their own aspirations based on the family situation. They do so by selecting from a list of rights, such as the following:

1. The right to visitation with grandchildren when there is a divorce.

2. The right to hear from grandchildren when separated by distance.

3. The right to express personal feelings, including child-rearing advice.

4. The right to live one's own life without having to rear another generation of children.

We hope parents will permit and encourage grandparents to assume significant family roles with these responsibilities:

1. To model the wise use of leisure time, including community service.

2. To help grandchildren know how their parents behaved as children.

3. To understand current child-rearing practices so as to participate more fully in family development.

4. To share knowledge of family history with grandchildren.

We also give grandparents "homework" questions like these:

1. How do you suppose your family looks upon you as a source of guidance?

2. How do you feel about offering child-rearing advice to your children?

3. How do you let your children know they're doing a good job as parents?

4. What topics of conversation most often lead to disagreement between you and your grandchildren?

EPILOGUE FOR PARENTS — AND EDUCATORS, TOO!

FORTY

HISTORY'S WISE LESSONS FOR EDUCATORS

BACKDROP: How really worthwhile are the gifts of ancient Greece to our society? What of Plato, Aristotle, Mao, Marx, Gandhi, Moses, Mohammed, Christ? Whose course should we follow? What should be our plan for action? More of Head Start? Earlier schooling? Can we afford the NEA's agenda for rushing little tykes into institutional settings? Financially? Physically? Mentally? Morally?

Ralph Waldo Emerson was right when he said that "the years teach much that the days never know." This is a line we would do well to repeat daily, for when you and I defy the wisdom of history we invite the collapse of our society. Some of us think the study of history has no value. And when we do study it, we often reason that what happened to Greece and Rome can't possibly happen to us. When we realize that it can, usually it's too late.

We educators in general are so out of touch today with the history of our profession that in many states legislators are a step ahead of us in determining what is educationally best for American children and the survival of our free society: These lawmakers are often giving us laws which strengthen families. How we respond will tell if America, her families, and the schools which we are determined to protect will survive.

Children of the State
In ancient Greece, Aristotle and Plato, both home schooled, somehow developed the idea that the state owned the family, and

271

advanced the philosophy of subjugation of children to the state. In his Book VI, Plato emphasized the importance of getting to the "young and tender mind." He wrote, "That is the time when the character is being moulded and easily takes any impress one may wish to stamp on it." And in *Crito* his perspective was clearly totalitarian: "Since you were brought into the world and nurtured by us [the state] can you deny in the first place that you are our child and slave?"

Plato's disciple, Aristotle, later declared in his *Politics* that "the state is by nature clearly prior to the family and to the individual since the whole is of necessity prior to the part." And he advanced the idea that the state should be in charge of the child at least by age seven.[1] When for several generations children lived away from their families, dominated by their peers, family values were not passed on. The social contagion of peer rivalry, ridicule, habits, manners, obscenity, drugs, and sex ruled, and before long that state collapsed.

Rome largely repeated Greece's folly, except that Caesar Augustus is credited with extending the life of his nation through his "Julian Laws" which called for family integrity. Quintilian, preeminent Roman educator, said home education with its influence on family integrity was superior to government schools. But convention prevailed, totalitarianism again won out, and Rome as an empire collapsed, its society handicapped by a weakened family base.[2]

The Julian Laws might well be a model for us, for among other things, they required young couples (1) to be married rather than live together out of wedlock, (2) to have children, and (3) to take care of their old folks. This latter practice has much meaning for today when so many children seem content to let their parents and grandparents languish unnecessarily in some state-funded care facility. Yet here is also a lesson for parents, for if you send your children away before they are ready, they may do the same to you.

Given the philosophy of Plato and Aristotle, their doctrine of *in loco parentis* was not surprising for, after all, the state was much longer-lived than the individual. Why shouldn't the state be the master parent? Later, Marx, Gandhi, and Mao Tse-tung likewise were willing to sacrifice the fabric of the traditional family for the economic welfare of the state. They reasoned logically from an atheistic perspective that an individual's life span was short, but the state was "forever."

However, Christ and the Judeo-Christian concept of personal eternal life flies in the face of such temporal ideas, and places much greater value on both the individual and the family. So did Moses. And our Muslim friends many times shame Christians in their devotion to sacredness of family relationships and the building of great children. Now, in the age of Marx, Gandhi, and Mao, socialism's history is repeating itself. There is increasing insistence by many that the state owns the child. This is why Carle Zimmerman predicts disaster for American society.

Plan for Action

Some of us, particularly in the United States and Canada, hear a lot of parents complaining about the schools, and a lot of schools finding fault with families. Why not take a mutual look at solutions, and not neglect history and research? Why not work together as many public schools and home schooling parents are doing today, to use these homes led by concerned parents — most of them very successful — as laboratories for better education?

Any plan for action should recognize that the family is the foundation and cornerstone of society. Yet, some states continue to encourage family decay by usurping parental authority instead of educating parents toward a better understanding of child development, constructive discipline, management of the home, and involvement in a moral, free-enterprising America. This education would build respect for the dignity and nobility of parenthood, so that mothers who choose to remain home with their young would enjoy as high a respect as society offers any profession.

It is time for educators to reevaluate their use of research and clinical evidence. We have brilliant child specialists who can tell you all about child development, but who seem unaware of the unique potential of the family. We have specialists in children's learning who know little about their physical development. We have readiness experts who apparently have given little attention to sociability. Some of these specialists are quite willing to surrender children to daycare, preschool, kindergarten, or early formal studies. It is high time to get these specialists together.

At the same time, there are thousands of educators, social workers, and state officials these days who join educational organizations in urging the mandating of part- or full-day kindergartens as socializing and readiness agencies. Here we have one of the two or three largest educational movements in the nation today.

No doubt there are millions of children whose parents can't or won't care for their offspring, who must have out-of-home care. Our analysis of more than eight thousand studies under federal and private grants over the last fifteen years has not turned up a single replicated study which verifies advantages of such care for children who have the option of full-time parenting.

We are well aware of the Ypsilanti studies of Head Start, but they have little meaning for average children.[3] Head Start's most successful efforts have involved more home contact than the norm. Meanwhile Head Start fathers hardly consider it the success it is commonly claimed to be.[4] Even Head Start staffers at the Department of Health and Human Services privately admit that it is probably not cost-effective except as a political device.[5]

Yet, strangely, in time of economic uncertainty, Head Start exponents not only somehow misuse these studies to urge more tax dollars for the disadvantaged and handicapped, but also get educators to apply Head Start to *average* youngsters. In an irresponsible use of research they urge *early schooling for all*. The National Education Association has since 1976 urged mandatory schooling down to ages three and four. This is like insisting that we hospitalize all children because a few have the flu, whether we can afford to or not. The burdens such suggestions lay upon families and the costs to the taxpayer are beyond our ability.

Resolving the Issues

In working out the issues, we must avoid straw men! We have found that both in legislatures and courts, school officials and social workers commonly suggest likely problems for home schoolers and society which seldom, if ever, exist. Among them: (1) readmission to conventional schools, (2) college or university admission, (3) child abuse, (4) unskilled care for handicapped children, (5) parent qualifications, and (6) relations with authorities and with conventionally oriented people.

We can quickly and honestly dispense with these by reviewing a few facts, in order, about home-taught children:

1. Most schools are eager to enroll them because of their generally superior achievement, behavior, and sociability.

2. College admission is seldom if ever a problem, unless officials are prejudiced, for most colleges and universities readily accept a good score on the GED, ACT, SAT, or similar measures.

3. We have not yet found the specter of child abuse among tens of thousands of genuine home schooling families. Home schoolers must not be confused with truant families or with conventionally schooling parents who care little for their children — where abuse will be more likely.

4. Home schooling parents are encouraged to utilize the best of clinical facilities and advice, to learn how to give the care needed and to provide handicapped children the best and most secure of all care — in the home.

5. Consistent with lessons of history and research, with the findings of the Smithsonian and other studies on genius, and with the findings of the Eight-Year Study, there is no reason to believe that parents who are warm and responsive and can read, write, count, and speak clearly will not be good tutors for their own children. In Chicago, blind parents are doing an excellent job, as are others who are hearing impaired. We often underestimate the potential of good parents in tutoring programs.

6. A Wisconsin education state official moaned that Horace Mann would turn over in his grave at word of the home schooling renaissance. We agree, but we also think he would likely be smiling, for one of the concerns he voiced the loudest was that of morality and character education. It will help a great deal if home educators remember that biases are best overcome by informing the opposition, and the critics do well to open their minds to this information. This attitude will be particularly enhanced if they do their own objective studies before they speculate or criticize.

Perhaps the biggest single issue involves parental rights versus state authority. It is fair to assume that both authority and responsibility for the education and welfare of children are vested in parents by the U.S. Constitution except as families are found to be derelict in the areas of the states' compelling interests. This assumes that the Constitution reigns over state and local statutes and policies in setting priorities for assumption of authority and responsibility in child rearing and education.

In the event of serious parental shortcomings, assumption of parental *authority* by the state should be limited to the extent of *responsibility* the state can assume for children's achievement, behavior, and social/moral development. The records of home-based educators clearly demonstrate the viability of educating and encouraging more parents to enter longer and more earnestly into the care of their children.

States should do their best to develop cooperative — rather than confrontive — relations with these concerned families. It pays for state officials to encourage more family closeness. In view of the high average home school success record, conventional schools can profit more by utilizing them as educational laboratories than by opposing, demeaning, or prosecuting home schooling parents. Homes often complement conventional schools, and school programs can supplement homes where their service is desired, as, for example, in many Northern California and Oregon counties. It's time for us to have more confidence in our home teaching parents. A recent Princeton University study on home schools suggests that they are well educated and financially and religiously stable.[6] They prefer to delay formal education — at home or school — until their children are ready. And most of them will not commit to any particular age for enrollment in conventional schools.

It is the hallmark of all ethical professionals — physicians, nurses, dentists, lawyers, engineers, educators — that they prefer the welfare of their clients over their own. In education, vested interests are set aside, and the welfare of children and families is placed ahead of dollars and jobs. The goal is noble children, admirable parents, and stronger families. Perhaps we'll be closer to that goal and have fewer burned out families when parents are honored instead of arrested for spending constructive time with their children.

FORTY-ONE

HOW HOME EDUCATION AS A MOVEMENT WAS BORN

BACKDROP: Many ask how the modern home education renaissance got its start. Throughout history there have been cycles of parental indifference or incapacity which moved control of children from the family to the state. Usually these followed devastating wars which divided families and left child care to others. Sooner or later the state would prove that its plan to take care of children — *en loco parentis* — was a poor substitute, and the family would rise again as the dominant force in children's lives.

Some of us were home teaching forty years ago, but the coalescence of interests from coast to coast took place between fifteen and twenty-five years ago. John Holt, Ed Nagel, Nancy Plent, Meg Johnson, Virginia Baker, and Pat Montgomery were among the many pioneers, most of these secular in orientation. Hewitt-Moore research gave the idea substance. Eventually independent churches got on board and now secular and religious *coalitions* cooperate in legislatures and courts.

When we were preparing to write the book *Better Late Than Early* for Reader's Digest, we learned how devious and bold prejudice can be when tradition is challenged. After Dorothy and I had submitted our preliminary manuscript and had our contract in hand, book editors Steven Frimmer and Bruce Lee said they would like to see the letters we had received on a June 1972 *Harper's* article entitled "The Race to the School House." The October 1972 *Reader's Digest* "Springboard for Discussion" department had republished it as "Dangers of Early Schooling."

Harper's editors told us it had drawn more letters than any article in their history. We received eight negative letters and over a hundred positive ones. So I brought copies of them and spent half an hour discussing them with Angela,[1] the researcher (who seemed friendly enough) whom Lee had assigned to the project. I left after I was satisfied that she was satisfied.

How wrong I was!

A week or so later Mr. Lee called.

"We have some questions about your book," he said in a worried tone.

"What seems to be the problem?" I asked, with visions of Reader's Digest attorneys managing somehow to stamp CANCELED on our precious contract.

"Angela's report suggests that the letters largely reflect doubts on your research. She questions your accuracy," he replied. "She says your conservative biases color your work."

"But there were more than ten times as many positive letters," I protested, "and one of the eight negatives was from John Holt who thought I was much too *liberal* with the schools."

"Oh?"

"Have you or Steve looked them over yourselves?" I asked. I invited him to check our analyses and accuracy with any reputable university faculty. I had done this a number of times.

"No, we're under deadlines on other projects."

"Could you?" I asked, "and see if there's still a problem?"

"Will do!" he agreed.

A week or so later, Bruce Lee called again, this time to say that editing was moving along well, and that they had had to fire Angela for deliberately misrepresenting the letters' consensus. "She didn't like your idea of keeping children longer at home."

Because of skillful and honest editing by Frimmer and Lee, *Better Late Than Early* was published in 1975.[2] These men gave us an exercise in editorial *objectivity* and *common sense* that is badly needed today among those who control laws and policy for schools.

We must add that the media have generally been not only objective, but also largely supportive of home education over the past fifteen to twenty years. One veteran reporter told us they are looking for "anything that will improve the behavior and literacy of the kids and avoid breakup of the family."[3]

Decline of the Family's Role in Education

Authorities as varied as King Solomon, historian Carl Sandburg, and Harvard sociologist Carle Zimmerman agree that wisdom, a nose for truth and common sense, could be learned through the pointing finger of history. And research and experimentation are the modern tools that verify the experience of centuries.

One of the lessons history has on the tip of her tongue concerns parents as educators, *both those who do most of the teaching at home and those who help with homework after school.* For more than three centuries America's children were educated mostly at home. The common schools were only open for a few months out of the year. Even then parents were intent on helping the young scholars, and the children helped parents with the chores — the productive kind of homework! The record of those eras in achievement, behavior, and sociability are history's legacy.

It is a sad commentary on many educators and laymen during the past twenty years that they have not learned from history, nor had the common sense to recognize a great record when they see one. Groupthink and vested interests have a way of blinding us. I confess that in all my years of studying, teaching, and presiding in colleges and universities — and even in a stint at the United States Office of Education — I hardly learned a nickel's worth about this greatest of all education — in the home.

After two world wars in less than a quarter of a century, children, further compromised by television, were reflecting the values of their peers more than those of their parents. And many parents, preoccupied with other ambitions and cares, were quite willing to leave most of the rearing of their children to the state via their public schools, recreational programs, and supplementary care such as Head Start. As these programs became widely used, they grew in political power. They were sacred cows which no politician dared criticize if he wanted to be elected. Eventually they also allied themselves with the labor movement, and seemed to become more concerned about perpetuating their own welfare than that of their charges — the children.

As it happened with ancient Israel, the Chaldeans, Greeks, Romans, and those of the French Revolution, so the Western family now took the back seat to the state. Americans were caught in the swim of history without a life jacket. And, according to pundit Walter Lippmann, the longer the state schools and colleges taught them, the more their religious and moral values declined, and the less they understood of their cultural heritage and Western civilization.[4]

Pioneers of Alternative Schooling

John Holt, a bachelor teacher, was not a researcher, but an uncommonly bright person with more than average common sense who became angry at the scars the schools were inflicting on the kids through the increased mechanizing and dullifying by mass education. He wrote eleven books on education where he became a respected voice. He had the rare courage to speak out while he was yet teaching in an effort to avoid the total stupifying of American children. He admitted that some schools were quite good, but in the great majority of them, especially the large ones, he perceived decline far beyond the ken of the average citizen.

A gospel of "unschooling" was his answer. He could have just as well called it "deschooling." But the myopic schoolmen and tradition-bound citizens failed to view it as a positive approach and invidiously criticized it as "antischooling."

The full blast of teacher association batteries only emboldened John. He quit his teaching job and went into full-time writing and speaking. When our article was published by *Harper's*, he was one of the first to write the editors—a two-paged, single-spaced typewritten letter voicing strong fears that I might be watering down his gospel. From his point of view, we were simply not conservative enough.

What John did not then understand, he later acknowledged as we became warm personal friends: Although we had a strong personal philosophy, our professional conclusions have been strictly research-based. At the time we could not afford the luxury of activism. We had to state our case without the flourish and freedom he could afford, for we must face the most incisive reactions from university scholars high in their ivory towers whose first impulse was to protect their own frontiers.

John was unique. Yet he did lay his mantle on others. First among those in his own organization was Pat Farenga, now president of Holt Associates, the organization John left behind when he died. He made it clear to close friends that Pat had "grown up" in the organization and explicitly shared in decision making. Meanwhile others became deeply woven into his network, among them Nancy Plent, a home teaching veteran whose free approach to home teaching is known far beyond her New Jersey limits.

In New Mexico Ed Nagel was working on a program of alternative schooling particularly directed to the disadvantaged. In Southwestern Michigan we began our home school-related research in 1969. And it was in Michigan that Judy Waddell went to jail in the mid-70s. And east in that state we found Pat Montgomery, a former nun, who developed another alternative program and became politically powerful as she confronted school officials and legislators. Other pioneers were Meg Johnson (New Jersey), Ginny Baker (Montana), the Harringtons (Idaho), the Larry Williams (California), and Mary Bergman (Missouri).

Early Research

While John was proposing unschooling and Ed and Pat were pushing their brands of alternative schools, Dorothy and I were researching school entrance age and work-study programs. Back in 1951 we began home schooling, even while I was president of a college with an elementary and secondary school. It was Dorothy's alertness fifty years ago to the damage done by early enrollments that sparked our interest. In 1937-38, her first year in California's South Whittier public school system, she established herself as its reading specialist. She found that children who entered school in their fives and early sixes, particularly little boys, had far more learning and behavior problems than older entrants. The absurdity of early school entrance bothered us for over thirty years.

While in Washington, D.C. in the late 1950s and again in the mid-1960s, we worked with university neuro-physiologists and scientists from the National Institutes of Health, and by the end of the decade we began full-time research. This was made possible by federal grants and by nearly $750,000 given to me by Carl and Ella Hewitt for arranging the sale of their California properties, but which we directed to a foundation we organized in 1964. Four federal grants came after the *Harper's/Reader's Digest* article caught the eyes of Oregon Democratic Congresswoman

Edith Green and New York Republican Senator James Buckley, whose aide, John Kwapisz, spearheaded the effort with the encouragement of Minnesota Republican Congressman Al Quie and Mrs. Green's aides.

When our teams in Michigan, at Stanford, at the University of Colorado Medical School, and at the National Center for Educational Statistics were finished in the mid-1970s, it was clear that children were being legislated into school at far too early an age. When we analyzed more than eight thousand studies variously on vision, hearing, taste, touch, smell, cognition (consistent reasoning ability), brain development, coordination, and socialization, we could not find one replicable study that supported six-year-old school entry. This was supported by our basic University of Colorado studies on the child's brain, by a fifty-state Stanford study on school entrance laws, and a massive survey of thirty-five hundred teachers and eighty-thousand students with the National Center for Educational Statistics (NCES) in Washington, D.C.[5] We were forced to conclude that no normal child should be forced into the classroom before eight to ten, especially boys who now occupy thirteen times as many slots in special education classes as girls and are eight times as frequently under treatment for emotional disorders.[6]

What we recommended was helping parents learn how to guide their children in free exploration and respond to them at home as suggested by the Smithsonian Institution's study on genius.[7] This process we nicknamed "home school," and it stuck, although we wish now that we could eliminate the word school. Many people somehow think we mean "school at home" or correspondence school.

Movement in the Making

Once we identified the home school, our *Reader's Digest* efforts and a few of our books caught fire along with those of John Holt, and a movement was in the making. Although our research was clearly secular, and carried out with the cooperation of many universities, we had a distinct advantage over John in numbers of "believers," identified as we were with Christian circles. He once estimated that 85 percent or more of all home educators were Christians, with most of his experience coming from the

East. Yet his figures jibed closely with enrollment percentages we had received from others in the West and Midwest. Although growth of the movement was rapid, John warned me that we should "keep the figure as small as possible lest the authorities [become] alarmed." But there was no hiding the figures: John Naisbitt used over one million in his book *Megatrends*, and one midwestern "authority" uses an even larger number. At this writing in mid-1988, we are convinced after discussions with officials of the Bureaus of Census and Labor that, including normal, migrant, and handicapped children, the total number of children schooled at home *most of each day* is well over a million, and there are increasing numbers of parents who are daring to supplement their children's conventional lessons.

The Formation of Support Groups

So in the face of hostile school officials, social workers, and even in-laws and neighbors, we at Hewitt Research began forming local home school support groups and regional and state coalitions, convinced that in unity there is both comfort and strength. And we began familiarizing friendly lawyers with home schooling.

The first support groups, to the best of our knowledge, were in Napa County, California, and Berrien County, Michigan, in the early seventies. Shortly they were sprouting up all across the nation, including Alaska and Hawaii.

Today there are thousands of effective local, regional, and state organizations across America, Canada, and around the world. At this writing we have requests from home school movements for books, and court or legislative help in Australia, Austria, Belgium, China, Denmark, France, Germany, Guam, Japan, Kenya, Korea, New Zealand, Norway, Philippines, Portugal, Russia, South Africa, Spain, Sweden, Thailand, Uganda, and an array of Central and South American countries.

We sponsored or shared the initiation of several meetings to open the possibilities of a national organization. This was a selfish gesture in part, for we were trying to unload some of the heavy burden which had accumulated over ten to fifteen years. But leaders from a number of states made it clear that *for now* home educators are a unique tribe under diverse state policies, and are not interested in supporting a national organization. The local support group remains the key organization, and the sound regional or state organization is a close second.

SUPPORT GROUPS:
HOW TO WIN FRIENDS
AND INFLUENCE PEOPLE

BACKDROP: If you need relief from fears of criticism or the law and the burnout pressures those fears generate, and still are a bit peer dependent, here is the the the safest place we know — *the home school support group reported by its own vital newsletter.* When we helped start the first such organization (that we know of) in Berrien Springs, Michigan, in the early '70s, and another in California's Napa Valley, we had no prophetic eye, no sense that one day there would be thousands of them across America, Canada, and Australia. Yet home education leaders made it happen.

The support group has given home schooling its power, as religious and secular leaders have joined forces in one of the world's most potent movements. And the support group is not through yet. From many points of view it remains an effective burnout preventive and cure. Yet the danger of carelessness and apathy is ever present.

Historians and scholars recall the terrors and amorality of Baal worship in which depraved men not only consorted in the groves with temple prostitutes, but frequently sacrificed children on the Baal altars to appease this sun god. Home schoolers, like Elijah of old, often feel as if they are completely alone in not bowing the knee to state "Baal" pressures to put their children in institutional settings before they are ready. Because of doubts, misinformation, uncertainty, and lack of information, many mothers and dads still keep children home unnoticed, some even in states friendly to home teaching!

A family which has chosen to cut across tradition may be unpopular with relatives, church friends, and neighbors. If one has determined to be "different," it often seems easier to be different with others.

Several years ago in Northern California one of four families home schooling in a particular church sought our help because of near ostracism by some of their fellow members. We tried to encourage them, suggesting that they make no attempt to persuade or argue, but only answer questions if asked, and keep research evidence handy just in case. By the next year they were happily surprised to be joined by seven or eight families. Now their support group has over a hundred members.

Starting a Support Group

If there is no support group in your area,[1] it is relatively easy to start one—perhaps with only one or two other families at first. Invite them to meet in your home and to bring any interested or potential home schoolers. Set the date far enough in advance to give them time to get word around, and to be sure, if possible, that both mothers and fathers are there. You may end up with twice as many as you expected.

At first you will find plenty to talk about without any special speaker. Yet, if there are any experienced home schooling families anywhere in the area, one or more will usually be glad to come and share their experiences. Just be sure that you know whereof your speakers speak, lest you mislead the whole group.

Most home teachers are stable people with a lot of common sense. Yet there are enthusiasts who occasionally are more visionary than people of vision. And, unfortunately, there are sometimes opportunists. Responsible support group and seminar leaders won't encourage nuisances who clutter more than enrich.

There are sympathetic home educators and other teachers who have done reliable research or who have had distinguished success who will speak to a larger group. Don't be afraid to take initiative, as long as you take counsel. There are now excellent leaders in nearly every state. There is also plenty of professional talent—careful child psychologists and educators who love home education yet who have no vested interests and are not out to get rich.

Most state and local support group leaders are selfless people who serve without pay, but a group is much more successful if the burden is shared. Everyone should have an active part—in contributing news or articles to your newsletter; in planning field trips, other activities, and interesting meetings; and in supporting the group financially. The most helpful and dynamic organizations we know about are those in which everyone does his share, as he is able.

Almost every family has some kind of creative talent or skill which can help to inspire other support group members. And if not in your immediate family, perhaps a grandparent, uncle, aunt, or friend may have something to share. One support group we know about had each family present a country of its choice, using different mediums to depict customs, food, costumes, and other information about the land and people. Another had a series on occupations or avocations which were presented by members of the group or invited guests. Still another had each family present a summary of some project they had been studying at home.

Some years ago we helped a Michigan home schooling father start a statewide association. We gave him forty names of interested people (with their permission), and he planned several meetings at regular intervals. In the meantime, we put a flier in each letter we sent to a Michigan family. And since the experience of home schooling is too good to keep secret, the news spread, and shortly the membership was in the hundreds. Eventually he invited us to a seminar of nine hundred at the state capital.

This leader's only mistake was in not expecting and asking larger financial support, either by encouraging contributions or by charging a minimal membership fee. It costs money to print and mail announcements and other information, not to mention phone calls, duplication, and other overhead expenses.

Those Valued Newsletters

Every regional or state body or coalition which expects to build power, initiative, and vitality into its membership should have its own organization, leadership, and newsletter. This is particularly important as the state group faces the need to develop legal and legislative strength.

By their very nature and flexibility these relatively small independent papers provide some of the most vital, lively, professional, dependable, and up-to-date materials and news which come across our desks. We exchange our *Moore Report*[2] for a number of newsletters from organizations all over the United States, Canada, and overseas, and many of them also exchange pieces with one another.

One of the advantages of such newsletters is the medium they provide for creative writing—a motivating power for both parent and child. Lee Gonet, editor of Alabama's brightly written *Voice*, says it has brought growth to her life, developed her own writing skills and even her patience with her family as they help her. Others could make similar statements about their improvement in journalistic or creative writing skills as they have "practiced and made more perfect" their articles for monthly newsletters instead of surrendering to the temptation to let somebody else do it. Our overriding appeal here, in avoiding stress, is that we all practice the Golden Rule. To the extent that we do not, we will inevitably be stressed, and will stress others. We say this because one of the most dangerous of burnout traps or stress factors is that of religious bigotry.

While some of us were sweating to develop legislative coalitions of all creeds to get laws that protected parents' rights, other writers and speakers viewed home schooling as essentially an organic Christian movement and set out to divide home schoolers in an effort that was harming home schools.

A statement by American hero Edward Everett Hale gives us words to close this chapter: *"I am only one, but still I am one. I cannot do everything, but I can do something; and because I cannot do everything, I will not refuse to do the something that I can do."*

Let us do it by the Golden Rule.

FORTY-THREE

THE BIG FAMILY-
STATE QUARREL

BACKDROP: Schools accuse parents these days, and parents accuse schools and the state. This is the pressure cooker into which the home teaching renaissance has dared to step. We will tell you stories in this chapter which will help you understand these home school dilemmas. Are children really our society's highest priority today as child-protection officials claim? Who gets priority with our schools and publishers? Do children? Or dollars and jobs?

Everywhere today people ask, Who is going to do something about the immorality in our society, decline in education, and the social contagion in our schools? Where does the responsibility lie? Are we a society of child users and abusers, selfishly satisfied with seat-of-the-pants wisdom and conventional practice? Are we open to sound research for our children as we are for our cars or our pets? Are parents more to blame for failing or are delinquent youngsters? Or are schools? Where change is necessary, what should we expect of parents? Professionals? The state? Parents clearly should have prior rights, but with this authority, according to top constitutional lawyers, goes a certain accountability to the state.

Our country and our world is made of many peoples, races, colors, national origins, and religions—from Buddhist, Christian, Hindu, and Jew to Muslim, Shintoist, and Taoist and many in between. There are astonishing differences *within* each of these groups. All these factors must be considered when trying to solve the puzzle we pose in this chapter. Just how understanding (not merely tolerant, but *understanding*) of others will we be, and how honest is our concern for others? When, at the University of Chicago in 1968, Dean Sol Tax and I joint-ventured the first World Conference on Mankind, I learned one of the great lessons of my life: Through every great religion of the world is woven, warp and woof, a strong and beautiful thread called "The Golden Rule."

Why do we bring this up here? In nearly every country of the Western world today we find less appreciation of children's freedom to grow within the family nest than we do in the Third World countries that were once called "heathen." They nurture children, as birds do their chicks, until they are ready to fly away. To the extent that the Western world has turned away from concern for our children and one another, the family fabric is becoming unraveled.

"The state is taking my authority, my domain," the parent protests. "It won't let me teach my own children, yet it holds me responsible for their behavior."

"What do you expect?" some officials retort. "After all, most of you can't wait to get your youngsters out from under your feet, and once they're with us, you have little interest in how they do!"

Of course this isn't the whole story. Many parents love their children dearly, and many school officials are sympathetic. Yet others are so consumed with preserving their power that they can hardly see the all-important forest (the children) for the trees (dollars, jobs, and influence in the community). Both argue, but sometimes we wonder how much anyone cares.

Constitutionally the parents are guaranteed rights of privacy to educate their children by U.S. Supreme Court decisions (some of which established bad precedence in other areas) ranging from 1923's *Pierce v. Society of Sisters* to 1977's *Roe v. Wade*, and possibly others before this book is printed. On the other hand, the state has a responsibility for the children of parents who don't or can't care for them. If the state doesn't assume this, who will?

The church once did, but seldom does now. And someone has to teach these children how to make a living and how to behave, or we will all pay. Is there a clear line of authority and responsibility here? Indeed there is! Think this through as you read these stories and you'll understand better why many are teaching at home.

Through a Parent's Eyes—A Case Study

A recent phone call from a frustrated Oregon mother suggests how far America has turned from her original educational system. We will call her Julie Bart. She lives near a dear friend of ours, and because of our research on school entrance age and generally strong support of parents, she mistakenly assumed our instant sympathy.[1] Instead I asked her to write out her family program and her complaints about schools, hoping that organizing her thoughts might help her—and us—to better understand her problem. It turned out that Julie's son Karl was failing in a special education class at age seven. Her psychologist advised that the boy was dangerously withdrawing, bordering on autism or a catatonic state. She had doubts about the psychologist, but vented rage on the local schools.

"Four years ago," she announced proudly, "Klaus and I upgraded to a larger house in a better area for the children's sake." Emphasis was clearly on the last four words.

Expenses had "since skyrocketed," so she "had to go back to work" after more than twenty years at home. She apparently failed to recognize that her returning to work had brought even more expense: taxes, daycare, household help, clothes, meals out, and transportation.

"My job simply requires a better second car," she said. "Besides, the older kids need the old one. Not one of them has given us a moment's trouble."

She adds that Karl is the last of four Bart children; the other three—a daughter and two sons—range from ages fifteen to nineteen.

When I asked if they have jobs, she answered, "No, because they're all too busy with school, especially the two oldest who are heavily into sports."

Then I asked how many of the children had even gone to daycare.

"I stayed home with all the kids except Karl," she responded proudly. "He was the only one we placed in daycare, nursery school, or kindergarten. We first enrolled him when he was three at the best child center in town—very informal." She knew my concern about early formal schooling. Julie appeared impatient that Karl "hasn't grown up yet." She added wryly, "So you've guessed we didn't plan on him?"

"Since my husband's on the road a lot, the load's heavy on me. By the time I get home, I'm exhausted."

Apparently no one in the family had much time for the little boy. When I mentioned the significance of her time and attention to her son, Mrs. Bart hardly heard me. Rather, she wondered if I had listened carefully enough to her "financial problems."

"I give Karl quality time," she insisted. Yet on careful questioning she admitted that this totaled only about an hour a week. And Karl's dad gets close to his son "perhaps thirty minutes or so weekly besides church and talking at meals several times a week." Neither parent considered family priorities at fault.

"Besides," insisted Julie, "Karl idolizes his friends at school." But the psychologist vowed that "Karl feels more rejected than appreciated."

Notice the sequence in the Barts' ties with Karl and the quality of his relationship with his siblings and age mates. Physically he had a home, but psychologically he had been homeless from age three. No matter how good the daycare and school programs, he was emotionally under the control of his peers. By now he is a peer-dependency veteran. But his dependency probably developed less from the attractiveness of his peers than from his feelings of parental rejection.[2]

His parents misread his feelings about his classmates. Neither parents nor siblings compensated. He was in almost every sense a social isolate. Withdrawal, delinquency, or violence was likely.

The last word we had on Karl is that he is under a psychiatrist's care by order of the court after petty thievery involving drugs. Yet he somehow seemed happier than we had seen him for some time! He had finally gotten some attention.

Another Case Study: The State's Ideas

In contrast with Julie Bart, let's see how the state operates. During the last several years a number of state and national studies have addressed parents' rights and obligations against the "compelling interests of the state."[3]

We don't use any case study as an indictment of either families or schools, but to determine what is best for American children. Nor does Pennsylvania, the focus of these instances, have a corner on this problem. By the time you read this, changes will likely have been made there and in other states mentioned in this book, such as Alabama, Michigan, Ohio, New York, and North Dakota, which have for years shared similar policies and practices. At this point we use a series of Pennsylvania cases, and use real names since they are of public record.

In Coraopolis the school superintendent charged the Metcalf family with violating the compulsory attendance statute. Although state law provides for home-based education, the official challenged the flexible spirit of the statute by vowing that he "does not permit home instruction to replace school instruction under any circumstances." He refused to consider test results, curriculum, or parental qualifications. At this writing an HSLDA attorney is defending the Metcalfs.

Concurrently in Butler, local school officials seek custody of the Hull children even though both parents have college degrees and Mrs. Hull has a Florida teaching certificate.

In a separate case a Scranton school is prosecuting the Jeffreys because the school board has added teacher certification to the state requirements for home educators. And in Grove City, Andy Peterson, a college professor and former school psychologist, fails to qualify as a home educator under local interpretations of state laws.

This alleged harassment has joined eleven embattled families in a federal civil rights action. They seek declaratory and injunctive relief and that the Pennsylvania compulsory attendance statute be declared void for vagueness in that it fails to define "properly qualified private tutor." The children in question are high achievers, are considered socially above average, and have outstanding behavioral records.[4]

Now for the Issues

It is crucial in any responsible society to determine who has authority and responsibility for the children: Do they belong to the family or to the state? If these powers — *authority* and *responsibility* — are divided, how are they best distributed in terms of children's welfare and the law? And which law sets priorities? Local? State? Or the U.S. Constitution? Should the state accommodate uninterested and uninformed parents and the increasing fragmentation of the American family by assuming more of the parents' historical authority and responsibility? Or should it work to educate parents and restore family unity as Caesar Augustus did when he faced the same dilemma in Rome?

Why must we have Pennsylvania-style confrontations? Why can't we join the family and school in an effort to build great children as many public and parochial schools are doing, particularly in Oregon and Northern California? The states' preoccupation with vested interests or tradition and conventional practice is considered by some laymen to range from "unprofessionalism" to "bigotry." We write this in the certain hope that Pennsylvania and other errant states will turn again to the generous and professional policies of the last generation. Yet each hostile state and school district seems to have its favorite issues. Some raise the specter of possible child abuse; others, of socialization, certification, possible parental ineptness, the *perceived* loss of opportunities to learn the sciences, sports, or such esoteric studies as gymnastics, music, and art. But they have yet to prove one of these allegations. Yet under pressure of social workers and schoolmen, judges too often fine or jail parents.

School and social service officials lean on weak sticks. The average performance of home schoolers in all studies exceeds the conventionally schooled child. In sports, world ski champion Tamara McKinney and the family of famed miler and home schooler Jim Ryun deny that home-taught youngsters are deprived. Untrue references to child abuse in home education do not reflect well on school officials who have too many troubles of their own to be throwing stones at parents concerned enough to teach their children at home. If officials will use home schools as laboratories as some do in Texas and California, both will profit.

FORTY - FOUR

WHAT DO WE *DO* ABOUT THE BIG QUARREL?

BACKDROP: This chapter is written to inform and to encourage you, not to scare you. There are reasons why home educators continue to feel legal and legislative pressure: Most people, including school officials and legislators, don't yet understand home education. What they are not up on, they're down on. Teachers' unions and allied groups work largely behind the scenes in their lobbying, handing out election money, and making "fear" talk to their members about loss of jobs. Educational ethics die.

We also face a big question in how to handle effectively a vast spectrum of indifferent or uninformed parents: Is it best to *accommodate* them by providing more daycare and other public or private services? Or is it better to *educate* them about how, why, and when their children develop? Under what circumstances, if any, should parents surrender their children to the state? What can we do? An understanding of these factors will give you courage and a desirable boldness.

Several days ago we received a telephoned plea from a Seattle, Washington mother whose little boy did not do well on a test. Although she pointed out that he was ill at testing time, the case was referred to Child Protective Services, supposedly a helpful, understanding, professional agency which, unfortunately, many home teaching parents have come to fear much like the Germans did their Gestapo of World War II. Not a few fear losing their children to foster homes.

To this extent overseas authorities agree that the American educational system has become totalitarian as the states gradually crowd the family out of its historic role.[1] The director of Hungary's Bureau of Child Care could not understand why America would want to inflict such care on its children unless under absolute economic necessity as in Hungary and Czechoslovakia.[2] Children (and their families), as Plato urged, have become slaves of the state.[3] To a certain extent, all of us are to blame for the conditions of our society. Without realizing just what was happening, we have allowed the state, the school, and sometimes even the church to take over our parental role.

What can parents do about this? Our outline consists of two major suggestions, the second of which has eight criteria:

A. Join the Home School Legal Defense Association.

B. Do what is right and be systematic about it:

1. Keep a reasonably clean and organized home.

2. See that children are reasonably supervised.

3. Work out your own systematic program or obtain curriculum help that *tailors the program to your child's needs,* so as to obtain the best results without burning you out.

4. Don't rush children into formal instruction.

5. Do not allow testing if your child is ill or other abnormal conditions prevail. And allow no achievement testing based on reading, etc., until at least age ten.

6. Work closely with your state home schooling coalition for better legislation that includes the option of evaluation by a certified teacher instead of tests.

7. Educate everyone you can, including neighbors, friends, school officials, judges, and social workers. Work and vote for candidates who understand and support you.

8. If you need solid data to do something about all this, contact the Moore Foundation, sending a self addressed stamped envelope to Box 1, Camas, WA 98607.

What can organized and unified home educators do? The most successful leaders have found that they best deal with the state: *first* by unified, tactful, intelligent but firm Golden-Rule negotiation with school officials; *second*, in that same manner of negotiation through legislatures; and *third*, through the courts with the most able and experienced home schooling lawyer they can find. If we sound hard-nosed about this, so be it. Our hearts are tender for parents who think this much of their children. In the last fifteen to twenty years, we have been intensively involved in legislatures and courts, beginning with attorneys who knew little or nothing about education and whom we literally had to train in our business. Today we have highly skilled, well-informed lawyers from coast to coast, including the Home School Legal Defense Association (HSLDA), the Rutherford Institute (which in the early years helped us pioneer court work), the Christian Legal Society and other groups and individuals who have gone to the bar for parents, many of them at sacrificial wages. In extreme cases some have charged nothing at all.

We have found that we could avoid at least nine out of ten likely prosecutions by doing one of four things: (1) educating schoolmen and courts on the nature and achievement of most home educators and on the probable legal outcome and its influence on the children, families, neighborhood, and town if they carry their case through court; (2) challenging the states and schools to do comparative studies on conventional schools and home education as Alaska, Arkansas, Oregon, Tennessee, and Washington State have dared to do; (3) stating in writing what you believe your options are, and making resourceful suggestions to which they may respond; (4) reminding them, if necessary, that you are prepared to institute a class action suit.

But basic to all these efforts, we have learned to become acquainted with our lawmakers in the state houses — inviting them and their families to visit home schools, to be our guests at picnics and potlucks, and accepting their invitations to visit them in the state capitals. On a few occasions, leaders collectively mustered from five thousand to twenty thousand parents in marches on their state capitols to let them know that we mean business and to show support for representatives and senators honest and heroic enough to stand for principle. Experienced, sympathetic lobbyists have been assisting and guiding their actions.

One of the most encouraging signs of all has been the *unity in diversity of religions* — *or no religion* — which have coalesced and demonstrated understanding of common freedoms. The only notable exception has been a few Christians who somehow applied a Bible verse to this movement—to avoid being joined unequally together with unbelievers. They apparently did not realize that this was a *movement*—just as anti-pornography or religious freedom may be a movement—and not a *marriage*! For the most part the activists who raised this false alarm have been silenced.

We, of course, must understand what many social workers face these days: thousands of parents who aren't much interested or who are actively uninterested in their children, and in many cases are outright abusers. Such unfortunate youngsters were once helped by neighbors, churches, and community agencies. Yet as we move surely toward a socialistic society, we leave their parenting increasingly to the state. Such children must have responsible care even as we must hospitalize those who are sick. Yet there is no more reason for states to provide such care for *all* children than there is to provide hospitals for all healthy youngsters.

Parents who are concerned enough to expend effort teaching their own do not deserve state interference. Do wise educators spend more effort indulging parents who place a better house or another car or a freer, more exotic lifestyle ahead of their children? Or do they educate parents to care for their own? When mothers of young children must work out of the home and away from their offspring, should the state handily take on the heavy responsibility which through most of America's history fell on relatives, neighbors, and the church? That may be the expedient way, but it also encourages the ethics of Cain—"Am I my brother's keeper?"

The state may be willing, but it has yet in any free society to prove its ability to become a universal parent. While claiming authority, it still holds mothers and fathers responsible for the behavior of their children! It will be an interesting day when another depression forces the state to give up some of these "services," and unemployed parents have once again to take over as they did after the Great Crash of 1929.

What meaning does this hold for a free democratic society? Students of Western civilization warn that parental dereliction, trends in public education, and state intrusion on the family threaten the survival of our free society.[4]

Comparative Studies

If educators are interested in truth, as all professionals should be, they should recognize that large numbers of children are suffering in institutional settings; values and achievement are being lost. Likewise, if research points to the home as the best educational nest, why should the state pick on those homes which are trying to solve this educational dilemma? Also if state officials do not trust current research reports on home-based education, why don't they authorize studies by objective researchers rather than pursuing vendettas against concerned parents and homes?

Alaska did this, comparing its Centralized Correspondence Course (CCC) home study students with conventionally schooled children on Alaska Statewide Assessment (ASA) tests for fourth and eighth graders in March 1985.[5]

Fourth grade home schoolers averaged 11 percentile higher in math and 16 percentile higher in reading. Eighth graders scored 12 percentile higher in both math and reading. A month later on the national Survey of Basic Skills, CCC students in *all* grades averaged well above their peers across the nation. The K-3 children averaged in the top quartile. This is the third consecutive year — since such comparisons were undertaken — that CCC students have scored high.

Alaska and a few other states are giving some attention to readiness, and a few are making changes in school entrance policies and finding better methods of coping with individual differences. Yet most states are bent on rushing children into school.

In Tennessee a state study found home-taught students to average 31 percentile ranks higher in reading than public school students.[6] We were at first disappointed when we found that math scores for Tennessee public schools averaged about the same as those of home schools. But a Tennessee public school teacher rose and quickly put our disappointment to rest: She described how they are instructed by school officials to teach to the standardized test instead of teaching for practical life as sound home teachers usually do. If home educators teach to the tests, they will substantially excel in math also.

There are bound to be exceptions to the high average achievement and sociability of home schoolers. But they are so few that they should not preoccupy busy educators who are daily faced with their own perplexities. The high standard of behavior should not be overlooked: home-educated children are seldom, if ever, involved in drugs, violence, sexual promiscuity, or similar conduct common to schools. Officials can also check out other perceived weaknesses of home school, such as a test to assure themselves that children schooled at home generally come out much better in self-concept and social adjustment.

If educators find home schooling effective, as has every state that has made such studies, why not help parents who are trying to find solutions to our moral and educational dilemmas? As public servants, shouldn't they also understand their obligation to encourage and support parental rights guaranteed by the U.S. Constitution?

Officials should not confuse home-taught youngsters with truant families. Surely they know the purposes of truancy laws which afford all the protection needed. In the event they have any trouble distinguishing between truant families and those who are truly home teaching, there is a nationwide network of thousands of home school support groups whose leaders can help them. Objectivity is, of course, an element of intellectual honesty. Recently the Wisconsin State Department of Public Instruction asked education staffers of the University of Wisconsin to do a study on home education. When questioned by state home school leader Diane Alme on the gross distortions and looseness of conclusions in the report, the university researcher replied that he was assigned to write "from a narrow perspective."[7] We need a broad and thorough education on tutorial home teaching, not a trading of biases.

Of course, there have been many demonstrations of understanding and large-heartedness by both legislators and state school officers. In Georgia, State Senator John Foster was at first skeptical about home schools and strongly supportive of a state school superintendent who was outwardly hostile to home educating parents. But the senator accepted the invitation of several Georgia families to visit their "genuine educational establishments," and he returned to write a strong law favoring home-based education. More parents would do well to befriend their legislators and inform them about the real home education.

Oregon Superintendent of Public Instruction Verne Duncan, in his tenth Annual State of the Schools Address, November 8, 1986, told the annual convention of the Oregon School Boards Association, "Public schools must cooperate with private schools and home schoolers. . . . let's not fight them, let's help them. They are our young people and part of our future. Whether we do it inside or outside the system, we must respond to the challenge of providing alternatives. . . ."[8] Duncan had found 76.1 percent of Oregon's tested home schoolers to be above average.

States and their institutions should also guard against pursuing vested interests. Precedent has clearly been set in the U.S. Supreme Court for cases where public officials and the state have a financial stake: they are required to have a neutral decision maker.[9] In our occasional teaching at the University of Nevada's College of Juvenile and Family Court Judges, these wise jurists suggest they must take care that they do not protect the financial or other interests of the states' schools at parents' expense. School officials seldom refer publicly to their fears of financial loss from losing students to home schools, although this is often a major concern. Yet because of the widespread success of home-schooled children across the nation—in achievement, behavior, and sociability—some officials are frankly reluctant to make local objective studies which compare home schoolers with conventionally schooled children. Unless states like Pennsylvania find a substantial number of home schoolers handicapped or abused, they perform an unjust service when they hinder good parents.

Tradition or Transition

The ideas in this book are neither radical nor new. They are educational principles and practices which, given the twentieth-century growth of the public schools, must be given substantial credit for America's greatness as a creative, free-enterprising nation. Home school is even more impressive considering the present decline of literacy levels and behavior.

I find it disconcerting after over half a century's work in schools at all levels, as a government educational officer and in-house consultant at the National Education Association, that (1) personally and collectively we are so dulled by the present that we resist learning from the past, and (2) we are guided so seldom by research and clinical evidence.

Morvin Wirz, who was head of the Division of Education for the Disadvantaged and Handicapped at the U.S. Office of Education when I served there, occasionally remarked about how we have research all around us, but are indifferent to it when it cuts across conventional practices.[10] If the proof of the pudding is in the eating, then how we interpret research is a measure of our intellectual honesty, our ethics, and our concern for children.

Given sound data on achievement, socialization, and behavior — along with the warnings of history — is it wiser or more professional for states to "help parents out" by taking over their rights or to encourage and educate mothers and dads to do what good families do best? Here is a crucial test of educational leadership and responsibility.

FORTY-FIVE

CERTIFIED
FOR WHAT?

BACKDROP: Nearly every state education department in the United States emphasizes certification of teachers as crucial to selection of employees in its school districts. Some bar anyone from a public, parochial, or private school job who is not certified. And countries in Europe and the Orient are not far behind. Germany and Japan, in fact, are stricter than most American states. Yet there is not a single basic study that supports this idea, and there are many that prove its error.

A few years ago a New Jersey high school hired a baseball coach who had been a big league star, and formerly had coached with the New York Yankee baseball team, one of the most successful in the history of major league ball. But he wasn't certified, so a few self-righteous professionals protested. Never mind that he was qualified: he didn't have a piece of paper certifying that he had survived a semester of student teaching.

The U.S. Supreme Court has supported the idea that teachers in elementary and secondary schools, unlike physicians, dentists, engineers, nurses, and lawyers, are not essentially qualified by certification. Experts say it is often counterproductive. Certification seems to be a means for vested interests — universities, education associations, school officials — to enforce closed shops, against research and sound practice.

Malaika Hakima, a Black Muslim, is one of the most beloved physicians in northeastern Alabama. She is mother and healer to all who come, and goes out, often without pay, in the old-fashioned way to make emergency calls. And her children are high achievers, as one might expect. She was even a certified

California teacher for ten years. But what Alabama school officials don't like is that Dr. Hakima has chosen to teach her youngsters at home. They have been harassing her for years because she is not certified to teach in Alabama. In Michigan, physician Ken Wenberg and his wife, Bonnie, who has a master's degree in maternal child care, were twice arraigned for keeping their seven-year-old son home because they didn't have a teacher's ticket from the Michigan Department of Education.

Does "Certified" Mean "Qualified"?

General education, such as elementary and secondary schooling, is so broad, so diverse in principle and method, so vast and unselective in diversity of students, that it is impossible to accurately certify that teachers can produce sound learning. In music, art, and other esoteric subjects, maybe; but for reading, writing, arithmetic, spelling, phonics, and understanding of health and citizenship, absolutely not. After he retired as one of Harvard's presidents, James Bryant Conant undertook a study of teacher evaluation.[1] He was generously financed by the Carnegie Corporation of New York. The program was administered by the Educational Testing Service of Princeton University. His collaborators were among America's most distinguished scholars.

Certification was central in his two-year study. He studied *emergency* credentials, *standard* credentials, *provisional* credentials, *permanent* credentials, and *emergency* certificates. Early in his book, *The Education of American Teachers*, he questions whether state certification policies "provide well-trained and competent teachers for the public schools." Less than fifteen pages later he asserts that "none of the present methods of teacher certification assure the public of competent and adequately prepared teachers," and asks, "What should be the basis for the state's certification of teachers?" In the next chapter he adds, "if accrediting agencies and state educational authorities tighten, by detailed prescription, the certification rules [as many try to do for private, parochial, and home schools], then neither my suggestions, nor those of anyone else (except him who writes the rules) can possibly be tried."

By the subject's very nature and his immense credibility, Dr. Conant seems forced over-cautiously, sometimes even ponderously, to proceed through subjects such as academic preparation, theory and practice, elementary teachers, secondary teachers, and in-service education, all the time seeking a "redirection of public authority." He ends up with several rather significant conclusions which most states apparently consider mere pontifications:

> A cynic might be tempted to define a liberal education as a four-year exposure to an experience prescribed by a group of professors, each of whom has prime allegiance to his own discipline. The programs in many institutions seem to have been developed not by careful consideration of a group but by a process that might be called academic logrolling. (I am not unfamiliar with the bargaining between departments when it comes to dividing up a student's time.) In any event, one finds a complete lack of agreement on what constitutes a satisfactory general education program for future teachers. . . .
>
> When one examines the courses in education, one finds almost as much confusion as exists in general education. Here the cynic might say that the professors are jealous of their share of the student's time but are ill prepared to use it. . . .
>
> In view of the great diversity of opinions and practices to be found in the leading institutions, I conclude that neither a state authority nor a voluntary accrediting agency is in a position to specify the amount of time to be devoted to either academic or educational courses.

I am certain that any professor, dean, president, or even student who is honest can't help but verify Conant's observations. In many, if not most, institutions, any given professor prefers to overstock most of his students with subjects from his repertoire. Furthermore, in teacher education most of the professional methods courses come *after* the teacher-candidate has been in college several years, without adequate screening in his freshman or at the latest, his sophomore year. So, after all that education, even when students do poorly in student teaching, professors are reluctant to refuse them credentials.

On his last pages Dr. Conant summed up in two words: *freedom* and *responsibility*. He asked for more institutional freedom to qualify their teachers, and challenged institutions to use that freedom responsibly. *This is precisely what we ask for home teachers* and for parents who teach their children part-time at home. By and large they have proven that they can handle freedom responsibly.

Professor Donald Erickson of the University of California, Los Angeles, is considered a leading authority on certification of teachers. His experience in teacher education at the University of Chicago, Simon Fraser University in British Columbia, the University of San Francisco, and now UCLA place him high among his peers. In the notable U.S. Supreme Court case, *Wisconsin v. Yoder*, which contested the rights of Amish parents to provide secondary education for their children at home, Dr. Erickson strongly questioned most teacher certification practices. I have testified as expert witness in several court cases with Dr. Erickson, and have heard him in each case testify that not only is certification seriously questionable as currently required in most states, but is often *counterproductive*. He confirmed this to me in a recent personal letter, adding that

> Teacher certification . . . requirements . . . should be regarded . . . chiefly as a device to ensure that schools of education will have plenty of students to justify their existence and growth. . . .
>
> . . .in the classrooms of . . . uncertified teachers . . . the enforcement of teacher certification laws might do much to reduce the level of teaching competence. If public school leaders wish to obtain their teachers through channels governed by certification and other techniques, I suppose we must grant them that freedom, but private school leaders should be permitted to capitalize on the special avenues of teacher selection and recruitment that have served so well thus far. One must remember, in this connection, that studies have shown with monotonous regularity that student achievement is generally higher in private schools than in public schools. It is highest, in fact, in that special segment of private education that has been least likely to hire state-certified teachers. . . . There is no evidence that justifies demanding that all teachers, in public and private schools and in home instruction, submit to our courses. . . . For these several reasons, and others, I am firmly opposed to laws that demand certification for private school teachers or for parents who teach their own children at home.[2]

Certification Procedures

Recently Harold Orlans, a guest scholar with the Brookings Institution, called me in response to an inquiry I had made of Brookings' librarian. Well aware of his reputation as an authority on institutional accreditation and his book, *Private Education and Public Eligibility,* I asked for a frank estimate of *current* certification procedures.[3] He unhesitatingly replied that he found little credibility in the process, then added, "It is clear that we must find something, but this [present practice] is not it. And no one seems to know for sure what that something is."

The situation is even worse than Dr. Orlans suggests. Even the common method of teacher evaluation-by-observation that many officials use has little or no support from careful research. Studies over the past fifty years have repeatedly urged that this practice be stopped. In a recent *Phi Delta Kappan* article, prominent teacher-evaluation scholars Donald Medley and Homer Coker urge that schoolmen discontinue the practice of trying to estimate teacher effectiveness by observing teacher and students in the classroom.[4]

Medley and Coker assert that "studies of the validity of principals' judgments . . . as reported in the literature have yielded consistently negative findings." They go on to define this as "no appreciable agreement between principals' judgments of teacher effectiveness and the amount students learn." They conclude with a sense of futility that "state legislatures [usually guided by state departments of education] continue to mandate statewide programs to evaluate teachers." And they speak of this as an exercise in "ignorance."

The extent of that ignorance is hard for anyone truly interested in children to believe. The last week of March 1988, we were called to the Syracuse, New York trial of the *Cato, New York School District vs. Randy and Alice Blackwelder.* The key *professional* issue in the trial was the claimed right of the school district to come into the Blackwelder home to evaluate by observation Alice's teaching ability; the Blackwelders insisted that there was no assurance that the school superintendent or his agents could reliably make such an evaluation. All the evidence as reported by the officials' main professional journal, the *Phi Delta Kappan,* has repeatedly shown such claims to be false. Judge Pederson found the Blackwelders innocent.

And about those court cases on certification: Dr. Hakima is still under state threat as we write this paragraph. The Wenbergs faced two court trials before Judge O'Brien threw the case out of the Pontiac, Michigan court; they have since moved to another state.

And the high school baseball coach? The last we heard, the New Jersey courts apparently had more common sense than the educators. We are not surprised, for every time to date we have been called to face New Jersey school officials at the bar, the courts have come through for the family. They quickly ordered the coach reinstated and decided that *quality of experience and results* are far better than a certificate or random inspection of teaching techniques. This is how most mothers and dads prefer to be evaluated, too!

FORTY-SIX

FOR THOSE ELITE WHO ARE INVITED TO COURT

The HSLDA Staff

BACKDROP: The idea for an association of home teachers for providing legal defense for home schools was born from a private attorney's conviction of a great need. He was Michael Farris, now President of the Home School Legal Defense Association (HSLDA).[1] In 1982, Mr. Farris became convinced of the value of home schooling his own children. At the time, home education in Farris' home state of Washington was in turmoil legally. Many home schoolers were being threatened with legal action by the various school districts. Because it became public knowledge that Mr. Farris was home schooling, he began receiving contact from home schoolers who were in trouble with their school districts. This has led to many interesting days *in* court and many exciting adventures keeping them *out of* court. He was joined by veteran California home school attorney Michael Smith and by attorney Chris Klicka.

While watching Tim and Beverly LaHaye taping a couple of television programs with Dorothy and Raymond Moore at the Osmun studios in Orem, Utah, attorney Michael Farris learned of home teaching. It was an instant conversion. Soon he also began to realize what hostile states were doing to home schoolers and to the Moores.

Meanwhile, Washington State parents were having problems. State law required parent-teachers to have teaching credentials. From contacts with home schoolers, it became obvious to Mike Farris that most parents couldn't afford attorneys to defend them. Although for years the Moores had been educating lawyers across the country, there were yet few who were familiar with the issues and even fewer who were willing to represent home schoolers on a reduced payment or donation basis.

Because of the issues' complexities, lawyers representing home schooling families must spend a considerable amount of time in research and writing briefs, not to mention the time in preparation for trial. It is unreasonable to expect lawyers in private practice to take most home school cases without any fee.

So Mr. Farris set out to make it possible for the average home schooling family to retain a laywer who is interested in their plight and who understands home education. His solution was to form home schoolers into an association dedicated to the preservation of home education throughout the nation. In this way the cost of hiring a lawyer would be shared by all members.

Facts About HSLDA

The association was founded in 1983. Soon it helped Washington State home educators influence legislation which was favorable to home schoolers and eliminated the certification requirement. Membership began with a small number and grew slowly the first couple of years. Now in 1988 the association has grown strong, with members in every state. It provides legal counsel and representation by qualified attorneys, including three full-time staff attorneys,[2] to every member-family who may be challenged in the area of home schooling. All attorney fees are paid by HSLDA on behalf of the members.

An HSLDA newsletter, the *Home School Court Report*, is sent quarterly to members. HSLDA is a clearinghouse for legal data regarding home schooling, including expert witness lists, synopsis of the fifty states' compulsory attendance statutes, sample legislation, briefs of cases handled by staff attorneys, and seminar and support group information.

Days In and Out of Court

In six years HSLDA has handled many exciting cases. In Kansas, the Jost family was charged with truancy and given four days to appear in court and present their defense. We hired a local attorney and prepared the Josts' defense over the weekend. The family presented witnesses testifying that they were legally home schooling.

The prosecutor called only one witness, the editor of the local newspaper, whom he thought would be unfavorable to the Josts. Yet, to the prosecutor's embarrassment, the editor, who had interviewed the family, testified to the sound quality of the family's home school program. He had previously been skeptical of home schooling, but had become convinced that it is a valid alternative. At the end of the one-day trial, the judge declared the Josts' home school legal, dismissed all charges against them, and dissolved a temporary injunction which prohibited them from home schooling.

We are glad to report that most HSLDA members' problems are resolved favorably without trial. One of these, described earlier in this book, is the Smeltzer case. We prepared a civil rights suit requesting damages from this superintendent personally, as well as the school district.[3] In order to resolve the matter short of having to file the lawsuit, a copy of the pleadings were mailed to the school district's attorney. The next day, the district dropped the charges and withdrew the disapproval of the home school program. The Smeltzers continue to home school today.

A similar situation occurred in New York for the 1986-87 school year. When the French family in Crown Point began home schooling for the fourth year, the superintendent wrote them a denial letter even though Mrs. French was certified, the children had scored high on the standardized tests the previous three years, and their curriculum met all state requirements. He had the family investigated by the Child Protection Agency (CPA). Chris Klicka, staff attorney and HSLDA executive director, persuaded the CPA to stay out of the situation. Then he sent a five-page letter defending the family, and warned the superintendent of his possible liability to the family if he continued harassment.

The night the superintendent received the letter, the school board met, and the French family was on the agenda. Mr. French attended the meeting and passed out copies of the letter to all of the school board members. The board went into executive session to discuss the situation and came out praising the family and their program. The superintendent even put his arm around Mr. French with personal congratulations on doing such a fine job!

As of this writing, HSLDA has four active federal lawsuits involving almost one hundred member-families in New York, North Dakota, Pennsylvania, and South Carolina.

Historical Home School Cases

What exactly are the sources of these legal conflicts? How are home schooling laws developed? In the early years of America's history, most education took place in the home. Public education in this country was not widely practiced for its first three hundred years. It did not become dominant until after World War I. Private, church, and common schools largely provided education and then only for a few months out of the year. Most of the teaching of our Founding Fathers was either by parents or by tutors in the home. At about the turn of the twentieth century, there began a nationwide legislative thrust to pass compulsory attendance statutes as public schools gained strength in their push toward national dominance.

It is interesting to note that the highest percentage of literacy in this country occurred prior to the advent of the public school. However, the state legislatures motivated by various reasons,[4] almost unanimously passed statutes requiring children to attend a public or private school. The first reported case of significance regarding home schooling occurred in Oregon.[5] Although this case did not involve a home schooling family, the principle of the case, as decided by the United States Supreme Court, established the right of parents not to have to send their children to public schools.

Oregon's compulsory education statute required all children to attend public school. The parents involved in this case were sending their children to a private school. The case was decided on the "liberty clause" of the Fourteenth Amendment. Therefore, it has become known as a parental liberty case,[6] and home schoolers argue that it stands for the proposition that parents have the constitutional right to choose the place and manner of education for their children.

However, opponents of home schooling argue that these cases only guarantee the parents the right of choice between public and private schools (outside the home).

For religiously motivated home schoolers, an equally important branch of constitutional law regarding this issue is the protection provided by the First Amendment's Free Exercise
Clause. In the case of *Wisconsin v. Yoder*,[7] the United States
Supreme Court held that the state violated the parents' right of
religious freedom by forcing Amish children to attend school
beyond the eighth grade. The Amish believed that attendance in
public school beyond the eighth grade violated their religious
beliefs and would destroy the religious values that they wanted
to instill in their children. The court found that the state's interest was not sufficiently compelling to require attendance in the
public school which would override the religious beliefs of the
Amish families.

These two constitutional principles — parental liberties based
on the Fourteenth Amendment and the Free Exercise clause of
the First Amendment — are the basis upon which most arguments are made supporting parents' right to home school. These
are not the only arguments that can be raised, but are the ones
recognized by our Supreme Court based upon the above decisions. The question we must ask then is this: Why are home
schoolers still in trouble? There is no single answer, yet courts do
not take a broad view of these rights and some courts look to
minimize the effect of the U.S. Supreme Court decisions, as well
as distinguish the facts of the decisions. If courts afforded the
same protection to home schoolers under the constitutional principles enunciated above as they do to pornographers under the
First Amendment, home teachers would have little trouble. But
such is not the case.

Fighting the Battle

The answer to this inequality is to obtain favorable legislation. While it is more difficult to home school in certain states,
it is HSLDA's position that home schooling is legal (although
circumstances vary) in every state of the union as a matter of
statutory law.[8] Also, as indicated above, home schooling is protected constitutionally in all fifty states because of our form of
government which recognizes the U.S. Constitution as its highest law. The key to obtaining favorable home schooling laws in

each state is to wage the battle on two fronts—the legislatures and the courts.

By and large, home schoolers are winning the battles in the state legislatures. HSLDA and the Moores work closely with local and state leaders, and with sound lobbying organizations to build sound bases. Legislation has been very favorable in states such as Georgia, Wisconsin, Minnesota, and Missouri, where statutes dealing with home schooling were declared void because of vagueness. Also, where the courts have ruled adversely, there has been a swift move to resolve the conflict by enacting legislation. This occurred in 1985 in Arkansas after the state supreme court ruled unfavorably against a religiously motivated home schooling couple whose child had achieved a 99 percent level on standardized tests and whom even the judge acknowledged was unusually well-behaved.

Since 1956, twenty-three states[9] have adopted statutes specifically dealing with home schooling. No state which has adopted a home schooling statute in the past thirty years has felt it necessary to require teacher certification as a sole requirement for families which teach at home. Several of these states formerly had laws requiring certification.[10]

All of the remaining states permit home schooling under some other statutory scheme which does not specifically mention "home education" or "home schooling." For instance, in ten states, home schools can legally operate as private schools or church schools which are not required to use certified teachers.[11] The remaining fourteen states all allow home schooling but the conditions vary from state to state. In some of these states if the instruction is "comparable" or "equivalent" to that taught in the public schools, the home school is "approved."[12] The key here is what is "equivalent instruction"? This term is so vague that several of these states have cases pending.

Current legislative battles continue in states such as Alabama, Colorado, Iowa, Ohio, Pennsylvania, and South Carolina. Generally speaking, the legislation that is being enacted requires little more than a notice of intent by the family, identifying the children who will be taught at home and the broad curriculum content that will be used. Noticeably absent is an educational level requirement for parents, although some states have insisted upon high school graduation or a GED as a minimal requirement.

States normally insist upon some means of monitoring progress, and the objective method normally chosen is some type of standardized testing or evaluation by a qualified person. Other variations have been reached after the legislative process has run its course and all sides have had their say. Usually the strongest negative voices heard in the legislative debate are directly or indirectly from the teachers' unions in each state.

Their most vocal argument for strenuous requirement and controls on home schoolers is based upon the assumption that there are parents who will neglect their children's education and that most parents are not qualified to teach their own children. At education committee hearings on home school legislation, a common preface to remarks by representatives of the teachers' union in opposition to reasonable home school legislation is: "The home schoolers that are in attendance here today, I'm sure are sincere and competent, but it's the children of those other parents 'out there' we must protect."[13]

Unable to cite examples, the proponents of these arguments make an assumption that many parents will educationally neglect their children. Therefore the NEA (National Education Association) has publicly stated its position that home schooling should be legal only if done by a certified teacher and then with tremendous monitoring requirements of the home schooling family.

However, historically our laws have presumed that parents are loving, competent, and act in the best interest of their children.[14] No law should be prefaced with the notion that most parents are incompetent to teach their own children or that some parents will educationally neglect their children. Even the notorious *Roe v. Wade* decision in 1977 by the U.S. Supreme Court approving certain abortion rights helps guarantee parents the right of privacy in educating their young.

Laws should not be so written that they treat all parents as child abusers because there are a *few* who do abuse their children. Furthermore, all states have truancy laws which handily take care of such problems. The sheep should not be trapped in laws designed to catch wolves. A good home school law will recognize that the vast majority of parents who desire to teach their children at home are sincere and will conduct a high quality educational program with the best interests of their children in mind. The home school record proves it.

One of the grave errors of this century has been delegating the responsibility of training children to the state or others outside the family. All understanding and conscientious home education attorneys are determined that this practice must be turned around so we can go on to other needs of society.

END NOTES

Introduction — How and Why This Book Came About

1. Harold McCurdy, "The Childhood Pattern of Genius," *Horizon*, Vol 2, p. 38. May, 1960.
2. Ibid.

Chapter 2 — Of Course You Can Do It!

1. Available from the Moore Foundation, Box 1, Camas, WA 98607.
2. If you can't readily find master home education teachers in your state or province who will share their wisdom and experience, and you would like such names, or if you are seeking information on learning methods or materials, send a self-addressed, stamped envelope to the Moore Foundation, Box 1, Camas, WA 98607.
3. Philippians 4:8.
4. Raymond S. Moore, et al., *Home Grown Kids, Homespun Schools, Homestyle Teaching,* and *Homemade Health* (all from Word Books, Waco, TX); *Homebuilt Discipline* (Thomas Nelson, Nashville); *Better Late Than Early* (Readers Digest) and *School Can Wait,* the latter two now available from the Moore Foundation, Box 1, Camas, WA 98607.

Chapter 3 — Home Schooling's Fifth Column

1. Matthew 22:21, KJV.
2. The Moores are now with the Moore Foundation, Box 1, Camas, WA 98607.

Chapter 4 — Getting Off the Trolley

1. Irving Janis, "Groupthink," *Psychology Today,* November 1971.
2. Parents' prior rights to determine the education of their children derive primarily from a series of U.S. Supreme Court decisions respecting the First and Fourteenth Amendments, for example: *Meyer v. Nebraska,* 262 U.S. 390, 43 S. Ct. 625 (1923); *Pierce v. Society of Sisters,* 268 U.S. 510, 45 S. Ct. 571 (1925) and companion case, *Pierce v. Hill Military Academy,* same citation; *Farrington v. Tokushige,* 273 U.S. 284, 71 L. Ed. 646 (1927); *Cantwell v. Connecticut,* 310 U.S. 296 (1940); *Martin v. Struthers,* 319 U.S. 141 (1943); *Wisconsin v. Yoder,* 406 U.S. 205 (1972); *Roe v. Wade,* 410 U.S. 113 (1973), and many others.

Chapter 5 — Why Are True Home Schoolers
So Balanced and Bright?

1. Wilfred Aikin, *The Story of the Eight-Year Study,* 4 vols; (New York: Harper, 1942).
2. "Larsen Makes Top Score in Mississippi." Unsigned article in the *Baldwyn [MS] News,* February 27, 1986, p. 9.
3. Maggie Rossiter, "Self-educated drop-out graduates summa cum laude from SVSC tonight," *Saginaw News,* May 1, 1987. Also, a personal note to Dr. and Mrs. Moore from Martha M. Holmes, Saginaw, MI, June 9, 1987.
4. First reported in an article by J'aime Adams, "Home Schooling, An Idea Whose Time Has Returned," *Human Events,* September 15, 1984.
5. Harold Skeels, *Adult Status of Children with Contrasting Early Life Experiences: A Follow-up Study.* Monograph of the Society for Research in Child Development. (Chicago: University of Chicago Press, 1966).
6. William D. Rohwer, Jr., "Improving Instruction in the 1970s — What Can Make A Significant Difference?" Address to the American Educational Research Association, 1973. Also, William D. Rohwer, Jr., "Prime Time for Education: Early Childhood or Adolescence?" *Harvard Educational Review,* August 1971, pp. 316-341.
7. Adams, *Human Events,* September 15, 1984; S. S. Greene, "Home Study in Alaska: A Profile of K-12 Students in the Alaska Centralized Correspondence Study Program," 1984, ERIC No. ED 255 494; G. A. Gustavsen, "Selected Characteristics of Home Schools and Parents Who Operate Them," Doctoral dissertation, Andrews University, 1981; N. J. F. Linden, "An Investigation of Alternative Education: Home Schooling," Doctoral dissertation, East Texas State University, 1983; Barbara Mertens, "Washington State's Experimental Programs Using the Parent as Tutor under the Supervision of a Washington State Certificated Teacher," The Superintendent of Public Instruction, Olympia, 1984-85; Dorothy N. Moore, ed. "On Home Schooling Figures and Scores," *The Parent Educator and Family Report* 4:2; Alan B. Rose, "A Qualitative Study of the Characteristics of Home Schooling Families in South Carolina and the Perceptions of School District Personnel Toward Home Schooling," Doctoral dissertation, University of South Carolina, 1985; Jon Wartes, Richard Wheeler, and Henry Reed, "Washington Home School Research Project," 1986, available from Jon Wartes, 16109 NE 169 Place, Woodinville, WA 98072; John Wesley Taylor V, "Self Concept in Home Schooling Children," Doctoral dissertation, Andrews University, 1986; Sonia K. Gustafson, "A Study of Home Schooling: Parental Motivations and Goals," Dissertation, Woodrow Wilson School of Public and International Affairs, Princeton University, 1987; Earl Wade Gladin, "Home Education: Characteristics of Its Families and Schools," Dissertation, Bob Jones University, 1987; Julie A. Bullard, "Characteristics of Montana Home Schools," Master's thesis, Northern Montana College, 1987; Jennie Finlayson Rakestraw, "An Analysis of Home Schooling for Elementary School-age Children in Alabama," Doctoral dissertation, University of Alabama, 1987.
8. David Quine, "The Intellectual Development of Home Taught Children," an unpublished paper done in connection with research at the University of Oklahoma, 1987. Resident at 2006 Flat Creek Place, Richardson, TX 75080; B. Tizard, M. Hughes, G. Pinkerton, & H. Carmichael, "Adults' Cognitive Demands at Home and at Nursery School," *Journal of Child Psychology and*

Psychiatry, 23:105-116, 1982; B. Tizard et al., "Children's Questions and Adult's Answers," *Journal of Child Psychology and Psychiatry,* 24:269-281, 1983a; B. Tizard et al., "Language and Social Class: Is Verbal Deprivation a Myth?" *Journal of Child Psychology and Psychiatry,* 24:533-542, 1983b.

9. "Math crisis predicted in U.S. classrooms," *The Denver Post,* Sunday, June 15, 1986.

10. Math-It, one of the most powerful home school arithmetic programs is very close to the Benezet principles, both in sequence of teaching and in maturity of the child. Math-It author, Elmer Brooks, recommends that no children take the course (which is really a game) until they have the concentration and reasoning ability to count from twenty to zero with their eyes closed while tying a bow knot. When they can achieve this level of coordination and concentration, he will shortly have them adding seven three-digit numbers in one breath, and doing cube roots in their heads. (He also endorses some standard math books for additional drill.) The average child needs little adult help to learn to do this, and students can teach other students—a hint to public and parochial schools whose busy teachers are troubled with failures in math.

11. Allan Shedlin, "What Is Enough? When Is Too Soon?" *Education Week,* April 16, 1986.

12. *The Adult Performance Level Project* (APL) (Austin, TX: University of Texas, 1983).

Chapter 6—When Are They Ready for Formal Learning?

1. Albert Bandura and Aletha C. Huston, "Identification as a Process of Incidental Learning," *Journal of Abnormal and Social Psychology* LXIII (1961), pp. 311-318. Albert Bandura, Dorothea Ross, and Sheila A. Ross, "Transmission of Aggression Through Imitation of Aggressive Models," *Journal of Abnormal Psychology and Social Psychiatry* LXII (1961), pp. 575-582; Albert Bandura and Richard H. Walters, *Social Learning and Personality Development* (New York: Holt, Rinehart & Winston, 1963).

2. David Elkind, "Early Childhood Education: A Piagetian Perspective," *The National Elementary School Principal,* December 1931, pp. 28-31. W. D. Rohwer, Jr., op. cit. Urie Bronfenbrenner, *The Two Worlds of Childhood* (New York: Simon & Schuster, 1970).

3. For a thoroughly scholarly treatment of readiness for learning, read the authors' *Better Late Than Early,* originally published by Reader's Digest Press or *School Can Wait* by Brigham Young University Press (both now distributed by the Moore Foundation, Box 1, Camas, WA 98607).

4. Torsten Husen, *International Study of Achievement in Mathematics, Vol. II* (Uppsala: Almquist and Wiksells, 1967), and subsequent studies in other subject areas.

5. Rohwer, op. cit.

6. James T. Fisher and Lowell S. Hawley, *A Few Buttons Missing* (Philadelphia: Lippincott, 1951).

7. John Dewey, "The Primary Education Fetich," *Forum,* vol. 25, 1898.

8. Arnold Gesell, *The Normal Child and Primary Education* (New York: Ginn & Co., 1912), pp. 118-119.

9. Marcelle Geber, "The Psycho-Motor Development of African Children in the First Year, and the Influence of Maternal Behavior," *Journal of Social Psychology* 47:185-195, 1958.

10. E. Mermelstein and L. S. Shulman, "Lack of formal schooling and the acquisition of conversation," *Child Development*, 38:39-52, 1967.
11. Unpublished data, January 1985, The Hoover Institution, Stanford University, CA.
12. John I. Goodlad, "A Study of Schooling: Some Findings and Hypotheses," *Phi Delta Kappan* 64:7, March 1983.
13. June 1972.

Chapter 7 — How Can They Possibly Be Socialized?

1. Bronfenbrenner, op. cit., pp. 101-102, 109, 152-153.
2. Bandura and Huston, op. cit.
3. Anne K. Soderman, "Schooling All 4-Year-Olds: An Idea Full of Promise, Fraught with Pitfalls," *Education Week*, March 4, 1984.
4. Taylor, op. cit.
5. Shedlin, op. cit. And Glen P. Nimnicht, as quoted by Betty Hannah Hoffman in "Do You Know How to Play with Your Child?" *Woman's Day*, August 1972, pp. 46, 118. Confirmed by personal letter from Dr. Nimnicht to Raymond Moore, September 29, 1972.
6. Dale Farran, "Now for the bad news . . ." *Parents Magazine.* September 1982; and the *Wall Street Journal,* September 5, 1984.
7. Larry Schweinhart, personal letter to Raymond Moore, Ypsilanti, MI, April 28, 1981, and April 1988.
8. Names changed in this true story.

Chapter 8 — Thinking: If You Want to Hurry It, Wait!

1. David Quine, "The Intellectual Development of Home-Taught Children," an unpublished paper presented to the faculty of the University of Oklahoma, 1987. David Quine, 2006 Flat Creek Place, Richardson, TX 75080.
2. John L. Phillip, *The Origins of Intellect, Theory* (San Francisco: H. W. Freeman, 1969).
3. Jean Piaget, *Psychology of Intelligence* (NJ: Littlefield, Adams & Co., 1976), and Piaget, "Intellectual Evolution from Adolescence to Adulthood," *Human Development* 15:1, 1972.
4. If you desire to study more of this phenomenon, much information is available from the National Center for Educational Information, Washington, D.C. and from the National Assessment of Educational Progress (NAEP).
5. Carol Simons, "They get by with a lot of help from their kyoiku mamas," *Smithsonian Magazine*, March 1987, pp. 44-52.
6. John Goodlad, op. cit.

Chapter 9 — Do You Want Super Babes or Super Children?

1. *Stranger Than Science* (Secaucus, NJ: Bantam Books, 1973).
2. Paul E. Mawhinney, "We Gave Up on Early Entrance," *Michigan Education Journal*, May 1964. (A more complete account may be found in the authors' book *Better Late Than Early.*)

3. Moore, et al., *Better Late Than Early*, op. cit. (Distributed by the Moore Foundation, Box 1, Camas, WA 98607).
4. "Panel: Superbabies may become burn-outs," *The San Bernardino, [CA] Sun,* November 14, 1987.
5. Ibid.
6. Gerald N. Weaver, "A Study to Determine the Approximate Age Level Most Effective for Initiating the Study of the Violin," *Lyons Music News,* November 1967.
7. 49:4, April 1968.
8. Selma Freiberg, *Family Happiness is Homemade,* 11:9, September 1987.

Chapter 10—Great Family Health

1. Available from the Moore Foundation, Box 1, Camas, WA 98607.
2. *Tufts University Diet & Nutrition Letter,* 6:2, April 1988, p. 3.
3. A. Keys, N. Kimura, A. Kusukawa, B. Bronte-Stewart, N. Larsen, and M. H. Keys, "Lessons from the serum cholesterol studies in Japan, Hawaii, and Los Angeles," *Ann. Internal Med.,* 48:83, 1958.
4. J. H. Howard, D. A. Cunningham, P. A. Rechnitzer, "Physical Activity as a Moderator of Life Events and Somatic Complaints: A Longitudinal Study," *Can. J. Appl. Sports Sci.* 9:194-200, 1984. D. L. Roth, D. S. Holmes, "Influence of Physical Fitness in Determining the Impact of Stressful Life Events on Physical and Psychologic Health," *Psychosomatic Med.* 47:164-173, 1985.
5. "Decision-making: A Boost for Thought," *American Health,* November/December 1983.
6. P. Curatolo, and D. Robertson, "The Health Consequences of Caffeine," *Ann. Internal Med.* 98:641-653, 1983. E. Boyd, et al., "The Chronic Oral Toxicity of Caffeine," *Can. J. of Phys. Pharm.* 43:995, 1965. M. Trichopoulos, et al., "Cancer and Coffee," *International J. of Cancer* 28:691, 1981.
7. Dr. Zane R. Kime, *Sunlight,* World Health Publications, P.O. Box 400, Penryn, Ca. 95663.

Chapter 11—How Well Do You Know Your Teenagers?

1. *Voice,* Vol. 4, Fall, 1987.

Chapter 15—Worried About Reading and the Basics? Try This!

1. J. Gilbert, "Projects not Textbooks Keep Engineers Current," *Electronics Design,* June 1986.
2. Penny Barker, "Later Literacy," *Home Education Magazine,* November 1987.
3. Letter from J.M., Texas, on file at the Moore Foundation, Box 1, Camas, WA 98607.

Chapter 17—The Real Homework: Family Industries and Service

1. 1 Thessalonians 4:11, 12.
2. *Phi Delta Kappan,* January 1976, pp. 322-327.

3. Penny Barker, "Education for Living," *Mothering Magazine*, Spring 1987.
4. Letter to R. S. Moore, March 29, 1988.
5. "Homework," *NEA Research Bulletin*, January, 1958. See also Raymond S. Moore, "Homework — Crutch or Panacea?" *The Clearing House*, April 1959.

Chapter 19 — Warnings from Disappointed Mothers

1. Sandra Thomas, Bothell, Washington, March 3, 1988.
2. Susan McKnight, Arlington, Texas, March 25, 1988.
3. Kathleen Creech, Kirkland, Washington, March 13, 1988.

Chapter 26 — The Navy Wife

1. This book is written from a Christian perspective and includes recipes.

Chapter 27 — A Single Mother and Her Washington Winner

1. J. T. Fisher et al., *A Few Buttons Missing* (New York: Lippincott, 1951).

Chapter 28 — The Former Assistant Attorney General

1. Published in *The Path To Home* by Reilly and Lee Company, Chicago, 1919.
2. Moore, *Better Late Than Early*.

Chapter 29 — The Physician on Leave

1. Proverbs 22:6.
2. Matthew 7:12.
3. Deuteronomy 6:7.

Chapter 31 — The University Kids

1. Ask your local librarian for suggestions and for leaders in their fields available from the Moore Foundation, Box 1, Camas, WA 98607. See *Math-It*, *Winston Grammar*.
2. Bonnie R. McCullough and Susan W. Monson, *401 Ways to Get Your Kids to Work at Home* (New York: St. Martin's Press, 1981).

Chapter 36 — Getting into College

1. April 10, 1988.

Chapter 37 — What Is a "Working Mother"?

1. P.O. Box 2001, Osterville, MA 02655. Phone 617/420-1010.

2. *Sacramento Bee*, February 23, 1988.
3. February 15, 1988.
4. For more on maternal attachment, see the authors, *Better Late Than Early* and *School Can Wait*, available from the Moore Foundation, Box 1, Camas, WA 98607.
5. Erma Bombeck, *Arizona Republic*, August 2, 1979.

Chapter 38 — Where Does That Leave Dad?

1. January 1988.
2. *Nebraska Home Educators Association News*.

Chapter 39 — The Grandparent Tradeoff

1. R. Butler & H. Gleason, *Productive Aging* (New York: Springer, 1985).
2. C. Hegeman, *Grandparents and Children* (Albany: Foundation for Long-term Care, 1986).
3. C. Tice, *The states speak: A report on Intergenerational initiatives* (Ann Arbor, MI: New Age, 1985).
4. B. Neugarten, & K. Weinstein, "The changing American Grandparent," *Journal of Marriage and the Family* 26:199-204, 1964.
5. A. Cherlin, & F. Furstenberg, *The New American Grandparent* (New York: Basic Books, 1986).
6. V. Bengtson, & J. Robertson, eds., *Grandparenthood* (Newbury Park, CA: Sage, 1985); G. Hagestad & L. Burton, "Grandparenthood, Life Context and Family Development," *American Behavioral Scientist* 29:471-484, 1986; W. McCready, "Styles of Grandparenting Among White Ethnics," in Bengtson and Robertson, op. cit.
7. A. Kornhaber, *Between Parents and Grandparents* (New York: St. Martin's, 1986).
8. Bengtson and Robertson, op. cit.
9. Kornhaber, op. cit.
10. R. Strom, H. Bernard, and S. Strom, *Human Development and Learning* (New York: Human Sciences, 1987).
11. U. Bronfenbrenner, "The Changing Family in a Changing World," *Peabody Journal of Education*, 61:3, 1984, pp. 52-70.
12. W. Peterson and J. Quadagno, *Social Bonds in Later Life* (Newbury Park, CA: Sage, 1985).
13. D. Fowles (Comp), *A Profile of Older Americans: 1985*, (Washington, DC: U.S. Department of Health and Human Resources, American Association of Retired Persons and the Administration on Aging); A. Pifer and L. Bronte, *Our Aging Society* (New York: Norton, 1986); D. Peterson, *Facilitation Education for Older Learners* (San Francisco: Jossey Bass, 1983); M. Wolf, "The Experience of Older Learners in Adult Education," *Lifelong Learning*, 88:5, 1985, pp. 8-11.

Chapter 40 — History's Wise Lessons for Educators

1. *Encyclopedia Britannica*, Eleventh edition, 1910, p. 952.
2. Carle Zimmerman, *Family and Civilization* (New York: Harper and Brothers, 1947).
3. L. J. Schweinhart, Letter to R. S. Moore, April 28, 1981.

4. Benjamin Bloom, *All Our Children Learning* (Washington, D.C.: McGraw Hill, 1980).
5. Ruth H. McKey, et al., *The Impact of Head Start on Children, Families and Communities*. DHHS Publication No. (OHDS) 85-31193. Superintendent of Documents (Washington, D.C.: U.S. Government Printing Office, 1985).
6. Gustafson, op. cit.

Chapter 41—How Home Education as a Movement Was Born

1. Not her real name.
2. Now distributed by the Moore Foundation, Box 1, Camas, WA 98607. Phone 206/835-2736.
3. Patricia McCormick of United Press International.
4. Walter Lippmann, "Education vs. Western Civilization," an address delivered under the auspices of Phi Beta Kappa at the annual meeting of the American Association for the Advancement of Science, Irvine Auditorium, University of Pennsylvania, December 29, 1940, *The American Scholar*, Spring 1941.
5. These included the NCES analysis headed by Robert Moon at Andrews University, an early childhood analysis directed by P. D. Forgione at Stanford, a children's neurophysiological study done by David Metcalfe at the University of Colorado Medical School, and analyses of more than eight thousand child studies, by R. S. Moore and the Hewitt staff, all under a four-part grant by the U.S. Office of Economic Opportunity under the general grant No. 50079,1973.
6. Soderman, op. cit.
7. McCurdy, op. cit.

Chapter 42—Support Groups: How to Win Friends and Influence People

1. If you need information about the nearest support group, want to get acquainted with key leaders in your state, or simply need basic information to start discussions in a new group, send a self-addressed, stamped envelope (SASE) to the Moore Foundation, Box 1, Camas, WA 98607. If you are in a hurry, call them at 206/835-2736. Please keep the Moores informed about your group either separately or through your state organization, and exchange your newsletter with the *Moore Report*. For the last fifteen or twenty years Holt Associates and Hewitt have been and still are the primary national clearinghouses for this type of information. If you know your state organization, these leaders can also help you locate support groups in your area.
2. You will often find some of the most impressive items reprinted or synopsized in our newsletter, which, along with John Holt's *Growing Without Schooling*, pioneered home school reporting. Our *Hewitt Report*, forerunner of our present *Moore Report*, was first published in 1969, nearly twenty years ago.

Chapter 43—The Big Family-State Quarrel

1. Moore, et al., op. cit.
2. Bronfenbrenner, op. cit. Glen P. Nimnicht, as quoted by Betty Hannah Hoffman, "Do You Know How to Play with Your Child?" *Woman's Day*, August

1972, pp. 46, 118. Confirmed by Nimnicht letter to R. S. Moore, September 29, 1972.

3. Eidsmoe, *God and Caesar* (Westchester, IL: Crossway, 1984). See also references in chapter 47.

4. Donald Erickson, supported by personal letter to the authors. See also "Certified for What" in Epilogue.

Chapter 44 — What Do We *Do* About the Big Quarrel?

1. Annikki Suviranta, "Home Economics Answer to the Problems Raised in Industrialized Countries," XII Congress of the International Federation for Home Economics, Final Report, Helsinki, July 23-29, 1972, pp. 92, 98-99.

2. Dale Meers, Statement in *Head Start, Child Development Legislation*, Senate Bill 3193. Hearing before the Subcommittee on Children and Youth and the Subcommittee on Employment, Manpower, and Poverty. Washington, D.C., March 27, 1972 (a).

3. Plato, *Crito*.

4. Ibid.

5. Alaska Department of Education, *SRA Survey of Basic Skills, Alaska Statewide Assessment Report, Spring of 1985*, Juneau. See also Alaska assessments for 1984 and 1986.

6. Letter dated February 10, 1987 from Betty W. Long, assistant to the Tennessee State Commissioner of Education, to Attorney Mike Farris, 731 Walker Road, Great Falls, VA 22066.

7. Diane Alme, letter to R. S. Moore, March 1987, and report from Henry Lufler, Associate Dean, College of Education of the University of Wisconsin to the Wisconsin Department of Public Instruction, February 1987.

8. Verne Duncan, *Tenth Annual State of the Schools Address*, November 8, 1986. State Superintendent of Public Instruction, Eugene, OR.

9. *Tumey v. Ohio*, 273 U.S. 510 (1927).

10. Morvin A. Wirz, Note to R. S. Moore, November 23, 1972.

Chapter 45 — Certified for What?

1. James Bryant Conant, *The Education of American Teachers* (New York: McGraw-Hill, 1963).

2. Personal letter from Donald Erickson, UCLA, to Raymond Moore, dated April 27, 1988.

3. See Harold Orlans, *Private Education and Public Eligibility* (Lexington, MA: Lexington Books, 1975), pp. 207-229.

4. Donald M. Medley and Homer Coker, "How Valid Are Principals' Judgments of Teacher Effectiveness?" *Phi Delta Kappan*, October 1987, pp. 138-140.

Chapter 46 — For Those Elite Who Are Invited to Court

1. The HSLDA home office address is P.O. Box 950, Great Falls, VA 22066. Telephone (703) 759-7577.

2. All three attorneys are home schooling their children.

3. A lawsuit that alleges that a public official in the course and scope of his employment has infringed upon the constitutional rights of the plaintiff. In this case, the allegation was, among others, that the superintendent was attempting to deny the family's right to freely exercise their religion, as the family was motivated by religious conviction at the time of the preparation of the law suit. Also, that the family's parental rights under the Fourteenth Amendment were being denied. The statutory basis for the last suit is contained in the federal statutes: 42 U.S.C. 1983.

4. Abuses of child labor and the education of the foreign born citizens was the primary motivation for passing compulsory attendance laws as well as the fact that, at first, the public schools were not well attended. This is where we first heard of the term "socialization." This was the argument that was made by public educators prior to compulsory attendance to attempt to convince parents to send their children to the public school, that is, the children are being deprived of the association with other children. The nation was a much more agrarian society at the turn of the century.

5. *Pierce V. Society of Sisters*, 268 U.S. 510 (1925).

6. Two other landmark U.S. Supreme Court cases stand for the parental liberty of parents to choose the place and manner of education for their children: *Farrington v. Tokushige*, 273 U.S. 284 (1927), and *Meyer v. Nebraska*, 262 U.S. 390 (1923).

7. 406 U.S. 205 (1972).

8. The laws on home schooling vary widely from very appropriate statutes like Missouri's, 167.031 Ann. Mo. Stat., to the archaic and unreasonable requirements of teacher's certification in Iowa, Michigan, and North Dakota, and sometimes argued in California.

9. These states are listed below with their respective dates of enactment: Arizona, Ariz, Rev. Stat. 15-802, (1982); Arkansas, Ark. Stat. 80-1503.4, *et. seq.*, (1985); Colorado, C.R.S. 22-33-104 (2) (i), (1963), see also Colorado Code of Regulations 2233-R-1.00 (1987); Florida, F.S.A. 228.041, (1985); Georgia, Geo. Code Ann. 32-2104 (b), (1984); Louisiana, LSA-R.S. 17:236.1, (1984); Minnesota, Minn. Stat. Ann. 120.101, (1987); Mississippi, Miss. Code Ann. 37-13-91 (3) (c), (1982); Missouri, 167.031 R.S.Mo., (1986); Montana, Mont.Stat. 20-5-102 (2) (f), (1983); Nevada, N.R.S. 392.070, (1956), see also Nev. Admin. Code Chap. 392 2-8, (1984); New Mexico, N.M.S.A. 22-1-2 (U), and 22-1-2.1, (1985); Ohio, Ohio Rev. Code 3321.04 (A) (2), (1976); Oregon, O.R.S. 339.030 (6), (1985); Rhode Island, 16-19-1 General Laws of Rhode Island, (1984); Tennessee, T.C.A. 49-6-3050, (1985); Utah, Utah Code Ann. 53-24-1 (2), (1957); Vermont, V.S.A. Title 16 166b, (1987); Virginia, Code of Virginia 22.1-254.1, (1984); Washington, R.C.W. 28A.27.010 (4), (1985); West Virginia, W.Va. Code 18-8-1(b), (1987); Wisconsin, Wisc. Stat. 115.01 (1r), 118.15 (4), 118.165 (1), (1983); Wyoming, W.S. 21-4-101, *et. seq.*, (1985).

10. See, e.g., Florida, F.S.A. 232.02 (4) (1982), and Florida Admin. Reg. 6A-1.951 (1974); New Mexico, N.M.S.A. 22-10-3 (1981); Virginia, Virginia Code 22.1-254 (1980); Washington, R.C.W. 28A.27.010 (1980).

11. These states are Alabama, Al. Code 16-28-1(2); California, Ca. Ed. Code 48222; Illinois, Il. Code Ann. 26-1; Indiana, Ind. Stat. Ann. 20.8.1-3-17; Kansas, Kan. Stat. Ann. 72-111(a); Kentucky, Kent. Rev. Stat. 159.030(b) or (g); Nebraska, Rev. Stat. of Neb. 79-1701(2)-(4); North Carolina, N.C. Gen. Stat. 115C-547 thru 554; Oklahoma, Ok. Sat. Ann. Title 70 10-105(A); and Texas, Tex. Ed. Code Ann. Title 2 21.033(a)(1).

12. These states are: Alaska, Ala. Stat. 14.30.010 (b) (1) (C) (10); Connecticut, Conn. Gen. Stat. Ann. 10-184 [local approval of equivalent instruction]; Delaware, Del. Code 14-2703 (a) [equivalent instruction]; Hawaii, Haw. Rev. Stat. 248-9 (6); Idaho Code 33-202 [comparable instruction]; Maine, Maine Rev. Stat. Ann. 5001 (2) (D) [equivalent instruction]; Maryland, Ann. Code of Md. 7-301 (a) [notice of intent]; Massachusetts, Mass. Gen. Laws Ann. Chap. 76 1; New Hampshire, N.H. Rev. Stat. Ann 193:1, also see N.H. Regulations and Procedures, ED 315.01-.04; New Jersey, N.J. Stat. Ann 18A:38-25 [equivalent instruction]; New York, N.Y. Education Law 3204; Pennsylvania, Penn. Stat. Ann. Title 24 1327; South Carolina, S.C. Code 59-65-40 [substantially equivalent instruction]; South Dakota, S.D. Comp. Laws 13-27-3.

13. These hearings are well attended by home schoolers who have been making very favorable impressions on the legislators.

14. *Parham v. J.R.*, 442 U.S. 584 (1979). In that case, Chief Justice Burger wrote for the majority: Our jurisprudence historically has reflected Western civilization concepts of the family as a unit with broad parental authority over minor children. Our cases have consistently followed that course; our constitutional system long ago rejected any notion that a child is "the mere creature of the State" and, on the contrary, asserted that parents generally "have the right, coupled with the high duty, to recognize and prepare [their children] for additional obligations." *Pierce v. Society of Sisters*, 268 U.S. 510, 535 (1925) . . . [other citations omitted]. . . . The law's concept of the family rests on a presumption that parents possess what a child lacks in maturity, experience, and capacity for judgment required for making life's difficult decisions. More important, historically it has been recognized that natural bonds of affection lead parents to act in the best interests of their children. 1 W. Blackstone, Commentaries 447; 2 J. Kent, Commentaries on American Law 190.

As with so many other legal presumptions, experience and reality may rebut what the law accepts as a starting point; the incidence of child neglect and abuse cases attests to this. That some parents "may at times be acting against the interests of their children". . . creates a basis for caution, but it is hardly a reason to discard wholesale those pages of human experience that teach that parents generally do act in the child's best interest. . . . The statist notion that governmental power should supersede parental authority in *all* cases because *some* parents abuse and neglect children is repugnant to American tradition. 402 U.S., at 602-604.

INDEX

MISSION STATEMENT

for Wolgemuth & Hyatt, Publishers, Inc.

The mission of Wolgemuth & Hyatt, Publishers, Inc., is to publish and distribute books that lead individuals toward:

- A personal faith in the one true God: Father, Son, and Holy Spirit;
- A lifestyle of practical discipleship; and
- A worldview that is consistent with the historic, Christian faith.

Moreover, the company will endeavor to accomplish this mission at a reasonable profit and in a manner which glorifies God and serves His Kingdom.

COLOPHON

The typeface for the text of this book is *Baskerville*. Its creator, John Baskerville (1706-1775), broke with tradition to reflect in his type the rounder, yet more sharply cut lettering of eighteenth-century stone inscriptions and copy books. The type foreshadows modern design in such novel characteristics as the increase in contrast between thick and thin strokes and the shifting of stress from the diagonal to the vertical strokes. Realizing that this new style of letter would be most effective if cleanly printed on smooth paper with genuinely black ink, he built his own presses, developed a method of hot-pressing the printed sheet to a smooth, glossy finish, and experimented with special inks. However, Baskerville did not enter into general commercial use in England until 1923.

Substantive editing and copy editing by Lynn Hawley
Cover design by Kent Puckett Associates, Atlanta, Georgia
Typography by Thoburn Press, Tyler, Texas
Printed and bound by Maple-Vail Book Manufacturing Group
Manchester, Pennsylvania
Cover Printing by Weber Graphics, Chicago, Illinois